The God of Yes

DAVID EDWARDS

The God of Yes

[LIVING THE LIFE YOU WERE PROMISED]

DISCUSSION QUESTIONS INCLUDED

HOWARD
PUBLISHING CO.

Our purpose at Howard Publishing is to:

- *Increase faith* in the hearts of growing Christians
- *Inspire holiness* in the lives of believers
- *Instill hope* in the hearts of struggling people everywhere
  Because He's coming again!

The God of Yes © 2003 by David Edwards
All rights reserved. Printed in the United States of America

Published by Howard Publishing Co., Inc.
3117 North 7th Street, West Monroe, Louisiana 71291-2227

03 04 05 06 07 08 09 10 11 12   10 9 8 7 6 5 4 3 2 1

Edited by Michele Buckingham
Interior design by John Luke
Cover design by David Carlson, David Carlson Design

Library of Congress Cataloging-in-Publication Data

Edwards, David, date
    The God of yes : living the life you were promised / David Edwards.
        p. cm.
    Includes bibliographical references.
    ISBN: 1-58229-285-X
      1. God. 2. Christian life—Baptist authors. I. Title.

BT165.E39 2003
231.7—dc21

2003047752

Judith Viorst once said, "Friends broaden our horizons.
They serve as new models with whom we can identify. They
allow us to be ourselves—and accept us that way. They
enhance our self-esteem because they think we're OK, because
we matter to them. And because they matter to us—for various reasons, at various levels of intensity—they enrich the
quality of our emotional life."

I would like to dedicate this book to just such a friend,
someone who is one of the great human beings, someone I
love and admire deeply...

To my very close friend,

_____

My Pastor, Father, and Friend

This book is dedicated to R. H., the man who has been "Paul" to me and who has allowed me the privilege of being "Timothy" to him. Through this relationship I have learned what true covenant friendship is about.

R. H., I can only hope that the mark you have left on my life will serve as a continuing testimony to the eternal value one life can have to another. Your work lives on in me.

Contents

CONTENTS

PART THREE: THE HOW OF YES

Acknowledgments

DR. JAY STRACK—For believing in me and letting me be your pizza guy at the beginning of my ministry days.

MS. FLO FLICKIE—You're my own personal coach. You left coaching an entire team to take on the daunting task of keeping me in line.

JOHN BULLARD—Forever is a long time, but that's the measure of our friendship.

CRAIG GROESCHELL AND DAY 3—Craig, thanks for dreaming the dream of Day 3 and having the courage and godly strength to make it a reality. Thanks also for showing incredible insight and quality judgment of character by asking me to be a lasting part of making it happen.

DR. ANTHONY JORDAN—Before I ever started ministry, you called me and encouraged me to walk the walk of agreement. Thanks for the phone calls.

KYLE MCDANIEL AND GENERATION REFORMATION—I wrote this book on your gift. Thanks to you, I'm no longer an outsider to technology.

JAY BRUCE—You are a true Amerikano.

ACKNOWLEDGMENTS

BOBBY MCGRAW—For working the late shift so many nights after you already worked the day shift for pay.

DR. JIM LYNCH (A.K.A. DOCTOR LAUGH-MASTER)—Thanks for reading the early versions of the manuscript and providing the much-needed prescriptions that helped cure many of the "early going ills."

TREY BOWDEN—When you first met me fourteen years ago, little did you know that one day you'd be spending twelve-hour shifts locked in a room, helping me craft my thoughts for this book. Thanks, bro.

THE SOUNDTRACK TEAM—The Allman Brothers, Shelby Lyn, Monty Montgomery, Miles Davis.

ALLIES IN AGREEMENT—Robert Routh, Mike Hutzell, and Chris Meduri. A lot of people talk about real friendship; fewer people come close to exhibiting real friendship. You guys embody the principles of friendship agreement.

THE BAND OF BROTHERS—Rick Lipsey, Stan Lee, Jeff Pratt, Doug Couch, and the Impact staff. Traveling twenty-seven days a month and writing a book is no easy task. In fact, it would have been impossible were it not for the generosity you showed me in allowing me to write during the day and speak at your camps during the summer of 2002.

DENNY AND PHILIS BOULTINGHOUSE AND JOHN HOWARD—Thanks for providing me the opportunity to get this message out to the masses. Yes, it was work. Yes, it was worth it. Yes, I hope many more people buy this second book than bought the first book, *LIT*. And Yes, I look forward to writing again for Howard Publishing.

MICHELE BUCKINGHAM—I spent hundreds of hours birthing the manuscript before sending it to you for editing. Now I know how a new mother must feel the first few times she has to leave her child with someone else while she returns to work. You cared for my baby, nourished it, and helped it become better than what it was when I entrusted it to you. Thanks.

Introduction

Most of us grew up learning about life from the word *no*.

"No, you shouldn't do that."

"No, that's not right."

"No, don't touch that."

"No, you can't go there."

"No, that's not good for you."

No is a restrictive term. It carries rejection with it. On a spiritual level, it conveys a lack of faith. Fear, worry, and doubt all flow out of no and into our lives. In many ways our perception of God has been predetermined by the no we grew up with. Many of us came to know God as the Great Restricter handing down and enforcing His list of things not to do. Our impression of church was shaped by the same no. The sermons we heard could all be boiled down to, "No, don't do that. You're doing it all wrong."

Yes, on the other hand, is an empowering word. When we hear *yes*, confidence, hope, and expectancy rise up within us.

I don't date a great deal, but every once in a while a godly woman catches my attention. I knew one such woman for about two years before she finally caught my eye. (I don't know what took me so long!) It was the final night of one of my Metro Bible Studies before the summer break, and as we walked out to our cars, I asked her, "Would you have dinner with me one night next week?"

Then came the suspense of waiting for her answer. She could say no, or she could say yes. She could just look at me and laugh. She spun halfway around, registering her genuine surprise at my question. Up until that time, she had only known me as the Speaker Guy. Finally, she turned back toward me and said, "Yes, I'd love to."

Yes. She said yes! I hardly ever ask anyone for a date, so I remember the moment well. When I heard that one word, I completely forgot all the negative feelings associated with her possible answer of no. I was living in the moment of yes!

Our relationship with God is a lot like that. Most of us live lives that work on some level. But each of us can identify specific core areas of life in which we always come up short; we just can't get them to work for us. God has extended to us an offer to live a life that works. Will we say yes or no?

Even now He is waiting for our answer. But most of us see God's offer as negative rather than positive. Our background of no has influenced our awareness of God so much that all we can see are the things we can't do rather than all the wonderful possibilities that His offer opens up for us. We've seen, firsthand, Christians who live extremely rigid and hyper-disciplined lives without much observable joy, and we know we don't want that. We perceive the life of Yes through our heritage of no.

If you're hungry for a life that works, you won't be satisfied until you make the personal discovery that the life God offers is much more liberating than it is restrictive. This is not to say that God is a pushover who allows us to live any way we choose without experiencing the negative consequences of poor choices. Rather, He sets before us a life of Yes that opens up a great many more doors of opportunity than it closes.

Unfortunately, the spiritual history of our world has been shaped by at least three strategic moments in which God's people have said no to God. The first moment occurred when God's first man and woman chose to live in a way other than what He had planned for them. God had intended for Adam and Eve to bear children and raise up a people whose king was God. But they said no to the dream of God, electing instead to create their own reality.

Introduction

The second moment happened when Israel, wanting so badly to be like other nations, chose to have a legacy of human kings rather than God as their sovereign ruler. God gave them judges to guide them with His messages, but the people rejected God's dream in favor of the world's ways. In that time, the Bible says, every one of God's people *"did what was right in his own eyes"* (Judges 21:25).

The third moment is today. Here at the beginning of the twenty-first century, the people of God have transformed God's dream of Christianizing the whole world into an enterprise that saves individuals and teaches them to behave in acceptable ways. Rather than pursuing the big picture and living out God's desire for a people who look to Christ as their Lord and King, much of the modern church has narrowed its focus and redefined God's kingdom as a future promise, not a present-day reality. By turning the kingdom into something that can only be realized in the sweet by and by, we have effectively said no to God's dream.

The Sunday after 9/11, America's churches registered the highest attendance of any time in history. Within the next several weeks, church attendance returned to the average. After 9/11 people came to church thinking they were looking for answers, when in reality they were looking for God. The problem is they found neither.

That's because much of the church has become an institution that has reconciled itself to the role of separating itself from the world and hanging in there until Jesus returns. We have become a people just trying to hold on until the end. God wants for us to live in a way that presents an observable reality of His kingdom to the seeking world. But instead of giving relevant help to seeking minds, we spew out the same answers as the solution to every problem that arises in our world. War: "These are the last days." Disease: "The end is near." Violence: "He's coming soon." 9/11: "I've read the end of the book, and we win."

As Bob Briner writes in his book *Final Roar*, "The fascination with popular end time prophesy has been very damaging to the Christian movement in this country....At best this is a huge distraction from the real and primary task Christians have been assigned to do."[1] We have abandoned our mandate—long before it's time to desert the planet.

INTRODUCTION

It's not that I don't care about the Second Coming. I'm looking forward to the day when I can ask God the really important questions of life such as, why do we have wars? Why, with all the wealth that's in the world, is there still poverty? And why the unexplained popularity of Capri pants for men?

But God's kingdom isn't something we can only know in the future. God's offer has always been a life lived in the reality of His kingdom, even while we're living in the midst of the kingdoms of the world. He has always offered a life that works in the here and now to anyone who will say yes to Him.

Our spiritual history bears out the truth that instead of saying yes to God and entering into the life He designed for us, we have tried to reproduce His life through our own efforts and disciplined behavior. The role of the children of Israel was to be God's light to the nations, but they chose instead to follow an ever-evolving set of laws and rules. The role of the church is to Christianize the world, but most of the church is content to simply conform people's behavior through manageable structures and multitiered institutions.

Meanwhile, our ever-vigilant God keeps on working out His purpose. He is not detoured or defeated by any of the choices people make. He continues to work to achieve His dream. As He says in Isaiah 55:11: *"My word...which goes forth from My mouth...will not return to Me empty, without accomplishing what I desire."*

God will accomplish what He set out to do, and He will do it the way He planned: through the lives of people who say yes to Him. He has committed Himself to redeeming mankind through the people of Yes.

It takes faith to say yes to God, and there is always an element of risk in faith. But from Creation forward, God has revealed Himself as a God we can depend on. In ancient times God delivered Israel from captivity, provided for His people in the wilderness, watched over them in exile, and brought them into the Promised Land. It was the dependability of God that Moses recounted to a new generation in the Book of Deuteronomy: *"Then you shall say to your son, 'We were slaves to Pharaoh in Egypt, and the LORD brought us from Egypt with a mighty hand'"*

(Deuteronomy 6:21). Moses used God's past actions to form the basis for a present faith. Israel had every reason to believe that God was the God of Yes. But when it came to living out the reality of their role as God's people, they repeatedly chose no.

From generation to generation, God has continued to give His people great promises that He always fulfills. He has continued to deliver them from their troubles and to abundantly provide for their needs. God has always acted on behalf of His people, and He always will. He is exactly who His words and actions show Him to be. Will we, like Israel, say no and reject the truth of what God has said and done, or will we say yes and enter into agreement with God, taking Him at His word?

This is the high drama of our faith. God has proven His faithfulness. He has shown us that His promises will never be broken. He welcomes us into a life of Yes, knowing full well that we will have many opportunities to say no to our faithfulness to Him. He has extended the offer. Now He waits for our answer.

I write these things out of a deep, abiding love for the church. Even though I travel a lot and I'm seldom at home, my membership remains at the church I grew up in. It's my love for Christ's church that motivates me to communicate the truths of this book. I'm convinced that, regardless of our denominations and spiritual preferences, we must bring our lives into agreement with the purpose of God. We must understand our role in God's kingdom and choose to live out that role in full agreement with God. We must live a life of Yes.

To do that we must understand the ways in which God has said yes to us. Throughout history God has made agreements with mankind that provide the strength, the power, the will, and the resources for us to accomplish the full extent of His purpose in the world. These agreements are eternal; they will never go away. The Bible calls them covenants. There are many different types of agreements, or covenants, mentioned in Scripture. In this book we will focus on the four eternal covenants God has made with His people. These four agreements represent God's eternal yes to us.

Typically, the topic of God's covenants is handled in a very technical manner. I have tried to present it here in a way that makes its application to our lives easy to understand. The first four chapters of the book explain the heart of Yes—what God's agreements are and why He made them. The next four chapters explain the hope of Yes—what those agreements can mean for our lives. The final five chapters explain the how of Yes—what we need to do to say yes to the life that God offers.

An entire generation is asking questions that can only be answered by observing the lives of people living in agreement with God. Ours is an age of fear, anxiety, and suspicion. Everyone has broken trust; everyone has had trust broken. The cry, Who can I trust? brings the most important questions of life to the surface: Is there a purpose for life? Is there a God? Is God for me?

In a recent poetry reading on the HBO program, *Def Poetry Jam*, Marty McConnell summarized the feelings of a generation. She said:

> We are the change generation. Fitted with the inconsistencies of a millennium influx. A vagabond lot, we skitter from one city to the next in search of an acceptable permanence. A home not in need of so much repair. See our inherited tools, they fit like a Phillips head in a slot-top screw.
>
> We are a generation of screamers. Silenced by this conspiracy of comfort that cradles us voiceless in our PC cities, where only the drunk and the dangerous spill what seethes in so many.
>
> I trade crusades like cards, flip issues like channels. Give me a God. Give me a rallying cry. Give me one good reason to die.

The Bible speaks with clarity: "*God is for us*" (Romans 8:31). He can be trusted. He is faithful. To be faithful, however, there must be a relationship; and relationship requires commitment. God wants to be in relationship with His creation, and He has proven His commitment over and over. He doesn't simply toss out promises without purposing to back them up with the full measure of Himself and His infinite resources. He is completely committed to seeing His promises fulfilled and His purposes come to pass.

God has already made His choice. He has said yes to us. Now the choice is ours. Will we look past all the static religiosity of our day and peer deeply into God in order to find Him as the meaning of all meaning? Or will we face life without God and lead others into that same life of rejection, doubt, and fear?

Will we say yes or no to God's offer of a life that works?

There is a God of Yes. Let's discover Him.

PART

THE HEART OF Y

The God of Yes

"It's not supposed to be like this!"

These are the words Samuel L. Jackson speaks to Ben Affleck in the movie *Changing Lanes*. He continues, "Our world is held together by an agreement or a covenant that keeps things from flying apart and us from hurting each other."[1]

As I watched the movie, I realized that Jackson's statement expresses exactly how most of us feel—as if we've been kicked in the teeth so many times that we could headline at any of the hillbilly shows in Branson, Missouri. But we're not all victims here. We're not without blame. Who among us, while playing fetch with a dog, hasn't faked throwing the ball just to see the poor pooch take off after nothing? Watching him search-n-sniff for the nonexistent ball is somehow funny to us. But the bottom line is we violated trust with the dog. We set up a certain expectation for the dog and suddenly changed it on him without letting him know—and then we laughed about it.

Or think about fishing. We cover a hook with a piece of food that a fish likes to eat and then dangle it in the waters of a popular fish hangout. The fish spots the tasty morsel and swims over to investigate. When he finally takes it in his mouth, we yank the rod and that sets the hook. We reel the fish in, wondering how in the world fish can continue to be so stupid. After all, they swim in schools. But they don't seem to be learning anything.

Dogs and fish may be trusting, but most people these days are not. In fact, when it comes to trusting in some of our national institutions, we've got more dents in us than a steel drum on a tropical island. Because I travel almost every day, people ask me if air travel is really any safer since the events of 9/11. I tell them it's not. What the authorities have done is create an illusion of increased security. Airport safety measures are so cosmetic that I'm surprised they haven't named Estee Lauder as chief of security.

Thousands of people who never graduated from high school have been hired by the federal government to serve as the primary line of defense against further terrorism in the skies. And what are they searching for when they scan our luggage? Usually pieces of metal. But not all pieces of metal are potentially violent. Recently, I saw a security guard take an elderly lady's pair of tweezers. Another time a man's fingernail clippers were confiscated. Personally, I'm glad they took those things away from them. There's no telling how many manicures they could have forced on unsuspecting passengers.

Because of the metal ban, the airlines no longer provide metal knives with their meals. Instead, the knives are plastic. Now I get to watch my knife melt into my chicken as I cut it.

In many airports armed military guards stand next to the x-ray machines. They have the uniform and the gun but no bullets. If something happens and they have to defend passengers against real terrorists, I hope there's a lady with an extra pair of tweezers around.

Trust is an intangible thing that is hard to gain and easy to lose. We trusted the airlines to protect us, and they didn't. We trusted the government to be there for us, and they weren't. Our ability to trust has become more fragile than a Fabergé egg filled with nitroglycerin. Weathered by one scandal after another, we've learned not to trust anybody or expect too much from anyone.

Our deteriorated trust has impacted our experience with God. After all, have any of us actually met the Homeland Defense Team or the

Airport Security Group? Yet, we're expected to blindly trust that they are doing their job. Eventually we realize that we're not any safer because of them, and we think, *Can God be any different?* And He's invisible!

Our perception of our world influences our perception of God. And our perception of God influences our real-life experience with God. Some of us picture God as Wilford Brimley riding along the fence line in a ten-gallon hat. Others picture God as Larry King frantically taking calls from all across the country. Still others picture God as Martha Stewart, there to put the finishing touches on any décor. Or…Urkel.

So often the church's message is "Trust God." And the response from most people is, "Yeah, right."

Who is God that we should trust Him? Or as King David asked, *"Who is this King of glory?"* (Psalm 24:10). You can't trust something you don't understand. You can't have faith in someone you don't really know. Before we can trust God and comprehend the weight of His promises to us, we have to understand who He is. Romans 8:31 says, *"If God is for us, who is against us?"* How can we know that God is for us? How can we know that He really is the God of Yes?

In Isaiah 46:9–11 God speaks for Himself:

> *Remember the former things long past,*
> *For I am God, and there is no other;*
> *I am God, and there is no one like Me,*
> *Declaring the end from the beginning,*
> *And from ancient times things which have not been done,*
> *Saying, "My purpose will be established,*
> *And I will accomplish all My good pleasure";*
> *Calling a bird of prey from the east,*
> *The man of My purpose from a far country.*
> *Truly I have spoken; truly I will bring it to pass.*
> *I have planned it, surely I will do it.*

In this passage of Scripture, God is speaking to Israel, a nation of people who was asking many of the same questions we ask today. Israel had a history of doubting God and worshiping different idols, and at this point they were caught in the middle of a decision: "Do we worship God as the one true God, or do we turn to our idols?" God responded by telling the people who He was and why they could trust Him.

How do we know that we can trust God today? How do we know that He will always be on our side? And what impact will this trust have on our lives? God's desire for us is the same as His desire for Israel. He wants us to know Him and trust Him. To help us do this, He tells us six key things about Himself.

HE IS PROFOUNDLY CLEAR ABOUT HIS AWESOMENESS

For I am God, and there is no other. (Isaiah 46:9)

God never second-guesses Himself about His own identity. He knows who He is. He doesn't need to take a personality test to determine if His temperament is more like a beaver or a rabbit. We're the ones who have the problem understanding who God is.

What are the barriers that keep us from really knowing God?

THE BARRIER OF SIMPLICITY

The way we speak about God reinforces our one-dimensional view of Him. For instance, some people call God the Man upstairs. God doesn't live upstairs. If He did, people in single-story houses would be in trouble. He's not in charge of building maintenance, and He doesn't run around His apartment in clunky shoes making loud noises that keep us up at night.

Some people call God the Big Kahunna. But isn't the Creator of the universe a bit bigger than a wave to be surfed?

Here are some other simplistic things we say:

- "Let go and let God." That's so vague. Let go of *what*, so God can do *what*? What if we let go of the wrong thing?

- "Everything happens for a reason." The problem is, if we say those words over and over long enough, "Everything happens for a reason" starts to sound like, "Anything can happen with a razor."

- "God is my copilot." If God is your copilot, then you're in the wrong seat.

- "My boss is a Jewish carpenter." This conjures up images of Bob Vila and *This Old House*.

- "God is in control." Many people use this phrase as the equivalent of a pacifier for the soul. When things happen in life that we don't want to face, we invoke it to avoid dealing with our problems. God is in control of all of life, but we suck the meaning out of these words when we hide behind them.

THE BARRIER OF SENTIMENTALITY

There is a trend in Christian culture to depict God in pictures of quiet, running streams of water and soft shafts of light coming out of the windows of beautiful homes. For many of us, that's how God resides in our lives—as a peaceful feeling drawn from a piece of art on the wall. For others of us, God is little more than a collection of songs sung years ago in old revival meetings (now revised and sung around a piano) reminding us of simpler days gone by. The danger of both of these views is that when something becomes sentimental, it is no longer relevant to the present; it's relegated to the past. A sentimental God is an impotent God.

God is not a soothing thought or a toe-tapping memory. He is a vibrant, proactive God giving every area of our life meaning and purpose. "Our awareness of God...must go beyond the warm fuzzy idea that He exists in an impersonal manner," Terry Crist writes in his book *Learning the Language of Babylon*. "The existence of God as a personal being is what frames the purpose of man. When you reject God as a personal being, you have eliminated the personal purpose of man as well."[2]

THE BARRIER OF SENSITIVITY

In many churches today, it's more important to be sensitive than to be truthful. Ministries, programs, and services are painstakingly designed not to offend anyone. As a result there is widespread misunderstanding about who God is and what He purposes to do.

Some things about God's personality will be offensive to us. He hates sin and opposes evil. He says, *"I am God, and there is no other"* (Isaiah 46:9). He is not one God among many other gods; He is the only God. He's a jealous God (see Exodus 20:5). And He makes promises and commitments that separate mankind into two categories: my people and not my people. These things are offensive to many of us because they run against the political correctness of our day.

THE BARRIER OF SPIRITUALITY

These days spirituality has become a search to discover one's own concept of God rather than a search to know God as He truly is. Store shelves are overstocked with books and materials to help us decide who we want God to be. Spiritual guides have opened shop and hung out a shingle in almost every town and city in America. It's actually vogue to discuss spirituality along with the latest movie and stock report. Spirituality has become popular, but our understanding and experience of who God is has reached an all-time low.

THE BARRIER OF SUFFERING

Some of us have gone through a painful experience and asked, "How could God allow something like this to happen?" The truth is, we have a hair trigger on our blame gun, and we too quickly blame God for things that are not the result of His work. We must not forget that God created a perfect world and that Adam and Eve chose to try to make it on their own. Sin entered the world because of their choice, not God's. Evil exists because the perfect world God created was de-created by the Enemy. Suffering is a natural product of the continuation of evil. If our focus is stuck on finding some logical rationale for all the suffering in the world, we will miss the reality of who God is.

HE IS PERSONALLY CONSISTENT IN HIS ATTRIBUTES

I am God, and there is no one like Me. (Isaiah 46:9)

When God speaks of Himself in Isaiah 46, He uses two names that reveal His attributes: *Jehovah*, which means "I am," and *Elohim*, which is translated "God." God uses the name *Jehovah* throughout the Old Testament to communicate that He is holy and righteous. This name demonstrates that God judges evil and calls His people to holiness and faithfulness, holding us accountable to live in agreement with Him. Jehovah is forever committed to one thing: the fulfillment of His purposes. He calls us to be completely committed to His purposes too. Jehovah is the God that makes the rules, sets the boundaries, and demands that His people follow and worship only Him.

Elohim is the name God uses to describe Himself as the lover of people. It is the name He uses when He makes agreements with mankind and enters into covenant relationship with His people. *Elohim* describes God as the one who is faithful to keep all His agreements. He not only makes agreements but works in mankind and in his creation to bring about their fulfillment. Elohim knows the heart of man and gently, lovingly guides His people to live in agreement with Himself. He is compassionate and long-suffering, even when His people rebel against Him. Elohim voluntarily binds Himself to His Creation and can never leave it. He is the God who cannot lie.

How can two different names describe the same God? Let me put it to you in a way we can all understand. Think of that animated cereal square on TV. One side of the cereal says, "People like me best because I'm frosted." Then it flips around, and the other side says, "That's ridiculous. People prefer me because I'm sensible and healthy." The truth is they are two sides of the same cereal. Get one, and you get the other. (Which side is best doesn't matter. I did my own survey and found that people prefer Count Chocula four to one over Frosted Mini-Wheats.) That's a silly and simplistic example, but it clearly communicates how God can be deeply in love with His people and at the same time completely committed to the accomplishment of His will.

Most of us understand the rule-making, demanding side of God (Jehovah), but we are not very well acquainted with the loving, committed, gentle side of God (Elohim). We've been told that God is the Big Policeman in the sky who swings a heavy club if we mess up. We've been told that He is watching, so we need to give Him a good show.

It isn't hard to understand God as the ultimate one we must please. It's a bit harder to understand that God is also our lover who is passionate about helping us succeed in everything He leads us to do. God relentlessly loves us in spite of all the mistakes we make. He is and always will be mankind's best and final hope.

God never changes who He is. He is always consistent. He is not fickle. He was not a different God in the Old Testament or to your grandparents. He is and always has been the same God. He is holy (He keeps His promises). He is righteous (He always does what's right). He is good (He loves us and is always working in us and for us). These things never change.

HE IS POSITIVELY COMPELLED BY HIS AFFECTIONS

Declaring the end from the beginning..."My purpose will be established." (Isaiah 46:10)

In this verse God is not talking about predicting the future; He is speaking about the intentions of His heart. He is less concerned with following a script or a map. He is more concerned with making sure we understand that all of His actions are motivated completely by the affections He has for us.

The ancient Greeks worshiped gods that were motivated by their own pride and arrogance. These gods were fickle and their behavior was impossible to predict. The Greek worshipers had to continually find new and creative ways to appease the gods and win back their blessing. The God of the Bible is nothing like this. He willingly made Himself a prisoner of His own affections for us. His affections compel Him to do everything possible to pursue us and win us back to His heart.

In the Old Testament, God repeatedly describes four main affections or intentions of His heart toward us. These four affections are the overarching motivation for all the actions He takes on behalf of His people and His work on the earth.

TO SAVE

The first chapters of Genesis tell us that mankind has been cut off from the person and presence of God by sin and is in need of salvation. Genesis 9:9–17 records the agreement God made with Noah. In this record God reveals His intention to win the world and all mankind back to Himself. Throughout the pages of the Old Testament, we see people trying old ways and inventing new ways to try to get back the unity with God that was lost in the Garden. On these same pages, God consistently shows Himself open and willing to forgive. *"In Your lovingkindness You have led the people whom You have redeemed"* (Exodus 15:13). God led the Hebrew children out of captivity in Egypt. He cared for them through the desert. He delivered them into the Promised Land and saved them from all their enemies. His heart toward His people has always been to save.

TO BLESS

Originally, God created a perfect garden and placed His creation of man and woman inside it. He blessed them by meeting their every need. Adam and Eve chose to rebel against God, but that doesn't mean that God changed His desire to bless His people. In fact, just before God led the Israelites into the Promised Land, He told them, *"But you shall serve the LORD your God, and He will bless your bread and your water; and...remove sickness from your midst"* (Exodus 23:25). The same God who made and kept all His promises to Israel is still compelled to bless all who will follow Him.

TO STRENGTHEN

Joshua was Moses' right-hand man, but he felt totally overwhelmed when God called him to take over the leadership of the Hebrew people after Moses died. So God told him, *"Have I not commanded you? Be strong and courageous! Do not tremble or be dismayed, for the LORD your God is with you wherever you go"* (Joshua 1:9). God was compelled by His affections to strengthen Joshua for the task that he faced.

There is no challenge or a trial that we'll ever have to face without the strength of God. He will always enable us to do whatever He calls us to do. He will never leave us in our weakness; His love for us will not allow Him to do that.

TO GUIDE

Even though the Hebrew people wandered in the wilderness for over forty years, they did so with God's constant guidance. He set up a cloud by day and a pillar of fire by night to show them where to go. The reason God did this is recorded in Exodus 19:6, *"You shall be to Me a kingdom of priests and a holy nation."* This is a part of the agreement God made with Moses and the Hebrew people. His intention was to guide them into the destiny He had planned for them.

Doesn't it seem strange that God would lead His people in a seemingly random path and call it "wandering"? The reason the Israelites wandered in the wilderness is the same reason we feel like we wander through life. We try to live life on our own terms and determine for ourselves which is the best path to take. It is so easy to get lost trying to make the most of life. In the process we miss life's real meaning and purpose.

CHAPTER ONE: *The God of Yes*

God, the author and giver of life, says, *"I will give them a heart to know Me, for I am the LORD"* (Jeremiah 24:7). God isn't hiding from us. The reason we can't seem to find Him is that we're looking in all the wrong places. If we will just ask, He will give us a heart to know Him, and He will guide us to find Him in all His living reality. He promises to lead us and work on our behalf in order to see that His purposes come about in our lives.

HE IS PERFECTLY CONFIDENT IN HIS ABILITY

My purpose will be established. (Isaiah 46:10)

God isn't nervous about getting His purpose accomplished. He is all-powerful and all-wise, but He doesn't have to micromanage the entire cosmos. He is infinitely bigger than His purpose, and He is so confident that it will be accomplished that He is not threatened when something happens that is contrary to what He wants.

I was speaking to a large group of singles not long ago, trying to help them understand this truth about God. I asked them, "Was anyone here in a marriage to a control freak or a micromanager?" Quite a few raised their hands, so I asked this follow-up: Did you like it? One of the ladies in the back responded, "We're here tonight, aren't we?" The room erupted in laughter. I continued, "Then why would we want to assign this attribute to God?"

Control freaks and micromanagers are either insecure about their ability to pull off their purposes, or they're insecure about the people they have entrusted those purposes to. God is neither.

Many people believe God is able to say confidently that His purposes will be established because His plans are written on a blueprint that cannot be changed. That's the same as saying that God sets certain things in motion and nothing anyone does can turn back the tide. If everything in life is already set, why did God work so hard to get

Israel to repent and return to Him? If God controls every detail, wouldn't He have controlled the responses of His people too?

God could micromanage everything if He chose to, but that would demean His character and degrade His position. It takes a greater God to lead people who have the power of choice than it does to lead a world filled with robots.

Once we understand that God has no desire to micromanage us, we can finally trust Him and embrace His purpose and plan for our lives. We can give Him our trust, because we finally understand that He first gives us His trust. He does not put His will in competition with our will. He is not looking for subtle ways to manipulate us so we will see things His way. He will not throw a temper tantrum if we choose our own way over His. He loves us and wants us to accept His plans. But His confidence in the fulfillment of His purpose rests in His own ability to make it happen, not in our fickle commitment to follow Him.

HE IS POWERFULLY CREATIVE IN HIS APPROACH

Truly I have spoken; truly I will bring it to pass. (Isaiah 46:11)

If God's plans are indelibly printed and incapable of being changed, we potentially could make one too many wrong choices and get to the point where it's impossible for God to bring us back in line with His purpose. Here's the truth: God's purpose never changes, but His plans to accomplish His purpose are completely flexible. He has more than one way to get something done.

When God sent Moses to Egypt to give Pharaoh the commandment, "Let My people go," He really was waiting for Pharaoh's response. If Pharaoh had agreed to let the Israelites go, Egypt would have avoided all the plagues. If he had let the people go after the frog plague, his country never would have experienced the infestation of gnats. If he had repented and let the people go after all the cattle died, the people wouldn't have been infected with boils. There were ten plagues because of Pharaoh's hard heart, not because God was following a script that would one day make a good movie.

What this account demonstrates is the creativity of God in the midst of human possibilities. God is powerfully creative in His approach to bringing about His purpose. There is more than one way for God to bring a dream to pass. You may have lost your job, or someone you love may have walked out of your life. No matter what has happened, it doesn't spell the end of God's ability to make it good. God is completely capable of taking leftovers and making a gourmet meal. He is never left without options. And He never leaves us hopeless.

You may be thinking, *Yeah, but what I lost was God's best, and now I'll have to settle for something less.* I'm not passing judgment; I'm just saying you're wrong! God's creativity is powerful and limitless. He never gives us second or third best. He always gives us His best. Life can throw us some pretty difficult curve balls, but even the most tragic events are no match for God's powerful creative ability to make everything work to achieve His purpose.

I meet people all the time who truly believe that God's plans are predetermined, like the levels in a PG-rated video game. They believe that if we want to follow God's plan for our lives, we must go through all the necessary phases of each level before we can move on to the next one. It's as if God is the game master with His hand on the cosmic joystick of our lives, gaining pleasure from making us navigate life's complicated labyrinth. With a flick of the wrist, He puts us through experiences designed to teach us the skills that will be necessary for succeeding levels. In reality there is no set number of predetermined steps that must be taken before God can bring to pass the next phase in His purpose.

A pastor friend of mine told me this story about a couple in his church who was without an income for several months after the husband lost his job. The couple prayed for God's leading and tried to live frugally on their savings; but after awhile, they were still without a job, and their money was running out.

As the wife was driving her car one day, she sensed God saying to her spirit, "Make blinds." A few blocks down the road, she passed a new housing development, and she made the connection that all those houses would soon need blinds. She turned into the development, found the contractor, and asked if she could present a bid to make all the blinds he needed. The contractor agreed but said that he needed the bid the very next day.

The woman rushed home and shared with her husband what God had told her. That evening they researched everything they needed to prepare the bid, and the next morning she delivered it to the contractor. Their bid was chosen, and they began making the blinds. God's creativity met their need.

HE IS PASSIONATELY COMMITTED TO AUTHENTICITY

Listen to Me, you stubborn-minded. (Isaiah 46:12)

God sees everything just as it is. He is not fooled by the games we play or the labels we choose to put on things. In the verse immediately following the passage we quoted in Isaiah 46, God calls the Hebrew people what they really are: stubborn-minded. He is more concerned that His words are authentic than whether or not they might offend someone. He is so passionate about authenticity that anyone who desires to know Him must relate to Him authentically.

God is not afraid of our responses and reactions to Him. He is not put off when we come to Him with legitimate questions and concerns. He is completely capable of taking our frustration and anger in stride without losing control and lashing out at us. He is patient and willing to take the time to help us understand Him.

God is the most responsive being imaginable. He is totally willing and able to adjust His plans and His emotions toward us in any way our relationship with Him requires. This is not to say that God has manic-depressive tendencies. He never changes. He doesn't have to. He is perfect in His character, and everything He does is consistent with that character. At the same time, He is authentic and responsive in His interactions with us. He understands and appreciates the things that make our life so real.

Life is full of possibilities, and those possibilities are a crucial part of the reality of life—even for God. Once we grab hold of this and believe it, we will more easily think of our lives in terms of what *might* be and what *could* happen. Then we can feel free to explore and pursue everything we could do and be in God rather than feel bound to the limited scope of a potential that was settled in eternity past.

We are created in God's image, and as such we are thinkers, feelers; we have the power to choose between the possibilities of life. We are fully alive when we identify and embrace the possibilities and seize the adventure they present us.

Perhaps you feel that you've missed out on God's purpose and plan for your life. You are well acquainted with a life that is limited and filled with disappointments. You crave the full and abundant life that Jesus promised but seem to always come up way short. You would like to discover how your life can be reenergized with hope and excitement. You want to know and understand God authentically rather than religiously.

You got on the right track when you picked up this book. The pages that follow are all about finding the life of Yes. They're designed to help you discover God in such a fresh way that you also discover the infinite hope and unlimited possibilities He has waiting for you. My purpose in writing is to show you how much God wants you to live a life in complete agreement with Him—and just how far He is willing to go to make this life possible.

The God of Yes is looking for real relationships with real people who are willing to make real choices to really know Him. You can be one of those people. You can say yes to God.

Hope, Not Hype

"New and improved!"

"Bigger and better than ever!"

"Too good to be true!"

These statements and many more like them are synonymous with the term *hype*. H-Y-P-E. This simple four-letter word means "to build something on nothing." Or, to put it in more hyped terms, "to create a reality that is entirely unsupported by the facts."

Our lives are influenced by hype much more than we may realize. Take computers, for example. The ads tell us that computers are fun because we can surf the net. Will someone please tell me how sitting in front of a screen and pecking away at a keyboard like a trained chicken has anything to do with surfing? I know what to do with a net, but where's the water? The most fun I've had in the few times I've been on the Internet has been waiting for a page to load so I could enjoy the disappointment of not finding what I was looking for.

Hype has provided the perfect solution to the boring wait in the grocery store checkout line: tabloids. Tabloids are to the news media what snake oil used to be to medicine. These rags are filled with overblown reports of the weird and the outrageous. They offer less truth than a sideshow barker. Do you realize that tabloids have subscribers? People actually pay to have these things delivered to their homes on a weekly basis. Yet, the papers are so bad, even pet birds won't use them. A few days after this trash arrives, it's hauled off to the landfill where it belongs.

On TV the late-night sell-evangelist du jour uses a paid studio audience, professional models, and an exaggerated foreign accent to hype the latest "must have" exercise equipment. This new machine promises you the body you've always wanted in just five minutes a day for the next twelve weeks, and it will only cost you fourteen easy-flex payments of $29.95. (*Hmm, let's see. The body I've always wanted in just three months for only $419.30, plus shipping and handling....*) The sell-evangelist claims the equipment is sturdy enough to pull a stranded truck from a ditch. Funny how when you unpack the box, it looks strangely similar to a mechanic's creeper and string.

And so the spin continues. There's the food dehydrator that never got used but brought $1.25 in the garage sale; the costume jewelry that turns your skin green; the cosmetic miracles that promise to cure the acne and remove the hair that doctors can't; the natural tan-in-a-bottle that makes you look orange. (What's so "natural" about dying your skin anyway?) And who can forget the knives that saw cans in half? When I got my set, no can in my mom's kitchen was safe, empty or full.

Of course, people who live in glass houses shouldn't throw stones. My windows may be made of stained glass, but they still don't filter out the truth that the cheap light of hype has found its way into Christianity.

For instance: I've seen the story of the prodigal son printed on Frisbees; shouldn't it be printed on a boom-e-rang? Then there's Easter: What does the death and resurrection of Christ have to do with a bunny and eggs? Wait, I've figured it out. The twelve eggs in a carton are the twelve disciples. And there's always that cracked one. That's the evil Judas egg.

Who hasn't clicked through late-night TV only to stop and listen to the unbelievable hype of someone promising that God will act on the viewer's behalf if only he or she would send in a generous donation for a genuine prayer cloth from the Holy Land? Too many preachers use words to paint a portrait of God as a short-order cook. I heard one preacher tell his congregation that if they needed a new car, an extra two-hundred dollars a month, or a new job, they should "order it up!" God would surely give it to them.

If we're going to "order up" a few tasty tidbits from heaven, maybe we should request a prayer tablecloth to put them on. I travel all across the country and speak in many churches with beautiful buildings. But I find that dressing up in nice clothes, driving new cars to beautiful buildings, and sitting on soft pews beneath stained glass windows does not eliminate the anger and bitterness so many people bring with them.

These examples are symptoms of the hyped, superficial Christianity and the shallow faith that permeates our churches. Is it any wonder that people who are looking for something genuine, something they can trust, look somewhere other than Christianity? The smoke and mirrors of hype have clouded genuine hope not only for the world, but for many of us in the church as well.

As Christians we need to reacquaint ourselves with the true elements of our hope in God. We need to reanchor ourselves in the truths of Scripture that produce hope in our lives. It is truth that produces the hope we so often seek through the cute sayings of hype. And hype is nowhere near adequate as a substitute for hope. Hype wears out. Hope endures.

Does your world right now seem hope*less* and hype*full?* No matter how little you have of real hope, God has His ways of reseeding hope and causing it to grow.

It can start with something as simple as the following story.

A LIFE LIVED IN AGREEMENT

Manasseh was the king of ancient Judah for fifty-five years. When he died, his son, Amon, took the throne. Both were idol worshipers, and over their combined reigns, the people of Israel made a critical choice: They allowed idolatry to replace their worship of the one true

God. The entire kingdom worshiped the gods of Canaan, along with many other idols and false gods.

In his book *The Mighty Acts of God*, Arnold B. Rhodes explains the significance of their decision. "The choice between the Lord and idols is a life and death matter," he writes. "Life is a qualitative word and stands for all the blessings of God. Death is also a qualitative word and stands for all the punishment of God. God's sovereignty never obliterates the responsibility of human decision."[1] Making the choice of who to worship was Israel's responsibility, and the people chose to trade the worship of God for the worship of idols. Their idol worship wasn't just the natural course of history or an innocent mistake; it was a conscious exchange of life for death.

Amon sat on the throne for only two years before he was killed by his enemies. Immediately, his eight-year-old son, Josiah, was crowned the next king.

Josiah turned out to be a good ruler. By the time he was twenty-one, he had gained the respect of the people. He'd led a successful military campaign and ruled the kingdom with confidence. All seemed to be going well for Josiah and for Israel. But during this time of relative success, Josiah's heart was challenged. God was at work in his life to bring him and Israel back into agreement with His will.

The voice of a prophet named Jeremiah tore through the morning air, delivering the words of God: *"For the sons of Judah have done that which is evil in My sight....they have set their detestable things in the house which is called by My name, to defile it"* (Jeremiah 7:30). In message after message, Jeremiah spoke words that were as intense as a trumpet's warning: "Oh, Jerusalem! Turn your heart from wickedness that you might be saved. How long shall evil live within you?"

Jeremiah continued speaking the prophecies of God over the next five years. When he spoke, the people of Jerusalem cringed; yet they knew that his messages were from God. Josiah also heard Jeremiah's words, and slowly the truth of those words changed his heart.

Josiah began to understand that the worship of other gods had ruined the kingdom and that Israel was in danger of receiving God's righteous judgment. To begin setting things right, Josiah ordered the removal of all the high places of pagan worship, along with their priests and prostitutes. He banned shrines to other gods as well as witchcraft and other forms of magic.

Josiah spent hours reading the journals of his renowned predecessor, King David. He longed to be a king like David. He craved God's blessings for himself and for his kingdom. One day, as the sun hung high over Jerusalem, he looked out over the entire city from his terrace. In the center of the city was the temple, which had been closed up for decades. Its great spires reflected the sun's rays as they pierced through the midday air.

That's it, he thought to himself. *The temple, the heart of worship, the place of God, the dream of David—I will open it once again.*

By the time Josiah turned twenty-six, the temple restoration was in full operation. It was during this time that a long scroll was found by one of the workers. Josiah's secretary, Shaphan, immediately brought the scroll to the king.

"Read it," Josiah said, and Shaphan proceeded to read the entire book aloud. It was the Book of the Law, the holy agreements God had made with Moses centuries before. Through these agreements God had said to Israel, "Follow Me as Lord, and My blessings will be upon you. Disobey Me, and you will suffer the consequences."

As the scroll was read, the entire Mount Sinai experience seemed to unfold before Josiah's eyes. At that moment he knew that the words given to Moses and the people of Israel at the foot of the mountain were still valid for him and his kingdom. He recognized that his father and many of the kings before him had allowed Israel to live in violation of God's holy agreements for many years, and Israel had suffered as a result.

Josiah gathered the priests, the elders, and all the citizens of Israel together and told the priests to read the scroll aloud. As everyone listened and watched, Josiah said yes to God's agreements, vowing to the Lord that he would keep His commandments and live a life of Yes before God. The people then joined their king and committed themselves to living out God's holy agreements as well. What followed was a forty-year renewal of those agreements in the hearts of the people. Once again God was the sole focus of worship in Israel.

The truths Josiah discovered about God's holy agreements are truths we need to discover today. Nothing will have a greater impact on the way we live than coming to an understanding of what it means to live life in agreement with God's purposes. Discovering life in agreement brings energy to the Christian life. It gives us the motivation to live with integrity, even when the forces of impurity pull at us in a different direction.

The simple, yet profound, principles of agreement increase our confidence that God is at work for good in every aspect of our lives. This confidence, in turn, enables us to have the day-to-day strength and power we need, even in the midst of the heaviest loads of stress, tension, and trouble. Through agreement God becomes our partner in every aspect of life. He promises, "I will work for you with all My heart and soul and strength."

Let's take a look at the truths Josiah discovered about living in agreement. These are the same truths that will bring about a renewal of agreement with God in our own lives.

THE DEFINITION OF THE AGREEMENT

The scroll that Josiah found was the Old Testament book of Deuteronomy. In Deuteronomy 29:10, 12 we read, *"You stand today, all of you, before the LORD your God…that you may enter into the covenant with the LORD your God, and into His oath which the LORD your God is making with you today."*

Covenants, or oaths, were an everyday part of life for the people of the Old Testament, but they are relatively unfamiliar terms and concepts for us. A simple definition of biblical covenant is this: God voluntarily binding Himself to His creation. In this book we use the term *agreement* to mean the same thing.

CHAPTER TWO: *Hope, Not Hype*

These days taking an oath is not a big deal. People perjure themselves all the time. For God to take an oath with mankind, however, is a big deal. God goes further than simply speaking the words; He takes on the responsibility of affirming the agreement as well as setting the consequences for breaking it. Unlike most of our agreements, God's agreements have three key characteristics.

THE AGREEMENT IS UNBREAKABLE

In the stories of John Grisham, the victim always seems to be found somewhere in Louisiana, and the trial ends up being held in Tennessee. Then there's always a scene in which the lawyer calls a witness to the stand; and before the witness testifies to anything, the bailiff makes the' person place a hand on the Bible and promise to tell the whole truth.

This is exactly what God was doing in Deuteronomy 29:12. God Himself took the stand, placed His hand on His Word, and swore by Himself to tell the whole truth and nothing but the truth, so help Himself. (*Hmm. If God sneezes, what does He say? Just wondering.*) By making this oath, God was binding Himself to the human race. If He should break it, all bets would be off; He could never be trusted again. In a very real and eternal sense, God's oath is the guarantee of our life. If He were to break His oath, the agreements we have with Him would be null and void.

Why would He do this? Why would the Creator of the universe willingly bind Himself to mankind? Why would He put Himself in such a committed position? For one reason: to remove any doubt or fear we might have about His trustworthiness. He made an unbreakable agreement with us so we can confidently put our trust in Him.

THE AGREEMENT IS UNCONDITIONAL

Deuteronomy 29:13 continues, *"In order that He may establish you today as His people and that He may be your God, just as He spoke to you and as He swore to your fathers, to Abraham, Isaac, and Jacob."*

Most of us are not familiar with unconditional commitments.

We've grown up with conditions placed on all our relationships. We've been told to make good grades so our parents will be proud of us. We've been given nice things when we've behaved the way the person giving the gifts wanted us to. We've had friends who loved us when we did certain things with them and wanted nothing to do with us when we chose to do other things. Many of us have had business relationships that were based solely on the condition of us being willing to do something illegal. Some of us have been in marriages that were based on some conditional aspect of security, such as a nice house, a sizeable bank account, or a new car every year.

These kinds of relationships are nothing more than conditional arrangements based upon performance. If one party breaks his or her word and doesn't act in the prescribed way, the relationship is over.

When God makes an oath, however, He makes an unconditional promise to love us and bless us and protect us. The guarantee for this promise is Himself. God swears by Himself that what He has committed to do will come to pass. God is the only one making the agreement, and God is the only one keeping the agreement. Regardless of our response, He has bound Himself to us. Nothing we do will cause Him to reconsider, change, or withdraw His commitment to us.

Every time Israel rebelled against God's will, God remained faithful to the promises He made. Today our state of spiritual anarchy is at least as advanced as any that Israel ever experienced. But just as God remained true to His agreements with Israel, He remains true to His promises to us, regardless of how rebellious we are. He remains true to His promises because He must remain true to Himself. He remains true because of His eternal love for us. He remains true for the sake of our lives.

The fact that God's agreements are unconditional doesn't give us the freedom to do whatever we please without facing the consequences. Rather, knowing that God will always remain faithful gives us the freedom to live life God's way, regardless of the pressures the world places on us. His faithfulness to us opens up infinite opportunities to experience, enjoy, and extend His will in our lives, no matter what obstacles we face. We can say yes to God and commit to living out His will without hesitation or question because we know His agreements are not only unbreakable, they're unconditional.

THE AGREEMENT IS UNLIMITED

Deuteronomy 29:14–15 says, *"Now not with you alone am I making this covenant and this oath, but both with those who stand here with us today in the presence of the LORD our God and with those who are not with us here today."* In this passage God was speaking about those people who would come to Him in the future through His Son, Jesus Christ. God extends His holy, eternal agreements to every generation everywhere in the world. No individual is outside its scope.

These words from Deuteronomy were first spoken when Moses led the Hebrew people out of Egypt. But as Josiah heard them being read eight hundred years later, he knew that God's promises were still available to him and to all the nation of Israel. He knew that the passing of years hadn't weakened the promises of God. He understood that years of rebellious living could never undo God's holy agreements.

Several years ago a Houston church put up billboards at major intersections throughout the city advertising its worship services. Most of the time church ads aren't very cool. The signs and symbols and cryptic Scripture references leave people feeling as if they're looking into the matrix. They're hard to read and not very good at getting across the message they're trying to communicate. But I have to admit, the billboards in Houston were the coolest signs I'd ever seen.

Each billboard was blue on the top and white on the bottom. Up in the left-hand corner, it said, "Jesus loves you," and in the bottom right-hand corner, it said, "No matter what." That's one of the best descriptions I've ever heard of God's agreements with mankind: Jesus loves us, no matter what!

God defines His own agreements and makes them unbreakable, unconditional, and unlimited. He has made a commitment to love us, protect us, and provide for us. He always has been and always will be true to His promises—no matter what.

THE DEMANDS OF THE AGREEMENT

Now that we understand the extent of God's holy agreements with us, we need to consider what we must do to live in agreement with God's purpose and plan. A life of Yes is not a complicated life, but it's not easy either. Remember, God made the agreements with us; we didn't make them with Him. Through His agreements God has bound Himself to us. This means He has the right to establish the demands of the agreements. And the demands are simple: Live in agreement with God. The benefits of God's holy agreements are limited to those who choose to live in agreement with His will.

There are four aspects to living life in agreement. Understanding them will help us live each day in greater agreement with God's will for our lives.

LIFE IN AGREEMENT SAYS, "IT'S ALL YOURS"

Deuteronomy 30:2–3 says, *"Return to the LORD your God and obey Him with all your heart and soul according to all that I command you today....then the LORD your God will restore you from captivity, and have compassion on you, and will gather you again."*

During Moses' encounter with God at Mount Sinai, God told him a time would come when the people of Israel would be scattered. That time finally came in 586 B.C. The people had chosen to live in disagreement with God for so long that God allowed them to be defeated by their enemy and taken into captivity. God's message to Moses was simple: "When you find yourselves scattered, remember whose you are and where you belong, and return to living in agreement with the Lord."

In Josiah's day the entire kingdom had given up their identity as God's people. Instead of living in agreement with the Lord, they'd chosen to "find themselves" in the worship of idols and deities manufactured by the pagan countries surrounding them. Rather than accepting and living out their God-given identity, they chose to create an identity of their own.

We live in a society with values that are similar to the ones in Josiah's day. From the time we are born, we grow up believing that we are the center of the world. We think that our schedules, our demands, and our dreams are the fuel that keeps the world spinning. We are tempted to take any job that brings us more money. We consider the pursuit of more stuff and bigger spaces to store it in one of our "inalienable rights."

We live with the illusion of ownership. We think we own our homes just because our names are on the titles. The reality is, if you have a mortgage, you owe the bank the money for the house—so the house really owns you.

We place a value on something based on how it relates to us: How does it affect me? How does it make me feel?

The bottom line of this kind of thinking is the self-centered belief that we can do whatever we want with whatever we have, and it doesn't really matter how it impacts anyone else—including God. We become the masters of our own destiny, the charters of our own course, the singers of "I Did It My Way." When this mind-set takes hold of us, our lives begin to scatter. The more we try to gather the control of our lives, the more everything in our lives falls apart. God did not create us to control; He created us to live in agreement.

Sometimes it's only when things are falling apart that we begin to see that the real Owner of everything is far bigger than we could ever be. The God of Yes is the only one capable of controlling the numerous and varied life circumstances that constantly threaten to destroy everything good He has for us.

The key to living a life of Yes is for us to take everything in our lives and say, "Lord, I choose to be in agreement with You, and my life is all Yours." No matter how far and wide we've been scattered by selfishness, pride, and materialism, God will restore us when we say yes to Him. He never forsakes His holy agreements with His people, and He reserves a place for each one of us within those agreements.

EACH INDIVIDUAL MUST CHOOSE TO BE IN AGREEMENT

When Moses and the Hebrew people stood by the shore of the Jordan River, looking across into Canaan and the Promised Land, they could see in both directions. Looking back, they could see the land they'd left; looking forward, they could see the land they desired. The scene was quite fitting. They were about to receive an ultimatum. They'd seen many miracles performed by God, yet they still doubted Him. Now they were in a position that was forcing them to face their unbelief—and challenging them to walk away from it.

They had left Egypt for the land God promised them, but a significant obstacle in the form of a river threatened to keep them from realizing God's promise. They had seen God work a miracle similar to the one they now needed. In their escape from the Egyptians, He had parted the Red Sea, and they had walked through triumphantly on dry ground. But this time, as they stood looking across the Jordan river into the Promised Land, their hearts lost hope.

That's when Moses said to them, *"You stand today, all of you, before the LORD your God....that you may enter into the covenant"* (Deuteronomy 29:10, 12). In choosing the words *"all of you,"* Moses was telling the people that their obstacle would be removed only as each one of them agreed to trust God to remove it. The decision to live a life in agreement is a personal decision. No one can choose to live in agreement with God for someone else. God had called Moses to lead "the people" out of captivity. Now God was calling every individual to choose the life of agreement for themselves.

The life of Yes has always had an *if* attached to it. You enter into agreement, Moses said, *"if you obey the LORD your God"* (Deuteronomy 30:10). Obedience is the caveat for agreement living. Without obedience we cannot come into agreement. Obedience requires submission of our will to the will of God. It requires us to admit that "Father knows best" and to act in accordance with that belief.

Submitting to God is hard for most of us for two reasons. The first is cynicism. For me, cynicism comes naturally. I learned it all by myself as a baby lying in a crib, watching that mobile twisting around over my head and thinking, *Yep, it's coming down on me*. Cynicism is a natural part of lives. It must be mastered, or it will saturate and control us.

This generation tends to approach God with calculated cynicism. Our cynicism comes out of a relationship with a world that seems to hand out more hurt than help. We carry an intense sense of despair and dismay into our belief system of who God is and how He will act toward us. Because our God-concept is jaded, we justify our decision not to move into agreement with Him. We not only justify it, we even come to feel good about it. All the while we lose more and more control over the important aspects of our lives.

The second reason we find it hard to submit to God and embrace a life of agreement is the secret sin we try to hide from God and from others. We try to strike a deal with God so we can continue to live nonagreeable lives and yet have the blessings that come from living in agreement. But God is not the emcee of a game show. He doesn't make deals when it comes to living the life of Yes. He requires complete surrender to Himself.

EVERY AGREEMENT GOD MAKES IS BINDING

God is not random. He acts consistently toward everyone. Some of us have grown up believing that God is inconsistent—that sometimes He's on and sometimes He's off. When He's on, He's really good; and when He's off, He's terrible. This fickle view of God makes it impossible to have a trusting relationship with Him.

I've learned through dating that randomness is inconsistent with any healthy relationship. The woman I dated yesterday probably will not be the same woman I'll take out tonight. Oh, her name will be the same. She will look the same and sound the same. But she will be someone completely different. Everything I thought was right yesterday will be wrong tonight. At least that's how it usually goes for me. Once I dated a girl with so many different personalities, she formed her own softball team. When I finally talked her into going to therapy, the doctor charged her group rates.

Unlike some of my dates, God is always completely consistent. He has made an agreement with us, and He has bound Himself to it. We don't have a choice in the way He acts toward us. We do, however, have a choice in how we relate to God. Based on our response to Him, we can relate to Him as a God of blessing—or a God of conviction.

BLESSINGS AND CURSES ARE IN THE AGREEMENT

When Moses stood before Israel, he presented a stark contrast: *"I have set before you life and death, the blessing and the curse"* (Deuteronomy 30:19). God's agreement had two sides: The Hebrew people could keep the agreement and experience blessing, or they could break the agreement and experience discipline and suffering. These same two sides are present in the new agreement brought to us and fulfilled by Jesus Christ. Follow God and there will be blessings; defy the agreement and life will not work.

To understand God's blessings, we need to understand that the focus of His activity in our lives is more than just getting us to heaven; it's also bringing heaven to earth through the lives we live. God loves us and wants our lives to work. When we order our lives to be in agreement with God, we find that He gives us the resources we need to live successfully.

That's the blessing side—the A side of the agreement. Now for the flip side. (Sorry for the reference to records—you know, those black vinyl disks that were once used to play back music?)

There is a popular myth among Christians that God is all grace. He is always smiling on us. We can do anything we want to during the week and confess it to God on Sunday, and we're all right. We love to sense His smile, and it's tempting to think that God is a pushover.

The truth is, living in agreement with God will bring His conviction when we are disobedient. Conviction may feel like a negative thing, but it's just as much a part of God as His smile. He is committed to making our lives work in Him, and He will use the strength and power of His conviction to let us know when we are outside of His will. It may feel bad, but conviction is God at work in us.

You may be saying to yourself (if you are, please don't move your mouth—that really looks crazy), *But the reference to "blessings and curses" is Old Testament, and we're New Testament people. We're not under law, we're under grace.* The apostle Paul addresses this issue in Hebrews 10:29. After talking about the consequences of breaking the Old Testament law, he writes, *"How much severer punishment do you think he will deserve who has trampled under foot the Son of God, and has regarded as unclean the blood of the covenant by which he was sanctified, and has insulted the Spirit of grace?"*

What should frighten us here is the possibility that we could become so presumptuous of God's grace that we'd feel safe enough to do whatever we please—and unintentionally place ourselves on the curse side of God's agreements. I have spoken this simple message to thousands all across this country; but for the sake of putting it in print, let me say it one more time: *Live in agreement with God, and good things happen. Live in disagreement with God, and bad things happen.* You and I get to choose. Which will it be, blessing or curse?

THE DYNASTY OF THE AGREEMENT

Moses concluded his presentation by telling the people the end result of their agreement with God: *"that you may live in the land"* (Deuteronomy 30:20). In the Bible the word *land* is always symbolic of the will of God. When we live in agreement, we find ourselves right in the center of God's will for our lives. The verse continues, *"...which the LORD swore to your fathers."* This last phrase reminded the Hebrew people that His agreements were nothing new; He had made them with their forefathers generations before. In this way God was revealing Himself as the creator of a dynasty—a dynasty of agreement.

Even today God is looking for people who will become part of this dynasty by living in agreement with Him. He is the God of Yes, and He desires a people who will say yes to Him. *"For the eyes of the LORD move to and fro throughout the earth that He may strongly support those whose heart is completely His"* (2 Chronicles 16:9). God is looking for people who will say, "I don't understand everything You want to do, God, but I'll agree with You and make the choices that will order my life and prioritize Your will over my own."

Many people think that God somehow randomizes the distribution of His blessings. If you get them, great; if not, well then, good luck. Others believe that God blesses those who deserve it the most. If that's true, I guess the two-thirds of the world's population who will go to bed hungry for the third night in a row need to work a bit harder in the deserving category. But God's blessings are neither randomized nor deserved. He gives them to people who choose to live life in agreement with His will.

To live a life of Yes, you only need to say yes to God. It really is that simple.

CHAPTER THREE

Lod's Four Agreements

Real estate has its own form of doublespeak. The other day when my mom and I were taking a walk, we spotted a For Sale sign on a house. Attached to the sign was a plastic box filled with fliers telling about the property. I took one of the fliers just to see how the house was being described.

My first surprise was the advertised price: $90,000. This was one of the older neighborhoods in my city. The house was in pretty good shape, but it looked very small, and there was only enough room for a garbage can between it and the houses on both sides. I read the flier aloud as we walked:

> Remember your grandmother sitting on the porch, listening to crickets on a summer evening while you chased fireflies? The yard with plenty of room to play but not too big to mow? The cool feel of the hardwood floor on your feet before you went to bed? The smell of rolls in the oven as you colored at the big kitchen table while Mom set the dining room table for dinner? Look no further! Call this house your home, and you can regain that feeling of stability and permanence.

The big closer of the ad nearly did me in: "This house is nestled in an interior lot in a sought-after neighborhood." This was a small house on a small lot crammed between two other houses in a neighborhood that had seen its best days about twenty-five years ago. Since that day I've put together a *Buyer's Guide to Understanding Real Estate Lingo.* Here are some of the highlights:

- When the house is described as "nestled," it means cramped.
- When the ad says it's "cute," that means it's something only a mother could love.
- If it's "charming," it needs repair.
- If it's "quaint," it's tiny.
- If it's "spacious," it's even tinier.
- If it's "airy"—the north wind is blowing through the cracked windows.
- If it's "must see to appreciate"—it's been condemned.
- If it's "simple"—it's a lean-to.
- If it's "conveniently located"—you share your driveway with three other neighbors, and the busiest street in town runs right in front.
- If it's "a view of water"—your neighbor's backed-up septic tank is within eyeshot of your den window.
- If it's "well lit"—that's the view at 11:30 P.M. when the police helicopter does its nightly neighborhood fly-by with a high-powered searchlight.

These are all good words or phrases describing something that you really shouldn't buy. Sometimes words can be used to sell something that should only be given away.

The offer God makes to mankind is not doublespeak. It's much more than just words. God offers His agreements by pledging Himself, not just making promises. He doesn't give us words alone; He gives Himself. He forever links Himself with the fulfillment of His agreements. They are the very soul of His commitment to us.

In this chapter I want to introduce you to the four eternal agreements

God has made with mankind by looking at four men who said yes to living in agreement with God. These four didn't understand everything God was doing in their lives, but they trusted Him to keep His agreements with them and to complete everything He promised.

These men are representative of all mankind. The things God promised them are the same things He promises us. The way He worked in their lives is the same way He desires to work in ours.

The promises you're about to discover are more spectacular than anything you have ever known. If you and I really grasped them, they would help us understand how history affects our today. They would change the very nature and purpose of our present lives. And they would change our impact on the future to such an extent that the entire world would come to know of God's great promises to mankind.

For the last two thousand years, God has been declaring His intentions and demonstrating His power to keep all His promises moving toward fulfillment, regardless of who or what is shaping history. He has done this by zeroing in and working through the lives of those people who come into agreement with Him. Only God could maintain such a grand commitment to a singular purpose. Only God could be powerfully creative enough to bring it to pass.

The four agreements we're about to discuss offer a more complete understanding of God's purposed intentions for us and for the world. Each agreement clearly defines His obligation to make certain that His promises are kept. God has always been positively compelled by His affections toward us. These agreements are His pledge that all of His purposes for us and for the world will be established.

THE AGREEMENT WITH ADAM: GOD PROMISES TO REMOVE SIN

And I will put enmity between you and the woman, and between your seed and her seed; He shall bruise you on the head, and you shall bruise him on the heel. (Genesis 3:15)

Early in the history of the earth, God's perfect creation was ruined by the one creature He had created in His own image. Instead of declaring vengeance on Adam and all his descendants, however, God chose to redeem them. Instead of striking out against His creation and punishing them, He chose to pursue them and make an agreement with them. Intent on winning His beloved creation back to Himself, God set in motion His eternal redemptive agreement, an agreement pointing ultimately to the One who would remove, once and for all, the sin that had come between Himself and mankind.

The plan He set into motion was offered to Adam under the single condition that he accept it. God provided the first animal sacrifice and gave the skins to Adam as covering for his body. In this action God was foreshadowing His willingness to sacrifice His Son to cover the sins of mankind. All Adam had to do was accept the free gift of God. Adam said yes.

When Adam and Eve were put out of the Garden, they knew for the first time the contrast between perfect unity with God and the evil that comes with separation from Him. They were filled with regret over their memories of what life used to be. We don't know this, but perhaps they never told their children about their failure and fall. One thing's for sure: They taught the kids how to keep the snakes out of the family garden (a skill they apparently never mastered).

We all know what it's like to have blown opportunities. We've all had to watch some of our dreams die. We've all had hopes transformed into regrets. Each of us has made decisions in relationships that ended up creating more problems than promises.

You invest heavily in the spiritual training of your children, only to watch them fail to grasp the real value of their inheritance. Your so-called friends show their true colors only after you have shown them your most vulnerable deficiencies. A new business prospect fills you with heightened expectation until you move your entire household to another state and discover the opportunity was a house of cards on a shaky table.

All too often *potential* married with *hope* meets unexpected *disappointment* in University Life. What is born is something you're still trying to make sense of (like those recurring monthly VISA charges and the Ab Doer in your closet that really doesn't). These are blown opportunities, life events you would just as soon forget.

Adam knew what it was to have something good and lose it. After he blew his opportunity, God came walking in the Garden and asked him, *"Where are you?"* (Genesis 3:9). Adam had to admit that he was naked and lost and hiding. It's easy to blame our circumstances or other people for the mistakes of our past. But in the end, like Adam, each of us has to be honest about where we are with God.

We don't have to fear God's response. His answer to Adam was to make a garment of skin to cover him. Adam did not die at that moment for his sin; instead, death was transferred to the animals as a picture of the Sacrifice that would one day remove the sin of the world. By covering Adam, God declared His agreement to voluntarily take responsibility for removing the separation between Himself and His creation.

Even at the place of our greatest failure, God makes a way for us to return to Him. The agreement He made with Adam promises all of us that sin will be removed. God intends to regain the intimacy with mankind that was lost—to recover creation and reconnect eternally with the creation He formed in His image.

THE AGREEMENT WITH ABRAHAM: GOD PROMISES TO RELEASE BLESSINGS

> And I will make you a great nation, and I will bless you, and make your name great; and so you shall be a blessing; and I will bless those who bless you, and the one who curses you I will curse. And in you all the families of the earth will be blessed. (Genesis 12:2–3)

Abram was seventy-five years old when God came to him and said, *"Go forth from your country, and from your relatives and from your father's house, to the land which I will show you"* (Genesis 12:1). Abram didn't know where God was going to lead him; he simply knew that God said, "Go." And so, without hesitation, he gathered his flocks, his herds, and his possessions and set out, along with his wife, Sarai, and his nephew Lot, for a land God had yet to show him.

At this point in history, God's purpose required someone who would simply take Him at His word. In Abraham God found such a man. Abraham's act of obedience made him one of God's original "yes men." Even though Abraham didn't understand everything God was telling him to do, he was willing to bring his entire life into agreement with whatever God spoke. He knew how to say yes and then stand behind the meaning of that little word.

As a result of Abraham's obedience and trust, God declared him "righteous" and brought him into His family. He promised to protect, promote, and provide for Abraham and to ensure the fulfillment of all of His promises to him.

By making this agreement with Abraham, God obligated Himself to make Abraham a channel through which He would pour His blessings into the world: *"I will establish My covenant between Me and you and your descendants after you throughout their generations for an everlasting covenant, to be God to you and to your descendants after you"* (Genesis 17:7). Abraham's obedience to the word and will of God unleashed the fullness of God's blessing, and God made him the spiritual father of all those whom He would bless from that generation forward.

As a result the agreement God made with Abraham still applies to us today. When we line ourselves up with God's will and choose to live a life of Yes, we become heirs of God's protection, promotion, and provision, just like Abraham.

Your life background doesn't matter. Neither does the size of your paycheck or the talents and abilities you have or don't have. It doesn't matter how many times you've failed. God isn't looking for someone with just the right skills or all the right contacts. He isn't looking for someone with a theological education who can understand and articulate the deep mysteries of the Bible. God's purpose hasn't changed since the time of Abraham; He is still looking for people who are willing to live in agreement with Him. He is still looking for men and women who know how to say yes and stand behind the meaning of that little word.

From the depths of His heart, God uses all His power and all His presence to do good for us in all the circumstances of our lives—when we say yes to Him. If God can bless and change the life of a man like Abraham and make him the spiritual father of the world, he can bless and change our lives too.

THE AGREEMENT WITH DAVID: GOD PROMISES TO REIGN WITH AUTHORITY

> *When your days are complete and you lie down with your fathers, I will raise up your descendant after you, who will come forth from you, and I will establish his kingdom. He shall build a house for My name, and I will establish the throne of his kingdom forever. (2 Samuel 7:12–13)*

God called David "A MAN AFTER MY HEART, who will do all My will" (Acts 13:22). In other words David was a man who said yes to God. As a result, when David sat on Israel's throne, God blessed the entire nation. He prospered Israel's harvests and flocks and expanded its borders. He also made this agreement with David: One of David's descendants would build a house for God's name, and this descendant's throne would be established forever.

Not many years later, David's son Solomon sat on the throne of Israel and literally built the first temple of worship—the first house of God. But while the temple was a magnificent structure, it was not the fulfillment of God's agreement with David. It wasn't the house God had been talking about. Rather, God intended to build a broader house within a broader kingdom. In the Bible a throne is a symbol of strength, power, and authority. God's intention was to establish an eternal throne of strength and power for all mankind—a throne that would serve as His seat of authority over heaven and earth.

After the rule of David, the history of Israel took a turn for the worst. The kingdom ultimately divided in two in a civil war, and the kings that followed on both thrones lived lives marked by personal evil and idolatry. They literally turned their backs on the God of David's agreement. God made sure they experienced the consequences of their sin, but because of His promise to David, He did not completely destroy them. God had obligated Himself to keep every part of His agreement.

Our lives are getting more complicated and stressful every year. We always have more demand on our time and money than we have supply. Today's computers make balancing our checkbooks one of the easiest things in the world to do. But the math isn't the problem. Balancing the job, the family, the friends, the responsibilities—that's the problem. Bill Gates and his billions can write software programs that automate just about anything, but they can't come close to helping us balance our lives.

Admit it: Don't you feel vulnerable when you can't find the strength to face the bad news of the moment? Of course, that news wouldn't be so tough if it weren't for the other seventeen pieces of bad news you received earlier that morning. Then, just as you feel you've reached your limit, your boss sends you an e-mail saying that your quarterly review scheduled for next Tuesday has been moved to 2:30 this afternoon so he can leave a day early for a long weekend at his condo in the mountains. Where does anyone get the strength to face these situations? In the same place David found it: the promise of God.

David found strength in knowing that his throne would be established forever—not because of his own abilities and power, but because God is faithful to perform everything He agrees to do. David found the same, exact strength that we can find when we bring our lives under the authority of God's throne. God has obligated Himself to establish a throne of strength in the lives of everyone who says yes to Him.

THE AGREEMENT WITH JEREMIAH: GOD PROMISES TO REDEEM NATIONS

"But this is the covenant which I will make with the house of Israel after those days," declares the LORD, "I will put My law within them and on their heart I will write it; and I will be their God, and they shall be My people....I will forgive their iniquity, and their sin I will remember no more." (Jeremiah 31:33–34)

When God spoke to the prophet Jeremiah, He said that He was going to make a new covenant, or agreement, with His people. The old agreement had been given through Moses, and it had focused on the people's adherence to specific laws and worship rituals. It was an external agreement made to demonstrate to the rest of the world that God's people were set apart, different. The nature of the new agreement, however, was going to be internal. It would provide a way for God to reestablish a personal relationship with mankind.

In the old agreement, God wrote His commandments on stone tablets. In the new agreement, He writes His law on our hearts. In the old agreement, God set up an exterior system of laws and required obedience. In the new agreement, God internally motivates us to follow Him.

In the old agreement, God's blessing was dependent upon the obedience of the people. They were often disobedient and missed the blessing of God, yet He remained faithful to them. In the new agreement, God's blessing is bound by His own obligation to fulfill His purpose. His blessing is completely available to everyone who chooses to live in agreement with His will.

In the old agreement, the sins of the people were covered by the blood of sacrificed animals. In the new agreement, our sins are removed and remembered no more. In the old agreement, the people went to a temple to meet and worship God. In the new agreement, we *are* the temple of God.

Let's look at the three main characteristics of God's promise to Jeremiah.

INTERNAL

> *I will put My law within them and on their heart I will write it.*
> (Jeremiah 31:33)

This part of God's agreement with Jeremiah is about the inner transformation God promises to bring about in us. We no longer have to be bound by destructive desires or addicted to bad life habits. The Spirit of God is alive and at work inside us, making all of God's power and authority available to set us free.

Before the new agreement, God's code of conduct was written down, clearly taught, and imposed on people's lives. Since obedience ensured God's blessing, each person's behavior became the measure of his or her compliance to the agreement. The law was one-size-fits-all, and everyone's behavior had to conform to it in the same way. Now, because of God's promise to write His law deep within us, His law is no longer one-size-fits-all. Instead, it's tailored to fit the way He is conforming each individual internally to His will. The Spirit of God Himself is our internal master tailor, fashioning and conforming our will to fit His.

INTIMATE

> *I will be their God, and they shall be My people.* (Jeremiah
> 31:33)

To interact with God under the old agreement, the people of Israel were required to follow specific worship rituals. They had to bring sacrifices and offerings to the temple and stand by as the priests offered those sacrifices on burning altars. All they could do was watch and pray as the smoke rose into the air. God was in His temple, and the people felt a sense of closeness to Him when they were there. Perhaps that's why God had them bring sacrifices to the temple grounds on a regular basis.

Under the new agreement, however, we don't have to bring sacrifices to a specific location in order to experience closeness to God. Through His Spirit, He lives inside us. He is no longer our God on the outside; He is our God on the inside. We are no longer His people because we come to His temple; we have become His temple because we are His people.

This intimate relationship allows us to cry out to God immediately whenever a crisis occurs. When the Hebrew worshiper entered the temple grounds, he could only go in a short distance—just far enough to present his offering to the priest. The priest would then present his offering before God in the inner courts. By contrast, our intimacy with God allows us to rush directly into the very presence of God, where we can find the full measure of His resources to help in our time of need.

INNOCENT

I will forgive their iniquity, and their sin I will remember no more. (Jeremiah 31:34)

Under the old agreement, when an animal was sacrificed, its blood was sprinkled on the altar to signify that the sins of the one who brought the sacrifice had been covered. This process had to be repeated on a regular basis because it was impossible for anyone to keep all the law all the time. There was no position of innocence; sacrifices had to be offered continuously. The temple system of sacrificial worship was a constant reminder to the people that their sin was always before God.

In the new agreement, however, our sins are no longer simply covered; they are removed. Blood sacrifices are not a part of the new agreement because we are declared innocent once and for all. When God's Spirit comes to live in us, He removes our sins and forgets about them forever.

THE AGREEMENT WITH US: WE MUST CHOOSE TO RECEIVE IT

When we align our lives with the four agreements God made with Adam, Abraham, David, and Jeremiah, we put ourselves in a position to experience the full force of all of God's resources. The more we understand these agreements, the more we grow in faith, confidence, and expectancy in the God who made them.

God does not automatically apply these agreements to our lives, however. He willingly binds Himself to us and promises to love us, protect us, and provide for us, but His promises are guaranteed only within certain boundaries.

Think about what happens when you walk into a football stadium to watch a game. From the opening kickoff to the last tick of the clock, specific rules are enforced. Both the players and the fans know what the rules are and how the game is supposed to be played. That's what makes it so interesting.

The rules keep everyone focused on the game's purpose. If one player refuses to play by the rules, a flag is thrown, and his team receives a penalty. If a team gets too many penalties, it doesn't win the game—and the object of playing the game, of course, is winning (unless you're the Dallas Cowboys).

A lot of money is paid by fans for the privilege of watching a game. Their money builds the stadium, pays the players' salaries, and provides the team owner with investment capital. The fans don't mind; they get their money's worth. Where else can they eat six-dollar hot dogs, drink five-dollar Cokes, and watch through rented seventeen-dollar binoculars as twenty-two millionaires purposely lose their tempers and try to hurt each other?

As soon as the game is over, the players and the fans leave the stadium and resume their lives. But for the few hours they are inside the stadium, everyone operates under a specific set of rules; everyone comes into agreement with the football rule book.

Life lived in agreement with God is similar. God has made unbreakable, unconditional, and unlimited promises with mankind. But while

He has bound Himself to us, He will not force His will on us. We can choose to live within the security and comfort of God's will and experience the blessings of His promises. Or we can choose to live in disagreement, outside the boundaries of His promises, and forfeit those blessings—just as a football player can choose to play outside the rules and suffer the penalty of his choice.

Deuteronomy 30:14 says, *"But the word is very near you, in your mouth and in your heart, that you may observe it."* To say that something is in your mouth means that you can repeat it; you can recite it; you can understand it with your mind. To say that something is in your heart means that you can react to it with your whole being. God has placed His agreements within you so that you can say yes to Him and live a life of Yes in total obedience to His will.

Being in a relationship of agreement with God always works to your advantage. The life of Yes is a winning life. The greatest thing that you can do is to embrace it with all your heart, mind, and strength.

Before you can do that, however, you need to learn one lesson. To begin this lesson, turn the page and read the title of the next chapter.

CHAPTER FOUR

There Is a God, and You're Not Him

Several years ago I spoke at a particular church in Missouri, and as tradition would have it, the pastor took the speaker out to dinner after the evening service. We went to a Chinese buffet called the China Bowl, a large restaurant that seated about four hundred people. A long trough ran down the middle of the room, and everyone pulled up their chairs and grazed. It seemed like a perfect choice to me; I'm single, and anything that's not quick-cook noodles looks beautiful.

The food tasted great, and I thoroughly enjoyed the entire meal. But about an hour or so after I went back to my hotel room, I was sick. If you've ever had food poisoning, you know what I was experiencing. I didn't think anything could be more painful than dating. I was wrong.

The only way I can think to describe it is this: Imagine that your body is a nightclub and your stomach is the bouncer. The stomach gets ticked off and begins to systematically kick everything out. "That's it. I can't take it anymore! The noodles in the corner, get out! The cabbage hiding under the Jell-O, you're gone! You, chicken, and you, peppermint ice cream, you're out right after the cabbage!"

Everything began to eject with force. I was unbelievably sick. The restaurant should have been named the China Blow, because that's what it made me do.

I called a buddy of mine in Houston and told him I was so sick, I was sure I was going to have to spend the rest of my life in one of those plastic anticontamination bubbles. He helped me book a flight out of Missouri early the next morning. When I arrived in Houston, he picked me up at the airport and drove me straight to the emergency room. It was about 11:00 A.M. At that point I was so white, I was transparent.

I crawled up to the ER desk and told the lady sitting there, "I have food poisoning, and I've been up all night." She took one look at me, handed me a clipboard, and said, "Here, fill this out."

Emergency rooms are strange like that. A fellow could walk in with his own head severed from his body and tucked under his arm, and they would make him fill out the paperwork before they did anything to help him.

I sat in a chair and started filling in the blanks.

Next of kin? "Jim Shorts."

Sex? "No, I'm not married."

Race? "Not until I feel better."

In case of emergency, notify? "Doctor." Was that a trick question?

When my name was finally called, I followed a nurse into one of those little doctor rooms—you know, the kind with the little cot covered with white deli sandwich paper.

"Put this on," the nurse told me as she handed me an extremely attractive, highly ventilated hospital gown.

Once in the gown, I knew I had at least forty-five minutes to kill (that's the way it is in these places), so I looked around to see how I could best use my time. I thumbed through the medical magazine that was on the counter, but not before I pulled the cotton off the ends of all the swabs in the drawer and licked all the tongue depressors and put them back in the jar. I was trying to decipher the origami I'd made with the deli sandwich paper when the doctor came in.

"Well, how are you?" he asked.

How was I? I wanted to say, "I'm just fine, Doc. I had an extra four hundred dollars to throw away, so I thought I'd come in and play with your cool toys." Instead, I looked at him and said, "My stomach hurts."

He told me to lie back on the table and began poking on my stomach. Now there's one thing you need to know about me. I'm made up of two things: fat and bone. I have no muscle. I have to wear boots just so I can stand up. As the doctor continued to mash and poke on my abdomen, he kept asking, "Does this hurt?" Through clenched teeth I responded, "If you press on me any harder, you'll be able to feel my spine."

Finally he stopped and asked me what I thought was wrong. I wanted to say, "You're the guy with the coat that closes in the front. Why don't you tell me?" Instead I told him about eating at the mega-trough at the China Blow the night before.

"It's either MSG or DOG, but whatever it is, I'm sick," I said.

I asked him if he could fix me up with an elixir or some pills, and he did. A few hours later, I got on a plane and went on to my next speaking engagement feeling much better.

The saddest thing about the entire episode was that through it all, I was mad. I kept thinking, *Golly, what a terrible time for this to happen. Of all the places, of all the people, why me, why here, why now? What did I do to bring this on? And God, let me point out that I'm working for You here.*

I was irritated—despite the fact that I had a friend who met me at the airport and drove me to the hospital. Never mind that the doctor had the abilities to make me well, and I had insurance to help pay for the expenses. I was irritated because this sudden illness interrupted my agenda, my schedule. It threw a kink into my plans.

It usually takes some kind of interruption, some kind of irritation, for God to get our attention and teach us an important lesson. When we make plans for the weekend and things unexpectedly change, we usually get mad and react badly. But let me tell you, when that kind of thing happens, we're in a full-on God moment. When something interrupts our dreams and plans, God is using that moment to teach us one simple lesson—the one lesson that will keep our faith in the practical rather than the ethereal. The one lesson that will lead us to change from our pattern of living for self to a pattern of living for God.

Here's the lesson: *The world does not revolve around us.*

PART ONE: THE HEART OF YES

We are not the center of the world. The world revolves around God and His purposes. There is a God, but we're not Him. Too often we make Christianity all about us. "How is God going to treat me? What am I going to get out of it? When is He going to answer my prayer?" We are children of God, but the world does not revolve around our plans. It revolves around God's purposes in our lives. He's not here for me; I'm here for Him.

In chapter 2 we talked about Josiah, a young man who became a king at an early age. Despite his royalty, he faced many of the same life situations we regularly face. Yet God taught him three lessons that helped him understand that he was not the center of his world. The same three lessons can help us understand that we're not the center of our worlds either.

Josiah was only eight years old when he was crowned king of Judah, following the evil reigns of his father and grandfather. For seventy-five years the temple—the place where the people of Israel went to worship the one true God—had been closed. All the gold had been stripped from it, and no one worshiped there anymore.

The temple had been built intentionally in the center of the city. It was supposed to be a constant reminder to the people that God was at the very center of their daily lives. It was the city's most dominant piece of architecture and could be seen for miles away. But by the time Josiah became king, it had been shut down for decades.

The temple is a type and shadow of Christ's presence in our lives. He is supposed to be at the very center of all we are and have and do. Yet how many of us do what the people of Israel did for those seventy-five years that the temple was locked up? We shut Christ out of our lives and go on building careers and families and futures, giving Him little or no regard. We pray, "God, I know it's all about You. Better is one day in your courts than thousands elsewhere." But we don't date as if we mean it. We don't spend our weekends as if we mean it. It's as though we know that the temple is there, but we have locked it shut. We keep it locked, powering on through life, business as usual. We say,

"I know God is in charge, but He's up there, and this is my life down here. I'm going to do with my life what I want to do with it."

When Josiah was twenty-six years old, his heart was turned toward God through the preaching of the prophet Jeremiah. He decided to reopen the temple for worship. During the restoration process, workers found a scroll of the Book of Deuteronomy in which God makes one central promise: "If you will obey Me, if you will follow Me, if you will put Me first, your life will work. But if you live for yourself, if you do your own thing, you will surely suffer the consequences."

As the scroll was read to him, Josiah began to weep. Like many of us, he had been a good church kid. He had grown up to be a good man. The Bible says that he walked in the ways of David. He was good king. But even in his goodness, he had been living his life for himself. He had established his rule his way, for his glory and benefit, not God's. As he listened to the words of the Scripture, he began to see that even though he loved God, he had put himself first. He had neglected the presence of God.

Josiah began to realize three things about God's central place in all of life—the same three things we must discover if we're going to live in a way that honors God in all we do.

GOD IS IN CHARGE
BECAUSE OF HIS CHARACTER

Second Kings 22:18 says, *"Thus says the LORD God of Israel..."* God commands respect and obedience because of who He is. God is not one more cosmic parent that we all have to listen to. He's not a guy who is just a little bit taller than the largest NBA player. If that's all He is, then we can get around Him. But He's so much more. He is God. He is different from us.

God is uncreated. He has no beginning and no end. *We* are created. We have a beginning, and we have an end. If we could break through the solar system and clear away everything but the pure presence of

God, all we would find on the other side is more of God. He is the original. You and I are the derivatives, the knockoffs, the ones made in His image.

There is no god like our God. We live in a culture that says all gods are equal, but that's just not true. God didn't win a lottery to become God. He didn't win on a ballot or in a popularity contest. No one elected Him, and no one gives their approval for Him to remain God. He is God. And because He is God, He can do what He pleases.

Every person down through history who has claimed to be God is dead. Everyone who has claimed to be God's son in our day and age has worn eyeglasses. That dude in Guyana wore prescriptions. The other guy in Waco, Texas—yep, he wore glasses too. All I'm saying is that if you're trying to convince the world that you're the Messiah, we'd better not catch you in LensCrafters. If you're Jesus, you better have good eyesight.

God is independent; we are dependent. We need food, shelter, warmth, clothing. We need to be shielded from the weather when it's stormy. We need protection from any number of things that are out of our direct control. But God is not controlled by the laws of time and nature. He isn't controlled by this world at all. He exists above and beyond everything we know. The Scripture says that God holds everything we see and can't see in the palm of His hand—singular. It all fits in just one hand.

God is God, and man is man. (*Thank you, Doctor Insight.*) No matter how hard we try, we can never become God. But we must never forget that God did have the power to become a man—and He did. He stepped into this world in the form of Jesus Christ. The intangible became tangible. The invisible became visible. Jesus came into this world and touched our sin, our screw-ups, and our struggles. He took them to the cross with Him. He was God in the flesh. Because God is not limited by the world, He was able to step into the world and bring salvation.

This message has to click on in our souls. We must come to realize that we are not free to spend our weekends any way we choose. We're not at liberty to do anything we like with our money and our time and our bodies. When we are irritated because something doesn't work out the way we planned, we need to recognize that God is trying to get our attention. He's saying, "This world doesn't revolve around you; it revolves around Me."

GOD IS IN CHARGE
IN THE MIDST OF OUR BAD CHOICES

For seventy-five years the people of Israel had been living selfishly, doing their own thing. They had not only neglected the temple; more importantly, they had neglected the very presence of God in their lives. Despite this, God was still God.

I grew up being taught that anytime I sinned, God withdrew Himself from me. He was offended and couldn't talk with me. So whenever I made a mistake, I freaked out and said, "God, I'm sorry. Really, I am." And I would imagine God responding, "I don't feel like talking with you right now." I really believed that when I sinned, God turned away from me and stopped being God in my life. I've talked to many people who have felt the same way.

What I've learned, however, is that only people who think the world revolves around them actually believe their sins can keep God from being God. To think we can rebel and show God who's boss by our choices, that we can somehow keep Him from being God in our lives, is completely wrong.

You can't do something so terrible that you catch God off guard. You'll never hear Him say, "Oh, my! I thought I covered everything on the Cross, but now you've gone and done something that I don't quite know how to deal with. You've found a loophole that I didn't cover. I resign. I quit. I can't be God anymore in your life."

Even when we do wrong, God is God. His plan is still in effect. He is still in charge. When we blow it, He isn't shocked. When we sin big time, God doesn't turn His head. He knew we had it in us all the time.

When God's people blow it, He doesn't change places. He is still on the throne. He doesn't stop being God—but He does switch roles. God is both a God of blessing and a God of conviction. We get to choose which way we will know Him at any given point in our lives.

In 2 Kings 22:17, God convicted Josiah of his nation's sin: *"They have forsaken Me."* He told Josiah that he and his people had lived their own way for over seventy-five years. Today His message to us is the same: If we choose to live our own way, we are guaranteeing ourselves the experience of God's conviction.

I love Wal-Mart. Anything that's for sale in this world for one thousand dollars or more is available at Wal-Mart for $19.95 or less. (Sure, it's an imitation, but it's close enough. It's just going to end up in a garage sale anyway.) Usually when I finish speaking somewhere on a Sunday afternoon and have a couple of hours to kill, I go to the local Wal-Mart to walk around and relax. But I'm always puzzled by one thing: Who proclaimed Sunday afternoons at Wal-Mart "Beat Your Kid in Public Time"? I've heard of time-out being used as discipline but not knock-out. I've seen parents not just hitting their kids but hitting for distance.

I can't bust on parents too much though. Every time I've seen kids being scolded at Wal-Mart, it's because they were begging for a toy. Have you ever seen kids begging for a toy? They are up and down those aisles like a drug addict looking for a fix: "Please! Pleeeease! Buy me this toy, Mommy! I haven't had a new toy in days! If you buy it for me, I'll be your best friend!" Parents have no choice. They can't always be givers of toys and blessings. (Sometimes they have to switch roles— for their kids' own good.)

Think back to the days when you were a small child and did something really bad. Your parents didn't come home from work and resign from being parents. They didn't throw in the towel; they just switched roles.

My mom would switch in midsentence. We'd be talking about something like what we wanted to eat for dinner, and she'd say, "David, what would you like for—*stop right now and look at what you're doing! What are you thinking? You know not to do that!*" At that very second, the phone would ring, she would pick it up, and, without missing a beat, she would sweetly say, "Hellooo?"

That's how God works. He doesn't change who He is. He simply changes roles. We make the choice of how we will know Him. If we say, "I know You are a God of blessing, but I choose to put myself first," then He switches roles and becomes the God of conviction.

GOD IS IN CHARGE
THROUGH HIS COMPASSION

Josiah began to weep when the scroll of Deuteronomy was read because he realized that he had been selfish. As good as he was, as right as his motives were, he had been doing things his own way, not God's.

His proper response to God's conviction brought the promise of blessing. In 2 Kings 22:19–20, God told him, "'*Because your heart was tender and you humbled yourself before the* LORD *when you heard what I spoke against this place and against its inhabitants that they should become a desolation and a curse, and you have torn your clothes and wept before Me, I truly have heard you*', declares the LORD. '*Therefore, behold, I will gather you to your fathers, and you will be gathered to your grave in peace, and your eyes will not see all the evil which I will bring on this place.*'"

Josiah discovered God's compassion only after realizing that even his well-intentioned plans to be a good king served his own ends rather than God's. Once he properly responded to that conviction and came into agreement, God promised to pour out His compassion on him by bringing peace both to Josiah's life and to the lives of his people. And true to His word, God unleashed forty years of peace and prosperity on the land of Israel.

Most of us are like Josiah. In fact, when we sit in church, we are surrounded by a room full of Josiahs. We may be good people. We may be looked upon as role models for others. We may even be church leaders. But when we take a closer look at ourselves, we realize that we are still selfish at the very core.

God will not let selfishness slide. He will confront it in our lives. He will point it out, put His finger on it, and remind us that we are not our own; we have been bought with a price. When we finally come to the end of our selfishness, we will discover the same thing Josiah did: the unreserved compassion of God. When God's control is unleashed in our lives, blessings flow through His unbridled compassion.

- To the ones who've been emotionally damaged: God declares them whole.

- To the ones who've made bad choices in life: God declares them forgiven.

- To the ones who've been rejected: God declares them loved.

- To the ones who've tainted their own private lives: God declares them pure.

- To the selfish ones: God declares them righteous.

Today God invites us to humble our selfish wills and say yes to a life lived in agreement with Him. As we do we'll find that blessings flow from the recognition of that one profound truth: He is God—and we are not.

PART TWO

THE HOPE
OF YES

PART TWO

A Promise Kept

"I know that's what you said, but I don't believe that's what you meant."

Most of us say or think that statement more times a day than we realize. Advertising has conditioned us to believe very little of what we hear, see, or read. Nothing ever measures up to the claims made.

In relationships we automatically listen for what's *not* being said. If we don't, we miss the real intent of any conversation, which is always found in the stuff between the lines. Sometimes a girl will tell the guy she's dating that she loves him, only to call off the relationship a week later. Then when he protests, "But I thought you loved me," she says, "Well, I do love you. But my love for you is the kind of love that ends when you leave the room."

People seem to have different meanings for the same words. Women might say, "I *like* him, but I really don't *like* him." "I *kissed* him, but I didn't, you know, *kiss* him." And the guys say, "Well, I spent money…MONEY!"

Relationships are complicated. They can be more difficult to figure out than the plot of a Fellini film. I'm not Doctor Relationship (or Dr. Phil for that matter), but I have managed to break the code guys and girls use to speak to each other. Knowing the code can simplify things immensely.

When she says, "Does this make me look fat?" what she really means is, "You'd better say no, or this will be the worst evening of your life."

When she says, "Wherever you want to go will be fine," what she really means is, "No matter what restaurant you pick, you'll be wrong."

When she says, "I don't want to talk about it," she means, "I don't know what's bothering me, but whatever it is, it's all your fault."

When she says, "You're such a good friend," she means, "There's no chance of us making out."

When he says, "I'm really busy," he means, "I can't right now. *Sports Center* is on."

When he says, "It's not you; it's me," he means, "It's you."

When he says, "I'll call you," he means, "Have a nice life."

When he says, "You're perfect for me," he means, "No one else will put up with me."

When he says, "Will you marry me?" what he really means is, "My roommates have moved out, there's no food in the kitchen, and I can't find the remote."

When it comes to our experience with God, we automatically assume that He's like everyone else we know. What He says, He doesn't really mean. We listen to Him, but we think that in order to really hear what He means, we must put His words through our filter of selective suspicion. But God always says exactly what He means, and He means everything He says. The bottom line is, we can believe God. When God makes a promise, He keeps it.

God has only one plan, and He has followed that plan since day one of Creation. The Old Testament is not God's first plan that didn't work out. The New Testament is not God's cosmic do-over plan. The plan of God has been unchanged since He made His first agreement with Adam and Eve. We're the ones who have the difficulty grasping His consistency. Each of the four agreements God made with mankind is a part of the one thing He's been doing since the beginning of time.

Paul begins the Book of Romans like this: *"Paul, a bond-servant of Christ Jesus, called as an apostle, set apart for the gospel of God, which He promised beforehand through His prophets in the Holy Scriptures."*

(Romans 1:1–2). In this brief passage, he lets us know that the prophets of the Old Testament were speaking the words of God for their time. The Old Testament was the Bible for the New Testament people, the people of Jesus' and Paul's day. One of Paul's tasks in his letter to the Romans was to clearly show the continuity and consistency of God's plan throughout Hebrew history. In the first few verses of Romans, he successfully lays out the beauty of God's singular plan for the redemption of the world and mankind.

A PROMISE MADE

Set apart for the gospel of God, which He promised beforehand through His prophets in the holy Scriptures. (Romans 1:1–2)

Finding people who say what they mean and mean what they say is harder than finding a phonograph needle in a CD Wherehouse. The way people communicate these days, it's hard for us to understand each other's words, much less trust that they're true.

I travel almost every day, and I have become quite good at figuring out from what nationality people originate. Talking with people from all over the world is really quite fascinating. Not long ago I was staying at a hotel owned by a man whose nametag had all consonants and one symbol that looked like a derivative of the periodic symbol for cobalt. The hotel was nice and promised 100 percent customer satisfaction. I had just about reached the 90 percent point when I went down to the front desk to get a couple of extra towels. It was late at night, and the woman at the front desk had a nine-inch-wide nametag with more of those strange symbols.

"Could I please have a couple of extra towels?" I asked.

The lady looked at me as if I was speaking a foreign language. Then she started speaking back to me in what sounded like Morse code: "Click, clickety, click."

It was obvious that she didn't have the foggiest idea what I needed, so I pretended to hold a towel with both hands and made a back-and-forth motion as if I were drying my back. "Towel," I said. "I need a couple of towels." Again she clicked her lack of understanding: "Click, click, clicky, clickety."

I made another attempt at hotel lobby charades and pretended to dry my leg, all the while saying, "Towel. I need two towels." She still didn't understand, but at least she stopped clicking and simply shrugged her shoulders. I pretended to roll up a towel and flick it as if I were popping someone in a towel fight. I looked at her with raised eyebrows, asking in silent, universal language, "Do you understand?" This time she just mimicked my facial expressions.

I thought for another moment and then began to make circular motions with my hand over my head, pretending to wrap my head in a towel. Her eyes instantly brightened and she pointed at me, crying triumphantly, *"Towel!"*

I'm not busting on any particular culture. And I'm sure not busting on people who are trying to learn the English language. The hotel lobby clerks who speak "good English" and have relatives who came over on the Mayflower still show signs of their origin. Once when I was checking out of a hotel, I attempted to make a reservation with the front desk clerk for a room two weeks later, since I knew I'd be returning to the same city.

"Fine, sir," she said. "What level would you like?"

Her question caught me off guard, and without thinking I answered, "Well, I travel almost every day and have gotten quite good at sleeping in hotel beds. So don't put me down as a beginner; you'd better sign me up as an advanced sleeper."

"Do you have a smoking preference?" she asked.

"I don't smoke," I said, "but I hear the ones with filters are better for you."

These days you have to qualify exactly what you mean by a non-smoking room. When I say nonsmoking, I mean a room that has never been smoked in, not a room that hasn't been smoked in recently. Nor do I mean a room that smells like someone charbroiled a curried rat on an open Hibachi.

CHAPTER FIVE: *A Promise Kept*

Fortunately, there's no misunderstanding Paul's statement in Romans 1. He clearly articulates the consistency of God's plan to win the world back to Himself. The four eternal agreements God made with mankind in the Old Testament form a common thread that can be traced from the beginning of time down to the heart of every man, woman, boy, and girl alive today. And these agreements are clear. God uses universal language we all can understand when He centers His promises on the concept of a simple seed. Let's take a look back at the four agreements and notice how God uses the word *seed* to communicate His promises.

GOD AND ADAM

God created a perfect place for Adam and Eve to live. Everything they could possibly need or want was provided for them for the taking. The Garden of Eden didn't require much in the way of work, just a bit of tending to. Perfectly balanced nutrition, clear water, always the perfect weather—God had thought of everything.

We don't know exactly how long it was before the first man and woman ate from the tree that God had forbidden them to touch. What we do know is that both Adam and Eve chose what they wanted over what God wanted. That evening, when God came for His daily walk with them, He found them hiding; their eyes had been opened, and for the first time, they knew they were naked.

God cast Adam and Eve out of the Garden and cursed them by limiting the number of years they would live; marrying them to survival through the production of their hands; causing pain in childbirth; and placing conflict and discord in their relationship with one another. God also cursed the serpent, Satan, for tempting them to rebel and promised that even though Satan would bruise mankind, God would bring Someone into the world—His *seed*—who would crush Satan's head: *"I will put enmity between you and the woman, and between your seed and her seed; He shall bruise you on the head, and you shall bruise him on the heel"* (Genesis 3:15).

In this one statement, God was pointing to His promise of salvation for all mankind. Just before expelling Adam and Eve from the Garden, He clothed them with animal skins: *"The LORD God made garments of skin for Adam and his wife, and clothed them"* (Genesis 3:21). This action was a type and shadow of the coming Sacrifice that would be required to bring salvation into the world.

GOD AND ABRAM

Even though he was old and his body showed the distinct signs of aging, Abram never gave up on the promise God made to him. Very late one night, God had met with Abram and promised to protect him, provide everything he and his family would ever need, promote him into a great nation, and prosper him and all his descendants: *"I will establish My covenant between Me and you and your descendants* [or *seed*, as the King James Version says] *after you"* (Genesis 17:7).

Abram's wife, Sarai, was past childbearing age, so Abram tried to help God fulfill His promise by having a son with Sarai's younger handmaiden. But God didn't need help. Instead, God supernaturally allowed Sarah to conceive, providing Abraham with the son He had promised. Through Abraham's *seed*, a great nation, Israel, was birthed; and through Israel, all the nations of the world have been blessed. Abraham's *seed* made it possible for every person in every nation to experience the salvation of God.

GOD AND DAVID

Although he was young, David was chosen by God to be the second king of Israel. God even had the prophet Samuel anoint David before the first king, Saul, was dead. David went to live in Saul's royal court and served as the king's court musician. Over the course of his life, he wrote many of the songs that are recorded in the Book of Psalms. After Saul's death David assumed the throne as God intended, and throughout his reign he conquered many enemies and amassed a great fortune. The nation of Israel was truly blessed under David's leadership.

One day David became burdened over the contrast between his ornate palace and the temple of God, which was a simple tent in the middle of town. David purposed in his heart to build a permanent house for God; but before he could get started, God spoke to him: *"When your days are complete and you lie down with your fathers, I will raise up your descendant* [again, *seed* in the King James Version] *after you, who will come forth from you, and I will establish his kingdom. He shall build a house for My name, and I will establish the throne of his kingdom forever"* (2 Samuel 7:12–13).

God made this agreement with David and promised that the One He would raise up, his *seed*, would sit on his throne forever. *"The LORD has sworn to David a truth from which He will not turn back; 'Of the fruit of your body* [literally, *seed*] *I will set upon your throne'"* (Psalm 132:11). God was telling David that He had a much larger plan than just building a house of worship in Jerusalem. His plan included establishing His rule over all mankind forever through the *seed* of David.

GOD AND JEREMIAH

For most of his life, Jeremiah carried out his ministry as a prophet being misunderstood and feared by the people he ministered to. His life was hard, but his relationship with God was stronger than the hardships he faced. He was faithful to proclaim every word God gave him, despite the lack of respect he received from the leaders and the people of Israel.

One of the messages Jeremiah spoke was this: *"'Behold, days are coming,' declares the LORD, 'when I will sow the house of Israel and the house of Judah with the seed of man'"* (Jeremiah 31:27). Israel had been unfaithful to God and had broken covenant with Him many times. Yet God declared to Jeremiah that He would remain faithful to His agreements and create for Himself a nation out of the *seed* of Adam and Abraham, under the rule of the *seed* of David. Then He added, *"I will put My law within them and on their heart I will write it; and I will be their God, and they shall be My people.... 'for I will forgive their iniquity, and their sin I will remember no more'"* (Jeremiah 31:33–34).

As we can see from these brief reviews of God's agreements with Adam, Abraham, David, and Jeremiah, from the time God closed the Garden of Eden, He has been doing one thing: bringing about His purpose of winning the world back to Himself. The four agreements are not human creations; they're God's creations—God's words revealing God's purpose for the world. God will accomplish His plan His way, in His timing.

People ask me all the time, "If God is all-powerful, why didn't He just put everything back the way He originally created it? Why go to all the trouble of making agreements with mankind? And why does He take so long to fulfill His agreements?" Second Peter 3:9 gives us the answer to that last question: *"The Lord is not slow about His promise, as some count slowness, but is patient toward you, not wishing for any to perish but for all to come to repentance."*

God's plan of redemption didn't begin with us. His faultless, perfect plan has been in place for thousands of years. God responded to the rebellion of Adam and Eve by beginning a process that would guarantee the completion of His divine purposes.

Throughout the Old Testament, God made promises and proved Himself faithful to keep His promises over and over again. In the same pages of Scripture, man's unfaithfulness stands in stark contrast. God uses perfectly timed and spaced repetition of man's inability to be faithful and of His own perfect faithfulness to demonstrate mankind's desperate and undeniable need of God. He uses the passing of years to establish His plan in the full view of all creation. He uses time to lock into our understanding that the fulfillment of all His agreements is found in one Person—one Seed. God has remained faithful to all four of His eternal agreements. His Seed truly fulfills the promises made to Adam, Abraham, David, and Jeremiah.

A PROMISE KEPT

His Son, who was born of a descendant of David according to the flesh, who was declared the Son of God with power by the resurrection from the dead, according to the Spirit of holiness, Jesus Christ our Lord. (Romans 1:3–4)

According to the Bible, Jesus Christ is God's Seed that came into the world. His arrival serves as the single most significant division of all of history. Jesus is the dividing point, the point of demarcation. Before Him all of creation looked forward to His coming as the promised Seed of God. Since His arrival all of creation looks to Him as the completion and fulfillment of God's eternal agreements with mankind.

Our world is filled with gods crying out for worshipers. A surprising number of people believe that all that's required of them is to choose which god they will worship and then stick with their choice for as long as they believe they have picked the right one. The name of their god is not important; what *is* important is their belief that the god they have chosen is the right one for them—at least for that time and season in their lives.

It's considered offensive these days to tell anyone that Jesus is the only way to reach the Father in heaven. Even many well-meaning church members rebuke their pastors for preaching the truth that Jesus is the way, the truth, and the life, and that no one comes to the Father except through Him (see John 14:6).

All world religions have value. They all contribute something. Buddhism will help you achieve a state of nirvana through the practice of its philosophy; Islam will teach you discipline through the study of its five pillars; Mormonism will make you a better bike rider. All religions have value but not for salvation. They don't impact eternity. Only Christianity offers the doorway into heaven. Only Jesus fulfills all of God's agreements and paves the way for the redemption of the world.

Jesus isn't one among many gods who can save us. He isn't who He is because He happened to be in the right place at the right time. As we said in a previous chapter, He didn't get to be the Son of God by winning a lottery. I mean, can you imagine the following scenario?

God wants to find a Savior, so He establishes a committee of angels who wade through the résumés of thousands of potential candidates and finally pick twelve finalists. After notifying the finalists, they set up twelve mock thrones on the platform of the universe. With more fanfare than the writer of "Pomp and Circumstance" could have ever conceived of, they introduce the finalists to the audience of the cosmos.

Each finalist makes his or her entrance to thunderous applause: Buddha, Mohammad, Joseph Smith, Confucius, the Dahli Lama, a few of the more powerful Greek gods, and finally, Jesus Christ.

The applause tapers off and the excitement mounts as the Plexiglas God-Lotto box is rolled to center stage. The finalists sit in all their splendor. *What must be going through their minds at this very moment?* the audience wonders. As the timpani drums roll, the spotlights move in unison from the farthest boundaries of creation to focus on the one small, clear box.

The smiling emcee begins to explain exactly what is at stake this night. Then a switch is thrown, and a powerful fan begins to move twelve Ping-Pong balls in random flight inside the box. They bounce against the clear walls, almost as if they are fighting against each other to be selected. The millions of spectators pray silently to the god of random order, making all manner of vain promises: "If you will just select my god, I promise to..."

Finally, after what can only be described as an eternal moment, one ball is swept up into the tube of decision. The tube has been blacked out, however, to ensure that no one knows the winner before the official announcement. The emcee makes his way over to the box and removes the one Ping-Pong ball from the tube, covering it with his hand. Again the timpani rolls, and the emcee holds up the ball in his clenched fist.

"And the winner is...Jesus Christ! Jesus, it looks like you win. Congratulations!"

The other finalists make halfhearted attempts at courteous applause but fail to hide their bitter disappointment. Jesus makes His way to center stage and stands beside the emcee. A beautiful angel hands Him a large bouquet of flowers. He wipes a tear from His eye as the music swells and the emcee sings, "There He is, God of everything!" Then Jesus begins his walk down the runway of the stars, where one of the spectators closest to the stage overhears Him whisper, "I can't believe I won. I'm the God of the universe!"

OK, so this scene didn't really happen. There never was a God-Lotto. It was actually a Scratch-N-Win. (Just kidding.)

CHAPTER FIVE: *A Promise Kept*

Jesus Christ is the one and only fulfillment of all the promises God made in the Old Testament. The writers of the New Testament recognized this. They identified Jesus as the Seed in each of the agreements made with Adam, Abraham, David, and Jeremiah.

THE SEED OF ADAM

For as in Adam all die, so also in Christ all will be made alive.
(1 Corinthians 15:22)

In this passage Adam and Christ are portrayed as representatives. This means they're acting for other people, and all who are related to them are affected by their actions. The first Adam gave up his right to be a son of God and opened the door to sin and darkness. Jesus, the second Adam, came to undo the work of the first Adam.

After their rebellion God promised Adam and Eve that He would send His Seed, the One who would crush the head of the serpent, Satan. God's Seed, Jesus, came and fulfilled this agreement through His death, burial, and resurrection. *"Therefore, since the children share in flesh and blood, He himself likewise also partook of the same, that through death He might render powerless him who had the power of death, that is, the devil"* (Hebrews 2:14). On the cross Jesus "crushed the head of the serpent" and conquered the one who held the power over death, the grave, and hell. After He fulfilled the agreement, He was able to say, *"All authority has been given to Me in heaven and on earth"* (Matthew 28:18).

THE SEED OF ABRAHAM

Now the promises were spoken to Abraham and to his seed. He does not say, "And to seeds," as referring to many, but rather to one, "And to your seed," that is, Christ. (Galatians 3:16)

Millions have been born from the seed of Abraham and his son Isaac. But even though the people of Israel have been the beneficiaries of God's faithfulness for thousands of years, they are not the fulfillment of God's agreement with Abraham. Jesus is the Seed. He is the fulfillment of God's plan to protect and provide, promote and prosper His people. All those who come to Jesus Christ are assured of receiving the protection, provision, promotion, and prosperity God promised to Abraham.

THE SEED OF DAVID

> Concerning His Son, who was born of a descendant of David according to the flesh. (Romans 1:3)

Jesus was a direct descendant of King David. In perhaps his greatest sermon, Peter picked up on this truth and spoke of David when he said, "And so, because he was a prophet and knew that GOD HAD SWORN TO HIM WITH AN OATH TO SEAT one OF HIS DESCENDANTS [literally translated, seed] ON HIS THRONE, he looked ahead and spoke of the resurrection of the Christ....This Jesus God raised up again....Therefore having been exalted to the right hand of God, and having received from the Father the promise of the Holy Spirit, He has poured forth this which you both see and hear" (Acts 2:30–33).

David is remembered as Israel's greatest king of all time. But even though David established Israel as a dominant world power in his day, he knew his reign would one day come to an end. His power, his rule, and his influence would fade, and ultimately, he would be replaced by someone else. He was able to look ahead and realize that God would fulfill His promise to him through God's own Seed, Jesus Christ, who was also from the lineage of David. The throne of Christ would not be over Israel alone, but over all of heaven and earth.

THE SEED OF JEREMIAH

> For this reason He is the mediator of a new covenant, so that, since a death has taken place for the redemption of the transgressions that were committed under the first covenant, those who have been called may receive the promise of the eternal inheritance. (Hebrews 9:15)

Our ability to know God and to experience the living presence of His Holy Spirit is made possible because God sent His Seed, Jesus

Christ, to become the mediator of a new agreement with mankind. The term *mediator* means that Jesus is the implementer and enforcer of the promises of the new agreement. He watches over these promises to make certain they are activated in our lives. Because Jesus is the fulfillment of God's agreement with Jeremiah, we can have our sins forgiven and know the indwelling presence of God through His Holy Spirit. God can write His law on our hearts, and we can have the full rights and privileges of being sons and daughters of God.

Not one single promise made by God in the Old Testament is waiting to be fulfilled. Every one of them has already been fulfilled by Jesus Christ. *"For as many as are the promises of God, in Him they are yes; therefore also through Him is our Amen to the glory of God through us"* (2 Corinthians 1:20). God made the agreements; Jesus is the content and the realization of those agreements. There's no need to guess about whether or not God has any unfinished business with mankind. Jesus is God's final act. God's plan is completely completed. Romans 8:31–32 says, *"If God is for us, who is against us? He who did not spare His own Son, but delivered Him over for us all, how will He not also with Him freely give us all things?"* God withheld nothing—not even His only Son—to ensure that His promises and agreements were kept.

A PROMISE RECEIVED

To bring about the obedience of faith…you also are the called of Jesus Christ. (Romans 1:5–6)

Jesus Christ is the Seed of God. He is the salvation promised to Adam; He is the success promised to Abraham; He is the strength promised to David; and He is the Spirit promised to Jeremiah, making it possible for anyone who believes in Christ to be called a child of God. By coming into agreement with God and placing our full dependence on Jesus, we receive the blessing and power of all of God's promises. We truly become God's people. And through us, God continues to propagate His plan to redeem mankind.

AS THE SEED OF ADAM, JESUS REMOVES SIN

Under the old agreement, priests used the blood of animal sacrifices to symbolically and temporarily cover people's sins. This was how God made a way for men and women to experience a relationship with Him. In the new agreement, Jesus' death on the cross completely removes sin once and for all. Only through the perfect sacrifice of Jesus Christ is our relationship with God made possible.

AS THE SEED OF ABRAHAM, JESUS RELEASES BLESSING

Every aspect of success that we experience—whether in relationships, careers, or any other arena of life—is a direct result of what Christ did in His death, burial, and resurrection. His victory enables us to win and be successful. We must never forget that our ability to succeed is not a function of our own talent. It does not rest in our own power, and it is not focused on our own purposes. Rather, it originates from God's resources that have been released to us through His promises, and it is focused on His purpose to win mankind and creation back to Himself.

AS THE SEED OF DAVID, JESUS REIGNS WITH AUTHORITY

The strength that we receive to overcome trials and temptations is a direct result of Jesus reigning with authority over heaven and earth. Our ability to persevere comes to us because the Ruler of the universe, the One who has unlimited power and strength, lives within us. His power reigns in our hearts and minds and ultimately finds its way into our choices and actions, impacting the way we think and act in our families, our churches, and our governments.

AS THE SEED OF JEREMIAH, JESUS RULES THROUGH PEOPLE

When we place our faith in Jesus, we become the beneficiaries of all the agreements of God. That means more than simply getting the blessings of the promises. It means that our status is changed. We don't just get something; we *become someone*. We become the channels God is committed to use to bring about His eternal purposes. Everything God wants us to be, He declares us to be in Christ. Everything God expects us to do to extend His presence in the world, He declares we are already able to do in Christ. We have been born again; He has recreated us to be the containers of His presence and the fulfillers of His purpose.

Because the indwelling Christ resides in us, God is literally establishing His rule in the world through us. As we say yes to God and live our lives in agreement with Him, He lives, rules, and reigns through us everywhere we go and in everything we do.

Sometime ago there was a young man in Houston who developed a revolutionary new business. The success of this business made him and his young wife extremely wealthy. They began to buy impressive homes, land, and furnishings, as well as many priceless works of art and sculpture.

Several years passed, and the man's wife became pregnant. *Finally,* they thought, *all the wealth we've amassed, all the properties we've purchased, and all the hard work we've put into the business will have real meaning and purpose.* They looked forward to sharing everything with their child.

The pregnancy proceeded without incident, and the night finally came when the man's wife woke him up and said it was time for the baby to be born. He drove her to the hospital, where the medical staff admitted her and whisked her into the delivery room.

He took a seat in an adjacent room and waited anxiously for news that his child had been born. Hours passed, and a doctor finally appeared. "Your wife is having quite a bit of difficulty giving birth," the doctor said, "but we're there with her, and we'll keep you informed."

The man paced back and forth in the waiting room and prayed. A few hours later, the doctor returned. He placed his hand on the man's shoulder and said, "You are the father of a baby boy." Ecstatic, the man breathed a sigh of relief. Then the doctor continued gravely: "Unfortunately, your wife died during childbirth."

The man's blank look mirrored the disbelief that registered in his mind and heart.

"I'm so sorry," the doctor said.

Silence filled the waiting room. The man closed his eyes as if trying to escape the reality of the moment.

"There's more," the doctor said. The man opened his eyes.

"Your son was born with Down syndrome."

It seemed too much for the man to bear. But over the next few days, as he went through the motions of burying his wife, he did his best to accept the truth: Life would never be the same.

The man brought his son home from the hospital and hired a nanny to care for the boy during the days. In the evenings he would come home from work and spend many hours with his son, playing with him and reading to him. He grew to love his son so deeply that over the years that followed, meeting the boy's special needs was never a burden.

As the boy neared his sixteenth birthday, the man commissioned an artist to paint his son's portrait. It was a very large painting, and the man put it over the mantel in his den. Everyone who came to visit couldn't help but notice the painting of the boy—the odd-shaped head, the childish smile. Somehow the very presence of the painting made most visitors uncomfortable. But the father loved his son, and he loved having the picture displayed in such a prominent place.

Not long after his twenty-fifth birthday, the son became ill and died. The grieving father stood by the grave and wondered what would bring meaning to life now that his only child was gone. He continued on with his successful business, but every accomplishment seemed empty without his son to share it with.

The man lived out the rest of his life alone, carrying his grief to his grave. After his death a large estate sale was scheduled in accordance with his will. His famous art collection was put on the auction block, and people from all over the country flew in for the sale.

The auctioneer called the sale to order, and everyone took their seats. The room fell silent as the auctioneer opened the first of two white envelopes handed to him by the estate's lawyer. The note inside was read aloud: "The painting of my son must be sold before anything else in the estate."

The disappointed whispers of the crowd dampened the enthusiasm of the sale. The auctioneer could actually see irritation on many faces. He placed the painting of the boy on an easel and began, "What am I bid for this painting?"

No one said a word. As serious art collectors, the bidders knew the painting had no value. They sat with their backs against their chairs, arms folded in frustration as they waited for the real auction to get under way.

Finally, the auctioneer asked, "Will someone start the bidding at five dollars?"

A woman in the back of the room raised her hand. It was the boy's nanny. "I loved the boy," she said. "I'll start the bidding."

No one else made a move, and the auctioneer counted down the bid.

"Five dollars going once, twice, sold!"

The rest of the bidders sat up in their seats, ready now to get to the real works of art. That's when the auctioneer opened the second white envelope and read the note: "To the individual who purchased the painting of my son, I bequeath all of my possessions. The auction is over."

The man had loved his son so much that he'd made accepting his son the prerequisite for getting everything else in his estate. The real value of his estate was not in the art or the properties; it was in his son. Whoever had the son had everything else his estate encompassed.

It's exactly the same way with God. Whoever has His Son has been born again and given full citizenship in His eternal kingdom. Whoever receives God's Son receives all that God has. The One who completed the singular task God has been about since the creation of the world brings into our lives the purpose and power of God. Whoever has the Son of God has life.

From the beginning of time, God has been drawing a line through human history. The line began with Adam and Abraham and remained constant through the lives of David and Jeremiah. God continues to draw His line through us today. And as He does, He says to the world: "I am the God of the universe, and I am your God. I have loved you, pursued you, and done everything necessary to bring you back to Myself. I have paid the highest price to ensure that you return to Me. I am seeking people who will say yes to Me. I am seeking those who will choose to live a life of agreement with My will."

At one time or another, God's line touches every individual, extending His personal invitation to come into agreement with Him through Jesus Christ. When you and I say yes to God, we become the beneficiaries of all of His agreements. We begin to live a life of Yes.

A Life of Agreement

Back in the spring of 1993, I received a call from a buddy of mine in Georgia, requesting that I come and do a summer youth camp on Jekyll Island. I was just beginning my ministry as a speaker and my calendar was free, so I accepted.

A few days before the camp was to begin, I left Oklahoma City and headed east in a 1985 Ford LTD. It was a huge car. About seventy could ride in it comfortably. If the trip went a bit longer than expected, I figured I didn't have to worry; the trunk could double as an efficiency apartment.

It took me three days to drive to Jekyll Island. When I crossed over the bridge from the Georgia mainland, I had about two hours to spare before I was scheduled to speak. That's when the LTD began to break. Things began to fly off—molding, bolts, belts, smoke. Stuff I never knew was on a car began to fall off mine.

I managed to coast into a little strip mall made up of several small shops and a Laundromat. I was scared. I'd never been in that part of the country before in my life. As I opened my door and got out, smoke poured out from under my car. I glanced up at the store signs and spotted a Shop-N-Lift (a Thrifty-Theft, a Rip-N-Run, a Stop-N-Steal—you know, a convenience store). I went inside and asked the clerk for a phone book so I could call a mechanic.

Thumbing through the pages, I found the number of a mechanic in a little town just a few miles away. When he answered the phone, I said, "Listen, man, I'm over on Jekyll Island, and my car is broken!"

"What's wrong with it?" he asked.

"Well, it's broken," I repeated.

"Can ya be a little more specific?"

"Yeah," I said, "when I go out and sit in my car, and I sit there for a long time, and then I get out, I'm in the same place I started."

"OK," he chuckled. "But Ah really need ya t' give me some idea of what the problem is."

I don't know anything about cars except where the gas goes, and that's only because my mom showed me when I first got my driver's license. But the mechanic was insistent that I give him at least a general idea of what was wrong. I hung up the phone and walked back outside to the LTD.

I really had no idea where to start, so I did the only thing I could think to do: I lifted the hood. The car had stopped smoking by now, so I had an unobstructed view of whatever it was that I didn't have a clue I was looking for. Maybe I could find an on/off switch? ("Oh, here's the problem—the switch is off. Who knew?") Finally, after several minutes of staring blankly, I closed the hood and went back into the store to call the mechanic again.

"Yeah, this is the guy on Jekyll Island with the car that doesn't run," I said.

"OK," the mechanic replied. "So what do ya think is wrong?"

"As best I can tell," I told him, "my propeller is broken." (I'm not making this up.)

There was a long silence.

"Excuse me?"

Like a dork, I repeated myself. "My propeller is broken. When I turn the key on, I don't hear any clicking, and nothing is turning."

He must have had pity on me, because he answered, "I'll be right out there."

A few minutes later, the mechanic pulled up in a tow truck. It was no ordinary tow truck; it was a *south Georgia* tow truck: candy apple red with huge chrome mag wheels, a custom eight-track in the dash, a rebel flag on the hood, and a horn that played the theme song from *The Dukes of Hazard*. Get the picture?

He rolled up beside my car and stepped out of the cab. This guy had the full-on mechanic's look: blue shirt with his name embroidered over the left pocket, ball cap with the logo of the local auto-parts dealer, and pants that were well below his...well, waist.

Finally, he hooked up my car and towed it to his shop. I called my buddy at the youth camp, and he came and got me. Amazingly, I made it to the camp just in time to speak.

A couple of days later, the mechanic called me with the news that my car was ready to be picked up. My buddy drove me over to the shop, and sure enough, there it sat, looking ready to go. The mechanic came out to meet me, and I asked him, "Does it work now?"

"It sure does," he said. "Lemme tell ya what Ah did to 'er."

He started reading off a list that was so long, my ADD kicked in. About halfway through, I interrupted him.

"Excuse me, but I really don't want to know everything you had to do to fix it," I said. "I just want to know if it works."

"Git on in and start 'er up," he said.

I sat down in the car and turned the key. The engine fired up and purred like a kitten. The LTD had never run so smooth. The mechanic motioned to me, so I left the car running and got out. He opened the hood and pointed to the engine.

"Looky here," he said. "Yer propeller works."

Does it work? That's the question most of us ask whenever we look at something that makes us wonder (a car engine, for example). I believe it's the same question people ask when they look at believers in Christ. The world wants to know, "This whole Jesus thing, this whole Christian-life thing—does it really work? If I take it on, will it really change my life? If I commit myself to it, will it make my life different? Will it make my life better?"

The Scripture says that God has *"set eternity"* in people's hearts (Ecclesiastes 3:11). This means we all come into the world with the supernatural knowledge that something is broken. We come into this world sensing that something is not right, that we have a hole in our hearts. The church claims to have the answers to life's biggest issues, but the one question the world is asking is, "Will it work for me?" The world is longing to meet just one believer whose life is living proof that a life in Christ really works.

We have to honestly ask ourselves, "Does the life I claim to live in Christ work for me? Is my life really different? Am I living a changed life? If I took the life of Christ in me and gave it away to someone else, would it make a clear difference in that person's life—something that he or she would be able to see?" If we can't pass our life on, if it wouldn't make a difference in another person's life, we may not have a life that works after all. Life either works for us, or it doesn't.

Shake your head and ask the obvious question, So how do I live a life that works? Simple: by living a life of Yes in agreement with God's will. That leads to the next obvious question: How do I live my life in agreement with God?

In Philippians 2 the apostle Paul points to the example of Jesus as he outlines steps for living a life in agreement. The Jesus who comes to live inside us knows how to make life work. While He was here on earth, He faced life exactly as you and I have to face it every day—and it worked for Him. He was born and took on the same limitations we have. He *"emptied Himself, taking the form of a bond-servant...being made in the likeness of men"* (Philippians 2:7). He became flesh and blood. Before coming to earth, Jesus spoke face to face with God. But while He was here, He had to talk with His Father the same way we talk with Him. His only communication with God was through prayer.

In the pages of the New Testament, we see Jesus living a life that every one of us can live. Jesus wasn't playing with a stacked deck or an insider's advantage. He set aside that advantage when He became a man. Now, because He lives inside us, we can live like Jesus. We can all live a life that works.

Paul tells us how: *"Have this attitude in yourselves which was also in*

Christ Jesus" (Philippians 2:5). The verses that follow detail the kind of life Jesus lived and identify the three major principles of a life lived in agreement.

CONTROLLED BY THE FATHER'S DESIRES

Being found in appearance as a man, He humbled Himself by becoming obedient. (Philippians 2:8)

Jesus was controlled by the desires of God. Remember when Jesus was a young boy and traveled to Jerusalem with His parents? After his family had been in Jerusalem for several days, they began their walk home. Somewhere along the way, Jesus' mother looked for her son but could not find Him anywhere. ("Great, now I've lost the Son of God. How's that going to look on Judgment Day?") So Joseph and Mary returned to Jerusalem and found Jesus in the temple, questioning the temple leaders. When Mary asked Him why He hadn't joined them on the journey home, He responded, *"Did you not know that I had to be in My Father's house?"* (Luke 2:49).

Jesus' entire focus was the desire of God for His life. When He was led into the desert for an in-person encounter with Satan, He responded to everything the enemy threw at Him with the same answer: "I must only do the will of My Father. I won't allow Myself to do the things you are laying out before me, because they are not My Father's desire" (see Matthew 4). While Jesus was traveling and teaching, He often communicated to His disciples that He could only speak and do what He heard and saw His Father doing.

Jesus invested His entire life to live out the answer to one question: What does God want? What difference would we see in our lives if we allowed the answer to that one question to guide everything we did? What difference would it make in our weekend plans if we asked, "God, what do You want?" What difference would it make on our dates if we asked, "God, what do You want?" What difference would it make in the way we handle life's problems if we asked, "God, what do You want?"

This desire to do God's will is the attitude of Christ described in Philippians 2. When we choose this attitude, we can't help but take on a new perspective toward the challenges life throws our way. We are no longer left to answer life's questions from our own limited resources; we can draw on the wisdom and knowledge of God and begin to live in a way that demonstrates His will on earth.

"God, what do You want?" The way we answer this question with our lives is important, because if we get to the point where we don't care about what God thinks, He is not obligated to bless us. God is not duty-bound to bless our lives simply because we go to church or serve Him in any particular way. Just because we give a certain amount of money to the church doesn't mean we're entitled to a regular dose of God's blessing. The blessing of God rests on people who are committed to doing His will. When we no longer care about living out His will in our lives, God is free to remove His blessing from us.

It is frighteningly easy to get to the place where we disregard God's will, even in the church. We can become so caught up in the maintenance of our church programs that we equate the good things we are doing with the will of God. I have been in churches where the focus had shifted away from finding and fulfilling the desires of God to developing ministry programs with measurable results. The programs had the outward look of success, but God's presence and blessing were noticeably absent. The people measured their ministry success by their own manufactured standards rather than by the measure of God's blessing that rested on the life of the church. Without the blessing of God, what's the point in a program?

The guiding principle for our lives must be, What does God want? The will of God is seldom known completely in all its detail. Our commitment must be to obey God's will regardless of how much we know or how comfortable we feel. I've discovered that the comfort comes after our unquestioning obedience.

CHAPTER SIX: *A Life of Agreement*

I've also discovered that the things that keep us from applying this guiding principle to our lives are usually things that give us some sense of security. We tend to hold on to our best abilities and strongest assets. If we are good at solving problems, we try to figure things out for ourselves rather than honestly ask, What does God want? If we can get people to follow our lead, diving in seems much easier than waiting to find out what God wants. The problem is, the security that our assets and abilities provide is only temporary. Sooner or later we find out we've been clinging to things that are unreliable—substitutes for real security that have deceived us into believing that what God thinks doesn't really matter.

One summer I spoke at a youth camp in West Virginia where the only thing to do for recreation was to go to the gym and play sports. After the morning and evening services, all the students would go there to play basketball and volleyball. Immediately I knew I didn't fit in. A gym is not a place I would choose to go for fun. Nevertheless, after one of the midweek services, I decided to go with a friend and hang out with the kids for awhile.

This gym was small, and it had those old wooden bleachers that fold up against the wall. The janitor had compressed the bleachers to make more room for the kids to play. That meant that the only place to sit was on the top bleacher, about fifteen feet above the ground. My friend and I scaled the bleachers and took our perch at the top.

The kids begged me to come and play, but I volunteered to be the team chaplain instead. "I'll watch the game and pray," I said.

After about an hour and a half, the camp director came into the gym and announced it was time for everyone to go to their cabins for the night. The kids dropped the basketball, threw the volleyball in the corner, and ran out of the gym in about fifteen seconds. My buddy took a quick jump and landed easily on the floor. Then he looked up, waiting for me.

It took a couple of seconds for me to plan my descent. But just as I started my way down the compressed side of bleachers, someone shut off the lights. The entire room went black. No light shining in a window or coming out from under the bathroom door. Nothing. Just complete darkness, with me hanging on to the bleacher wall.

The last thing I'd seen before the lights went out was that the ground was quite a distance below my feet. For a few moments, I thought I just might have to hang there until sunrise. My buddy stood nearby in the darkness, trying to convince me that the gym floor was only a few inches from my feet. I refused to believe him. Instead, I painted Technicolor pictures in my mind of me falling to the floor, breaking both legs, and finishing the rest of my summer speaking schedule in a motorized wheelchair.

Over and over my friend tried to convince me that I was close to the floor, but I had already convinced myself that his voice sounded far away. Finally, after about ten minutes or so, I let go, dropped two inches, and touched the floor.

Every one of us has something that feels too secure to let go of. So we hang on, not knowing that the very thing we're gripping so tightly is the one thing that keeps us from real security. It doesn't matter how many people tell us we would be better off without it. We choose to believe our own convictions about our own comfort.

If we want to experience a significant move of God in our lives, we must release the comfort and security we've chosen to hold on to. We must let go of anything we've allowed to keep us from being committed to God's purpose. We must say no to that thing and give God our ultimate yes.

Many people are in toxic relationships that others can easily see are only a poison to the life God has for them. People in such relationships feel the heartache and sometimes bear the physical marks of abuse. Instead of abandoning the toxicity, they choose to hold on to it, convinced that anything else will be less secure, less comfortable, or worse. To get out of this type of relationship requires saying yes to God. To change a financial situation or job track record, to improve a marriage or a relationship with children or parents, we must give God the go-ahead to work in these situations. If we want God to change our lives, we must give Him an ultimate yes.

This shouldn't be a problem for us. Jesus Himself was faced with having to give God His own ultimate yes. In order for Jesus to complete the destiny for which He had been sent to the earth, He had to say yes to God. The Bible is clear that by the time His parents found Him in the temple questioning the temple leaders, Jesus knew His destiny. I'm sure there were days when Jesus would walk to the edge of town to watch criminals being crucified, knowing that someday His life would end on a similar cross.

CHALLENGED TO FULFILL A DESTINY

To the point of death, even death on a cross. (Philippians 2:8)

The night before His crucifixion, Jesus knelt beside a rock in a garden called Gethsemane (which means "wine press") and begged God for a way other than the cross to fulfill His destiny. This night was a time of ultimate challenge for Him. After He prayed He knew there could be no other way; so He surrendered Himself to death on the cross, saying, *"Not My will, but Yours be done"* (Luke 22:42).

Jesus' example demonstrates the price that's involved in choosing a life of agreement. His surrender to God's will shows us four things that we, too, must face when we give God our ultimate yes.

IT WILL BE FRIGHTENING

And He was saying, "Abba! Father! All things are possible for You; remove this cup from Me." (Mark 14:36)

The cup Jesus spoke of is not a literal cup. It's symbolic of two things. First it symbolizes the sin, the scars, and the screwups of the entire world. Every one of us has felt isolated from God. That isolation causes us to panic and creates an intense sense of being alone.

Imagine feeling this way for every person in the world all at once. This is what Jesus felt that night in the garden. The cost of the Cross was painfully real to Him. Jesus suffered mentally, spiritually, and physically for us all.

The second thing the cup symbolizes is the wrath of God. God the Father hates sin; He hates Satan and everything that evil has done to the world. All of the hatred God has for sin and the Evil One was about to be poured out on Jesus on the cross. It's no wonder Jesus sweat drops of blood in the garden. For the first time in His life, Jesus felt the full weight of His destiny.

Anytime we give God an ultimate yes, it will be frightening. The consequence of releasing our hold on what we have chosen as our security seems uncertain and filled with hidden costs. For some of us, giving an ultimate yes is more of an emotional struggle; for others it is physical, and for others it is spiritual.

When I was a student in college, I filled my time with things that were valuable to me. I studied, worked a job at a Mexican restaurant, and made extra money doing commercial art projects in my spare time. Many of my friends spent their "nonclass" time drinking and partying. The way I looked at it, they had made their choice and I had made mine. I enjoyed the schedule I'd created for myself, and I enjoyed having money.

God began speaking to my heart about ministry, but I wasn't exactly sure what He wanted me to do. One day I was at the restaurant, checking out my schedule for the week, when the truth hit me: If I was going to follow God in His call to ministry, it would cost me my time. Following God would cut into everything I had arranged my life around. At that time I had no premonition of what my life would be like today. For all I knew, God was going to have me minister in the ghetto. Giving God complete and ultimate control of my time was a frightening thought.

When we are faced with the decision to give the ultimate yes, the cost of letting go may seem too high. So we hold on—like the death grip I used to hold on to the bleachers in that dark gymnasium. In reality we are just inches from the floor. It's not that big a deal. Letting go means falling into the arms of God.

IT WILL BE FRIENDLESS

And He came and found them sleeping. (Mark 14:37)

Three times Jesus asked His friends to watch and pray with Him, only to come back and find them asleep. Here He was, facing the most serious challenge in His life. He wanted and needed the support of His closest friends. But they couldn't keep their eyes open.

When you and I give God our ultimate yes, we must give it on our own. We can't expect anyone else to stand with us or make the decision for us. Jesus brought His closest friends with Him to the garden at the most critical time in His life. But at the moment He needed them the most, they were not there for Him.

To say yes to God may mean that we miss out on things that other people do. It may mean that we make choices about the use of our time, our money, and our bodies that others don't understand. This is the cost of friendlessness.

It's easy to spot Christians who haven't given God an ultimate yes. They are the ones who say, "I'm seeking the will of God." "I'm just a seeker." "I'm going to different churches to figure out where God is and what He wants to do in my life." These statements are smoke screens covering up the lack of an ultimate yes. As long as people remain seekers, they don't have to make a decision. The truth is, they are still seekers because they don't want to say yes. They don't want to live differently from others. They don't want to pay the cost of surrendering to the will of God.

When we finally say yes to God, we must do it alone. No one can make that decision for us. In that moment we will be friendless.

IT WILL BE A FIGHT

Yet not what I will. (Mark 14:36)

Jesus struggled with the will of God in His spirit. He prayed, "I've known for My entire life that I am destined for the Cross. But if there is any other way for Me to fulfill My destiny, please, Father, show me how." While Jesus' spirit was telling Him that He was to go to the Cross, His flesh was screaming, "I want out!"

To give an ultimate yes is always a struggle. The fight we feel is between our spirit and our flesh as they are challenged by the will of God. This is the same fight Jesus felt. Jesus could have said no. His flesh could have won out. He could have slipped out of the garden, traveled to India, gathered followers, and taught for the rest of His days on earth.

We tend to see Jesus' life as if it were a PowerPoint presentation: There He is in the manger. Look, there He is at the temple, asking questions. Oh, look, He's beginning his ministry. Isn't the sea where He chose His first disciples beautiful? Do you see those pitchers of water—the ones that contained the water He turned into wine? There's the blind man; there's the leper; there's the lady who gave the two small coins. Listen to this sound clip of Jesus telling the parable of the prodigal son. Watch this video clip of Him walking on the water. There He is on the cross. There's the empty tomb. Look at that; He's ascending into heaven.

We think God handed Jesus a script in heaven and then sent Him down to earth to live it out. But Jesus could have exercised His own will and told God no. In His time of struggle, He had the power to choose. God's entire redemptive plan came down to that one crucial moment: Would Jesus give God His ultimate yes?

God's plan for redeeming the world still relies on whether or not you and I give our ultimate yes to God. When things get hard, we have the freedom to exercise our will and walk away. We also have the freedom to say yes. Either way, God's purpose will be accomplished. He is always looking for people who will say yes to Him—and He always finds them.

IT WILL BE FINAL

Yet not what I will, but what You will. (Mark 14:36)

When Jesus spoke these words, He was saying, "Yes, God. I will do what you want, not what I want. I will follow Your plan, not My own." From that point on, there was no turning back.

Once we give God our ultimate yes, every fight we face on the other side of that decision is a fight inside the will of God. For example, when we say we're going to get free from an addiction and we're going to do it God's way, we fight every step of the way inside the will of God. From our point of decision, every battle is a fight to bring that ultimate yes to pass.

After His garden experience, Jesus faced every battle in the spirit. When He came and found the disciples asleep for the third time, He had already given God the ultimate yes. He woke them up and told them, "Get up. Let's get going. We have a job to do" (see Mark 14:42). He could face His destiny because His decision was final. He had said yes, and He would not turn back.

COMMITTED TO FAITHFULLY DISCIPLE

> *Do nothing from selfishness or empty conceit, but with humility*
> *of mind regard one another as more important than yourselves;*
> *do not merely look out for your own personal interests, but*
> *also for the interests of others.* (Philippians 2:3–4)

Most of us go to church for what we can get out of it. In my discussions with single adults, I've found that the reason most give for coming to church is to find a date. The church has become the number one place to hook up.

Coming to church to find a date changes the way you work a room. It even changes the pickup lines you use.

"Hey, what translation do you read?"

"Your name must be Grace because you're so amazing."

Every week, no matter where I'm speaking, I see people walk into the room and look around expectantly. I know what they're thinking; it's written all over their faces: "Is she (or he) here? Is this the night I meet the one I'll spend the rest of my life with?" People are so focused, I often don't know how to break the news to them that those flesh colored objects in their peripheral vision are...other people.

When we say yes to God, we agree to take on Christ's attitude toward others. We agree to communicate through our words and actions that their needs are more important to us than our own. Such an attitude is so rare that it's often met with disbelief. But a life of Yes is committed to giving life away.

Let's say you've had a long day at the office, and it has finally come to an end. On the way to the elevator, you notice that your coworker Bob is struggling to finish a project on deadline. The stress hanging over Bob is nearly visible, and his frustration is more than obvious. If you take a moment to ask how the project is coming along, you might hear him say, "Well, I'm almost finished, but time has just about run out." You might also hear a silent invitation from God to communicate His life to Bob in a very practical way by offering to stay for a few minutes to help him finish the project. Go ahead—it won't take long, and I promise you it will be worth the look of disbelief on Bob's face when you treat his needs as if they are more important than your own.

Jesus communicated to everyone that His needs were less important to Him than theirs were. He lived His life simply to fulfill one purpose: to love the Lord with all His heart, soul, and mind, and to love everyone He met as Himself.

I receive lots of cards during the holiday season. Some come from vendors wanting me to sample their products. Others come from friends and acquaintances around the country. Once I got a card from a friend who is obsessive-compulsive, and it was neatly signed several hundred times…but I digress. One card I received had the James Allen Francis essay, "One Solitary Life," written on it. I've printed a portion here and italicized some of the words for emphasis:

ONE SOLITARY LIFE

He *never* wrote a book.

He *never* held an office.

He *never* had a family or owned a house.

CHAPTER SIX: *A Life of Agreement*

He *didn't* go to college.

He *never* visited a big city.

He *never* traveled two hundred miles from the place where he was born.

He did none of the things one usually associates with greatness.

He had *no credentials* but himself.

There are many things Jesus never did. But what Jesus did do was find twelve men and pour Himself into them in such a way that the very life He had come to bring to the world was deposited in them. He invested Himself in them in such a way that they never forgot the impact of His example. They never forgot that the purpose of receiving life is to give it away.

Jesus' investment in the Twelve is the clearest example we will ever have of discipleship. Unfortunately, the definition of discipleship has undergone more changes than Michael Jackson, and most of the time it looks nothing like the original.

Let's be clear about what discipleship is not. It's not traveling and singing. It's not building buildings. It's not dressing up like a clown and making balloon animals. It's not serving on a leadership committee. It's not putting dramatic interpretation to popular songs. It's not puppets. It's not reshelving books. It's not parking cars or taking up the offering. It's not buying the refreshments for the after-church fellowship or taking the attendance in Sunday school. It's not singing in the church's Christmas extravaganza-skit-thing. It's not volunteering to drive the church bus or to serve as cook for summer camp. It's not even speaking and writing books. (I put that one in for myself and everyone else who does what I do.)

And here's the one that might be the hardest to accept: It's not coming to church every week and listening to the sermon. We will never truly understand discipleship; we will never know what it really means to invest in another person's life until we stop hiding behind our church offices, responsibilities, and chosen duties.

The question is, who—not what—are you investing in?

Discipleship is a focused investment of yourself into the life of another person (or, at most, a few others). It's continuing to make this investment over what can seem like an incredibly long period of time. Just how long you are to make the investment is not for me to determine. I am only pointing out that this is the example of Jesus that the Bible shows us. Jesus was committed to discipleship.

It would not be fair for me to tell you to do something that I'm not doing myself. For the past several years, I have taken different young men with me on the road. These young men are sensing God's call on their lives, so they fly with me, keep the same schedule I keep, and help me wherever I go. These discipleship experiences have been some of the most rewarding and challenging times of my life.

These young men see me at my best and my worst. They see my highs and lows. They see me succeed and fail. I talk honestly with them about pursuing God's call on their lives both on and off the stage. I do my best to let them see how they can live on the road and remain committed to what God wants. I do this because of the example Jesus gives me.

All the sermons we've heard, all the Bible studies we've attended, all the retreats and camps we've been to, all the seminars and conferences we've sat through, all the notebooks we've filled with teachings and principles—all these things point us to a single question: Why would God make certain that all this information is revealed to us and deposited into our lives?

What's the purpose of knowing all these things? Is it just so we can be smarter about God? Is it so we can feel "deep" because of all the knowledge we possess? No! It's so we can give it away. It's meant to be deposited into someone else.

Christianity is caught more than it is taught. Each of us must ask ourselves the question, Who is catching the life of Jesus from me?

Jesus invested Himself in those twelve disciples because He knew that after He was gone, they would be given the responsibility to carry out His work throughout the earth. He knew they were the ones God would use to bring Himself glory throughout all the earth.

CONSUMED BY A FUTURE DREAM

So that at the name of Jesus EVERY KNEE WILL BOW, *of those who are in heaven and on earth and under the earth, and that every tongue will confess that Jesus Christ is Lord, to the glory of God the Father.* (Philippians 2:10–11)

Jesus had a future dream. His dream was that one day every creature in heaven and earth would bow and give honor to God the Father. Jesus' dream is still for the whole world to give honor and praise to God the Father. He came into this world with this dream inside of Him. He felt it, craved it, and became so consumed by it that He willingly gave up His life on the cross in order for it to come to pass.

It is this dream that keeps you and me from getting blown out of the water by the daily grind of life. Without a future dream, the distractions of life become the ultimate maze of confusion. Troubles that would ordinarily be little more than speed bumps become blockades to our life direction. Problems that would be detours at worst become blind alleys with no exits. Our future dream is what keeps us stable in an unstable world.

Ask yourself, "What is God's dream for my church?" "What is God's dream for my job?" "What is God's dream for my family?" "What is God's dream for my life?"

Each of us is unique, and we all have distinctive things to offer. Living a life in agreement with God doesn't mean that we lose our individuality. On the contrary, God places within each of us specific abilities and shortcomings that He desires to control, fill, and use to accomplish His purpose in the world. Our dreams and desires are most fully realized when we're committed to seeking and doing whatever God wants.

There are people reading this book right now who, at one time or another, have known God's dream for their lives; but for whatever reason, they gave up on it. There are others who want desperately to find God's dream so they can abandon themselves to it. I've met hundreds of people in churches all over this country and around the world who have dared to ask God to birth His dream in their hearts. They have sold out to that dream and have seen God accomplish more in their lives than they ever thought possible.

The dream begins with a desire and grows through our simple steps of commitment to see it become reality. When we take one step, a door opens. As we step through that door, another way is made clear; and with it, things that were once hopeless become hopeful. A small piece of the dream becomes reality. One step leads to the next, and that reality births an even more "impossible" reality. God has a dream for our lives. It's real, and it fits exactly into His big picture.

For some of us, God's dream is to transplant us somewhere in the world, far from our hometowns, for the purpose of giving our lives away. For others, God's dream is to use the talents and knowledge He has gifted us with to transform our homes, our communities, our places of business. For still others, God's dream is to provide us with the ability to make money to finance His ministries throughout the world.

Several years ago I had the privilege of speaking to 35,000 people at the Youth Evangelism Conference at the Alamo Dome in San Antonio, Texas. It was a great night, but it was also the same night the Spurs won the National Basketball Association championship at Madison Square Garden. The entire city was in gridlock. Traffic was bumper to bumper in every direction.

After the conference several of us decided it would be best to walk back to our hotel through downtown San Antonio. For the entire twenty-minute walk, all we saw and heard were thousands of noisy, drunk Spurs fans honking and screaming, "We won!" It looked like live footage from *Cops*. People were running up and down the street and hanging out of car windows, yelling the same thing over and over: "We won!"

All I could think was, *No you didn't. They won. You watched.* The only people who truly won were the players in the game. The real winners were the San Antonio Spurs players who'd been completely committed to following the playbook the coach had developed. They were the ones who'd experienced the coach's daily leadership and learned things from him they never could have learned on their own. They caught the dream of winning the national championship, and through the exercise of their commitment, they made it happen. They were the real winners; everyone else was just a spectator. They knew the real thrill of victory; everyone else just had a new excuse to party.

It's the same for most of us in Christianity. We sit in our pews and celebrate the victory we read about in the Bible. "Amen, brother. We win! We read the end of the book, and we win!" No we didn't. The ones who win are the ones who are controlled by the Father's desire. The ones who win are the ones who are challenged to fulfill their destiny. The ones who win are the ones who are committed to faithfully disciple others. The ones who win are the ones who understand that their dreams are best realized when they dream the same dream as Jesus: to bring glory to God the Father.

The challenge for all of us is to get off the bench and into the game, to get out of the stands and onto the court. We won't begin to make a real difference in this world until we say yes to God—until we say, "Father I don't know everything I have to offer, but I'll give everything I have. Just put me in and give me an assignment. I'll do my best. Put me in, God!"

At the end of your life, God won't ask:

"Did you write a book?"

"Did you hold an office?"

"Did you have a family and raise children?"

"Did you own a house?"

"Did you graduate from college?"

"Did you travel extensively?"

"Did you earn the credentials that men applaud?"

He will, however, ask if you lived your life in agreement with Him. Were you controlled by the Father's desire? Were you challenged to know and fulfill His destiny for you? Were you committed to faithfully disciple someone else? Did you live out your dream in harmony with the eternal dream of Jesus? Did your life give glory to God the Father? Did your dream fulfill the dream of God?

Did you live a life of Yes?

Times of Refreshing

The airports around the country have become my neighborhood. They're like little cities. In most airports you can find just about anything you need except space to stretch out and nap between flights. So instead of napping, I walk around the terminal and shop or watch people.

A few times each year—mostly during vacation season and holidays—the airports are extremely overcrowded. This past holiday season, the airports were filled with families and little children. Whenever I see a family with screaming kids sitting at my departure gate, I automatically introduce myself because I know they're going to be sitting next to me on the plane. That's just the way it is. It never fails.

When it comes to children, the only thing I know to do is to bend over, pat them on the head, and say, "Helloooooo." After that I'm completely lost—count me out! Moms and dads have my greatest respect. They deserve medals. I often speak to groups of parents, and whenever I do, I don't talk about the Apocalypse. I figure with two-year-olds in their homes, they're already living through the Tribulation.

I live in Oklahoma, right in the center of tornado alley. Every year we have several twisters that cause quite a bit of property damage. If you live in a part of the country where tornados are rare and you would like to see some of the devastation up close, you have my personal invitation to pay a visit to Oklahoma. If that's too far to travel, then take a quick trip through the home of a friend who has a two year old. You'll get the general idea.

Kids have it pretty good though. Once I walked into an airport men's room and saw a dad clapping for his little boy because he had gone by himself. I thought, *I miss those days when people clapped for me when I did even the simplest things right*. ("Yeah, Son, you got the food in your mouth without sticking the fork in your eye. Way to go!")

You can get away with a lot of things as a kid that you can't get away with when you're an adult. As a child did you ever hold your breath to win an argument? If you're a grownup in the business world, you can't do that anymore. Say you're on a sales call, and the prospect tells you he doesn't want to buy what you have. You can't pout, stick out your bottom lip, then take a huge breath of air and hold it until he agrees to buy what you're selling. The guy will just look at you and your puffed-up cheeks and tell you to get out.

These days if you want to resolve a problem at work, you have to go through the company conflict resolution committee or talk to the corporate mediator. When you were a kid, things were much simpler. All you had to do was say, "I'm rubber, you're glue, whatever you say bounces off me and sticks to you." Here's an idea: The next time your manager calls you into the office and tells you, "Your level of performance fails to meet the established minimum of acceptable behavior," try saying, "Sticks and stones will break my bones…," and see what happens.

The best thing about kids is the way they enjoy simple pleasures. The other day I was walking through an airport and noticed a family just in front of me. The mom and dad were in conversation, and their five-year-old son was playing an imaginary game. Every eight or ten steps, this little boy would jump into the air, spread his arms out, and proudly announce, "I'm Superman!"

Even though they weren't going to my gate, I followed them just to watch the little boy. The parents made a quick pit stop at one of the food courts and bought their son a soft drink. Have you ever seen a young child drink? He grabbed the cup of soda with both hands and put it up to his mouth. He made all sorts of slurping and popping sounds as the soda dripped from his chin onto his shirt. This was followed by some really loud swallowing noises. Then he threw his head back and let out a huge "Ahhhhh!" It was as if he was saying, "Thanks for that drink. I've been thirsty since birth!"

I couldn't remember when I'd enjoyed anything as much as that little boy enjoyed that cold drink. I'd forgotten what it was like to be that thirsty, to enjoy a simple pleasure so much that I became completely immersed in it. And I thought, *Isn't that just like our relationship with God?* Too often we lose our deep thirst for God and forget the pleasure of His presence and the fullness of His life.

In Acts chapter 2, Jesus' disciples experienced the outpouring of God's Spirit. They were present when the prophecy recorded in Joel 2:28 was fulfilled: *"It will come about after this that I will pour out My Spirit on all mankind."* The fulfillment of this prophecy was the first evidence that the kingdom of God had been established.

Jesus had come to earth as the Seed that God had chosen to fulfill the four agreements God had made with mankind. Through His death on the cross, Jesus completely fulfilled every one of God's promises. Then, before leaving the earth, Jesus promised His disciples (and us) that He would send His Spirit to us: *"And He, when He comes, will convict the world concerning sin and righteousness and judgment"* (John 16:8).

Jesus explained, *"If I do not go away, the Helper will not come to you; but if I go, I will send Him to you"* (John 16:7). Everything Jesus did was done to get His Spirit into our lives. He knew He had completed His role in God's plan to win the world back to Himself. He was the complete fulfillment of both the old and new agreements. He also knew that the coming of the Holy Spirit was the beginning of the fulfillment of a new agreement with mankind.

It was the Spirit that empowered Peter to preach his first sermon and lead three thousand people to trust Christ as their Savior. In his message Peter quoted the prophecy from Joel, saying, "'AND IT SHALL BE IN THE LAST DAYS,' God says, 'THAT I WILL POUR FORTH OF MY SPIRIT ON ALL MANKIND'" (Acts 2:17). Peter was declaring for all to hear that this was the first of the last days. God was already pouring out His Spirit on mankind.

We all have times when we dry out. We forget what it's like to enjoy the presence of God. We get used to doing things a certain way. Or life throws us so many punches that we feel completely damaged in our souls, and we end up going flat. The good news is, seasons of refreshing also come into our lives, initiated by the Spirit of God. God knows what we are going through. He knows exactly how we feel, because He lives inside us.

Some of us have been through the deepest valleys life has to offer. We have experienced failure in business and relationships. We have lost people and things that are important to us and to life as we know it. We have seen our dreams dashed, our hopes halted, our faith flattened. We may have grown up in church, but for some reason we've been out of church for years, and we're just now taking baby steps back into fellowship with God.

For others of us, it's not that we've drifted out of fellowship with God. Nor have we lost someone or something that is critical to life. We've just become anesthetized by the mundane, everyday repetitions of preparing lunches, delivering kids, keeping a boss happy, helping our parents with their special needs—all the while wondering, *When will there be any time for me?*

Many of us look at the world around us and think, *We're losing the battle*. The world seems to be getting darker all the time, and we can't help but wonder, *Just how much difference can one Christian make?* We feel powerless, spiritually flat. God understands all of this, and His Spirit initiates the refreshing we need.

Shortly after delivering his first sermon, Peter healed a man who had been known to be sick for quite some time. The people of the city came to Peter, asking, "How have you done this? Are you a magician or something?"

Peter responded, *"Now, brethren, I know that you acted in ignorance, just as your rulers did also. But the things which God announced beforehand by the mouth of all the prophets, that His Christ would suffer, He has thus fulfilled. Therefore repent and return, so that your sins may be wiped away, in order that times of refreshing may come from the presence of the Lord; and that He may send Jesus, the Christ appointed for you"* (Acts 3:17–20).

Peter answered their question in a way that usually doesn't win friends or positively influence people. He told them that they had acted in ignorance, that they were the killers of Jesus. He called them to repent of their sins and clearly reminded them of who Jesus was. In doing this Peter outlined the way the Holy Spirit would enable them—and us—to live in agreement with God.

THE SPIRIT OF GOD
SHATTERS OUR TRADITIONS

I know that you acted in ignorance. (Acts 3:17)

Peter was hard on the people who asked him how he could have healed the lame man. No doubt some of them were religious leaders who had spent their entire lives studying the Old Testament. They saw themselves as the very elite, the sons of Abraham, the chosen ones. To their minds, if anyone was a part of the "in" crowd, they were. Their role, after all, was to be the keepers of the agreement with God. They were the ones entrusted with the laws and the agreement tradition.

This elitist attitude was the reason they had turned on Jesus and had Him crucified. Their tradition taught them that God would send a fleshly Messiah, one who would establish a physical rule on the earth. In reality God had always been about the establishment of a spiritual kingdom. They saw circumcision as an outward sign that the nation of Israel was chosen by God to be the base for His earthly Messianic rule. In reality God used circumcision to symbolize that His agreement was always spiritual. Circumcision was given as a seal of the nonfleshly, spiritual agreement God made with Abraham.

Jesus didn't come to town to lead a revolt against the Roman government. He came to establish God's kingdom in the hearts of mankind. Instead of clearing the Roman oppressors out of Jerusalem,

He cleared the moneychangers out of the temple, healed the sick, and raised the dead. This type of Messiah was an offense to the religious leaders because their traditions and their positions of authority were threatened. Together they conspired to have Jesus killed.

Isn't it interesting that the only people Jesus had any serious trouble with were the religious leaders? They ultimately nailed Jesus to a cross because He shattered their religious preconceptions. Looking through the lens of tradition, they couldn't recognize that the old agreement was completed and a new day had come. They misunderstood the single most important event in history.

Even though they were students of the prophets, they failed to understand the meaning of Jeremiah's prophecy: *"'I will put My law within them and on their heart I will write it; and I will be their God, and they shall be My people...for I will forgive their iniquity, and their sin I will remember no more'"* (Jeremiah 31:33–34). Their tradition required that God's law be literally written on parchment and carried in little boxes on their wrists and foreheads. Their tradition also demanded that certain ceremonies be regularly reenacted at the temple, including making sacrifices and giving offerings. They didn't see that Jeremiah was declaring something much more significant: that God would complete the old agreement through His Seed, Jesus, and write His law on their hearts by the Holy Spirit.

Many of us miss the presence of God today because we tend to look at God through our own traditions. If you were raised in a formal church, you probably talk in "thees" and "thous" whenever you encounter God. If you were raised in a liturgical church, your encounters with God are probably quite structured, and you count on the repetition. If you were raised in a contemporary church, you probably limit your encounters with God to seventeen minutes—and only when you're in shorts and a T-shirt.

During times of refreshing, God pours Himself out on us to get us to understand that there is more to Him than we are currently experiencing. If we're not careful, we can take God's presence for granted. After all, He did promise that where two or three are gathered in His name,

He will be there (see Matthew 18:20). We can become so entrenched in the way we look for God to work in our lives that we miss the "much more" of Himself that He wants to show us. We can become not so much *unable* as *unwilling* to recognize that God is bigger than the way we have come to experience Him. Life becomes completely one-dimensional when we only accept God if He relates to us through our preconceived beliefs about who He is and how He works.

The life of the Holy Spirit in us shatters our traditions and expands our vision of God. The Spirit of God opens our eyes wider than our traditions and prejudices have allowed, and inevitably, we come away with a larger picture of who God is; a deeper faith in His ability to handle life's problems; and a renewed passion to live a life of Yes in agreement with Him.

THE SPIRIT OF GOD
SATISFIES OUR THIRST

The things which God announced beforehand...He has thus fulfilled. (Acts 3:18)

It is amazing to me that the religious leaders of Israel spent so much time studying the Scriptures and yet missed this obvious truth: God has always been more concerned with the spiritual things of life than the fleshly things. These religious leaders and their ancestors took their responsibilities very seriously. Throughout Israel's history they developed a thirst for greater physical adherence to the law; and in order to try to satisfy that thirst, they developed hundreds of new laws that "devout" Jews had to keep. But their focus on physical enforcement of the law kept them from seeing God's focus on spiritual adherence to the law. Isaiah prophesied that God Himself would satisfy a person's thirst: "*The afflicted and needy are seeking water, but there is none, and their tongue is parched with thirst; I, the LORD, will answer them Myself, as the God of Israel I will not forsake them*" (Isaiah 41:17).

Long before you and I were ever born, God promised to come to us when we were parched and thirsty and pour Himself out on us to satisfy our deepest thirst. We are in the last days of Joel 2:28, and God is pouring out His Spirit on all mankind. Anyone who is thirsty today can come to Him and find satisfaction and refreshment.

"Ho! Every one who thirsts, come to the waters; and you who have no money come, buy and eat," God said through the prophet Isaiah, *"Come, buy wine and milk without money and without cost"* (Isaiah 55:1). In other words, it doesn't matter what you're thirsty for or what your needs are; God will satisfy every thirst. Jesus echoed that call in John 7:37: *"If anyone is thirsty, let him come to Me and drink."* Regardless of your need, no matter how often or how badly you have been beaten up by life, you can satisfy your thirst by coming to Him and drinking from His unlimited source of *"living water"* (John 7:38).

Most of us are seekers of one thing or another. The searches in our lives are simply signs that we are thirsty. We switch jobs, we switch hobbies, we switch friends and other significant relationships, not realizing that all we're doing is searching for something to satisfy a thirst. The reality is, a new job or hobby or relationship will not satisfy our thirst any better than whatever we left behind. There is never enough money to satisfy our thirst for material things. There is never that "exactly right person" to satisfy our thirst for companionship.

God has called us through the prophets and through His Son to come to Him when we are thirsty. He knows what so many of us are unwilling to admit: No one, no experience, no thing other than God Himself is capable of satisfying the thirst we have.

I speak somewhere just about every day of the year, and there are times when I simply go flat. I burn out. I wonder how in the world I will get up and say one more word about God or Jesus or the Bible. I have found myself standing before a crowd and hearing something that is completely annoying, only to find out it's the sound of my own voice. There are times I go completely numb. I get in my rental car, drive back to my hotel room, and cry out to God, "I need to be refreshed!"

There's no need to feel guilty about going flat. Sometimes we go flat not because of sin, but because we have used up everything God has given us. These are the times we need to take our thirst to Him and wait for Him to satisfy us once again.

Sometimes when I preach on this topic, I hold up a paper cup filled with water and read Ephesians 5:18b: *"...be filled with the Spirit."* Literally translated, this verse tells us to be "continuously being filled" with the Spirit. If God says we need to be "continuously being filled," the implication is that it is possible to become empty.

I explain to the audience that we rely on the Spirit for strength to face temptation, to engage in spiritual warfare, to witness, to pray, and so on. With each item I mention, I allow a small stream of water to spout from the cup. I keep listing ways that we rely on the Spirit until the cup is empty. Then I make the point that we must constantly bring ourselves to God for refilling. He pours out His Spirit on us to satisfy our thirst and meet our every need.

THE SPIRIT OF GOD STRENGTHENS US FOR THE TASK

He may send Jesus, the Christ appointed for you. (Acts 3:20)

The day before Peter preached his first message and three thousand people were saved, he and the other apostles were hiding, trying to figure out what they should do. But then God poured out His Spirit, and they were empowered. Immediately they went out and demonstrated God's strength for the entire city of Jerusalem to see. In the days and weeks that followed, they continued to preach, heal the sick, and establish the beginnings of the New Testament church, which continues to this day. They could never have done these things on their own; it was completely beyond their abilities. It required the strengthening of the Spirit of God.

The ministry of the Spirit of God strengthens us, too, for the task that He knows lies ahead of us. We cannot survive or complete this task using our own abilities. Like Peter and the apostles, we need God's empowerment. We may not know what lies ahead, but we do know that God is preparing us for the future He has planned for us. He has sent His Holy Spirit to empower us for that purpose.

There are six ways the Spirit of God deposits His strength into our lives:

HE CONVICTS

> *Now when they heard this, they were pierced to the heart, and said…, "Brethren, what shall we do?"* (Acts 2:37)

It is the conviction of the Spirit that leads us to receive Christ, and it's through conviction that He matures us. The Holy Spirit leads us to feel the same way about things as God does.

One evening I was speaking at the Metro Bible Study when a young man who had just become a Christian came up to me and said, "I think God is mad at me." I asked him why he thought that, and he said, "This past weekend I went out and did the stuff I've always done on the weekends, and I felt terrible. I've never felt bad about doing that stuff before. I think God's mad at me."

I smiled and looked him straight in the eye. "Bro, God's not mad at you," I said. "What you felt was conviction. That's one of the ways the Spirit of God ministers to you."

HE REGENERATES

> *Jesus answered, "Truly, truly, I say to you, unless one is born of water and the Spirit he cannot enter into the kingdom of God."* (John 3:5)

The Holy Spirit always brings the life of Christ into our lives. Recently I spoke at The Cove, the Billy Graham training center in North Carolina. For the four days I was there, I kept hearing that a New York City fireman was at The Cove too. He had been a part of the rescue effort of 9/11, and he'd spent the past several months on the cleanup crew. Apparently he'd reached a breaking point and felt he just had to get away from New York.

CHAPTER SEVEN: *Times of Refreshing*

Only God knows why he chose The Cove for his retreat. He wasn't a believer. Instead of coming to hear me speak, he went hiking and rappelling, then had the shuttle-bus driver take him back to his room so he could get drunk. People told me that he was on the campus, but for the first couple of days, I never saw him.

He finally came to my third, fourth, and final sessions. As everyone was packing up to leave, he approached me on the porch of the meeting room and introduced himself.

"I sat through the last three sessions," he told me, "and I heard what everyone sang and what you said. I want you to know, I believe all this stuff is real. There's just something about it that speaks to my heart."

This was a man whose life had been forever changed by the terrorist attacks of 9/11, yet the things he saw in the lives of the believers at The Cove had made a dramatic impact on him. I asked, "Are you at a place where you are ready to receive the Spirit of God? Are you ready to ask God to step out of heaven and into your life?" He said he was.

I raised both hands, and when he gave me a double high-five, I held his hands over our heads. I said, "If you're ready, you're about to receive the Spirit of Christ. He is about to come and live inside you—not because I say so, but because the Bible promises it." Then I quoted Romans 10:13: *"WHOEVER WILL CALL ON THE NAME OF THE LORD WILL BE SAVED."* I led this man to Christ, and the Spirit of God came to live in him right then and there.

HE SEALS

> *Who also sealed us and gave us the Spirit in our hearts as a pledge.* (2 Corinthians 1:22)

God put His mark on us as a guarantee of His ownership. The Spirit of God doesn't come on and off of us. His presence is permanent and indelible. It's that permanence that makes His power consistent in our lives.

Traveling all the time makes weight management a constant challenge for me. I've been on the road for the past eleven years, and that's exactly how long I've been on a diet. (I tried the SlimFast diet products and gained weight. I really like the way their shakes taste, especially mixed with about six scoops of Häagen-Dazs.)

If the Holy Spirit flew in and out of my heart, I would never be able to count on His strength to face the challenges of life. But because I'm sealed in Him, I can always count on His strength being there for me—even when the challenge of the moment happens to be a buffet line.

HE PLACES US

> *But now God has placed the members, each one of them, in the body, just as He desired.* (1 Corinthians 12:18)

The Holy Spirit has a task to accomplish through each of us. He gifts us, empowers us, and places us as He desires, so that work He has for us can be completed.

For the past two years the Metro Bible Study has grown, and so has its impact on the city of Memphis. I consider it a privilege to be a part of it every week. I've watched as the Spirit of God has raised up twenty-five leaders who fully cooperate with Him in the positions He has given them. Some serve coffee; others handle the prayer requests that come in; others set up and tear down the entire facility. These people weren't enlisted by anyone other than the Holy Spirit. They have done their jobs faithfully over the past two years, and they still passionately look forward to serving each Monday night.

HE GIFTS US

> *But to each one is given the manifestation of the Spirit for the common good.* (1 Corinthians 12:7)

Each of us has an active ministry given to us by the Spirit of God. Have you found your gifts? Are you using them in a way that builds the kingdom?

I know a young man who grew up in a youth group in my hometown of Oklahoma City. When he was a teenager, he fell in love with playing the drums. He had the talent and worked hard at developing it.

With the help of his youth minister, he recognized that the Spirit of God had gifted him, and he began to cultivate his gift by playing drums in the youth ministry. Several years have passed now, and this young man is married. He continues to utilize his gift in his church's worship services each week.

HE EMPOWERS US TO WITNESS

> *But you will receive power when the Holy Spirit has come upon you; and you shall be My witnesses.* (Acts 1:8)

My best friend in the whole world lives in Oklahoma City. Every time I'm there, we go to a little Mexican restaurant for dinner, and the same girl waits on our table. One day this girl came up to our table and announced, "I just got engaged!"

While we were admiring her ring, she started telling us about her fiancé. "He just got out of prison, and he's recovering from a drug addiction," she said. "He's not really a Christian, but he's a good man."

I couldn't count all the red flags that were waving in my head at that moment. I didn't know the girl well enough to say, "This marriage sounds like a horrible idea," so I mumbled, "Well, I'll be interested to see what happens in the future."

Every time I was in town, my friend and I would eat at the same restaurant, and I'd always ask our waitress, "Do you still have the ring, or have you called it off yet?" She would always smile and say, "No, I'm sticking with it."

One day I asked, "Is the wedding still on?" and she answered, "We had a horrible fight. He was so rude! But I'm going to give him one more chance."

In a poor attempt at humor, I asked, "So has he started flicking lit cigarettes at you yet?"

"No," she said, "like I told you, he's not a smoker; he's a drug addict!"

"I'm sorry. I can see how that would be better," I said weakly.

Our conversations always took place between her passing out chips and salsa and taking orders from four or five other tables. Before we left that night, I motioned her over.

"So, you're going to give him another chance," I said, picking up where we left off.

"Yeah, I'm just going to hang in there," she replied.

We had this same basic conversation for several years. This woman was engaged for a very long time! Then one day she came over to our table and said, "Well, you're the minister guy. What would you say to me?"

With considerable excitement I asked, "You want me to tell you what I think about you and your boyfriend?"

"No."

"Oh." I could barely hide my disappointment.

She continued, "What would you say to me about my life? I feel like my whole life is in chaos all the time." She told me that she had grown up in the Catholic Church and still went to mass.

"I'm glad you were raised in the Catholic Church and go to mass," I said. "But what I would say to you is that the presence of God needs to be real to you. Until God reveals Himself to you personally, no religious routine can possibly help you."

"Someone told me one time that to become a Christian, you couldn't just check off a box on a card. You had to go through something. Do you know what I'm talking about?" she asked.

"Yes I do." I reached into my pocket for a little book I was carrying called *How to Make Life All Good*. It's basically an outline of the gospel message.

I asked her if I could show her the booklet. She still had tables to wait on, but she said, "Sí."

Pointing to a picture of a man on the left side of the outline, I said, "We enter this world separated from God. We try whatever we can to get into the presence of God. We try to be good. Do you ever try to be good?"

"Yeah," she said. Then she excused herself for a few minutes to take some fresh chips to another table. We continued this way through the entire booklet. I would show her a page and tell her a truth from

Scripture, and she would wait on a table or two before coming back for more.

After a few more rounds of sharing the gospel between waiting tables, she asked if she could sit down with us. This woman actually sat down at our table in the middle of this Mexican restaurant and gave her life to Christ! I led her in a simple prayer, and she prayed it line by line. I looked up, and she was weeping. My best friend was weeping too.

Do you know why this happened? Not because I'm a great speaker. Not because I know how to close a sale. It happened because Jesus is the Son of God, and with His presence comes power. This girl stopped in the middle of serving tables to say yes to the God of Yes.

The Lord Jesus is King, and He pours out His Holy Spirit to bring new life, wisdom, guidance, and strength to individuals, families, and nations. The Spirit of God calls, holds together, and sends out a new reconciling community into the world called the church, designed to lead the world back to God. As the church is empowered to fill even the remotest part of the earth with the gospel, the Holy Spirit creates a completely new race of people living in agreement with God and filled with righteousness, peace, and joy. In this way the work of the Holy Spirit fully succeeds.

THE SPIRIT OF GOD
SUMMONS US TO TURN AROUND

Therefore repent and return, so that your sins may be wiped away. (Acts 3:19)

The Spirit of God doesn't call us to make more promises and try harder. He calls us to *"repent and return."* But repentance has negative connotations for many of us. When we think of repentance, we think of a two-week spring revival where Brother So-n-So from First Church of Bucktooth comes in and tells some scary bus crash stories, frightening everyone down the aisle to the altar. That kind of scenario is contrived and really has nothing to do with repentance.

Repentance simply means to come back. It means to show up. Peter told the people in Acts 3:19 that if they would come back to God, if they would show up before Him, their sins would be taken away, and God would bring times of refreshment to them. Every prophet throughout the Old Testament had given this same message of repentance to the nation of Israel. Now Peter was offering hope to a new generation, reassuring them that it wasn't too late to repent. And if they did repent, he told them, they would receive the blessing of the new agreement.

Peter's message was simple: Get out of the old agreement and get into the new agreement with God through Christ.

The key question of the new agreement is, are you in the Spirit? If not, repent and return. The new agreement never asks us whether or not we have completed a class, signed a card, or given regularly in the offering. The new agreement is more concerned with position than performance. What is your position in relation to the Spirit of God? Are you in or out?

Any one of us can perform, but that doesn't mean we're living in agreement with God. The new agreement is the place of returning. It's where we find ourselves when we choose to repent and return to a life of Yes. Only in the new agreement can we receive the constant refreshment that comes from saying yes to the Spirit of God.

CHAPTER EIGHT

The Power Line

We live in a world that gets its baseline for reality from a TV show called *The Real World*. The show documents the most pathetically fake reality there could ever be. Seven beautiful people live in a rent-free luxury house, complete with every cutting-edge electronic device available. They are allowed to do anything they want to do and have it all captured on videotape. Does this sound like your real world?

To make sure the reality is preserved, the producers of the show hold auditions for upcoming episodes. These "nonactor" people are so busy playing to the cameras that they don't have time to be real. But we watch it—and why? Because we don't care that it says it's real when it's not.

Integrity has disappeared from our national landscape. It's been replaced with tolerance and its subtle twin, political correctness (otherwise known as PC). In the language of PC, truth is bent to whatever degree is necessary to make sure no one is offended and everyone feels comfortable. These days our society is so touchy, we all have to use our eyeteeth to watch what we are saying. Speaking the truth without offending anyone is harder than putting pajamas on a three year old.

In our PC world, a word can't simply mean what it means anymore. The truth is too...well, *true*. And sometimes the truth can hurt. PC blurs the lines of reality just enough to keep everyone happy and feeling good about themselves. Who cares if integrity is undermined in the process?

Here's a sample English-to-PC dictionary for those of you who are outside the PC loop:

English	PC
Smart	cerebrally advantaged
Hunting	stalking nonhumans
Ugly	visually inconvenienced
Liar	reality stylist
Gossip	issuing a misstatement
Dead	really late for work
Adultery	progressively minded marriage, or user-friendly marriage
Mean	kindness impaired
Racist	colorless thinking
Lost	unchurched
Sin	adult entertainment
Hell	a temperature-intensive location

Let's see if you can translate this sentence: When the unchurched, visually inconvenienced reality stylist is really late for work, we can know that he is paying for his adult entertainment in a temperature-intensive location forever. (Answer: When the lost, ugly liar dies, he'll pay for his sin in hell forever.)

What happens when PC finds its way into the church? The Bible becomes "the processed tree carcass of celestial information." The Ten Commandments become "the Ten Suggestions, which, in an ecologically sound move, God put on stone, thus saving paper and affirming the life of trees." The following scriptures would read differently too:

- "Their eyes were opened, and they were both in a clothing-optional state."
- "We saw it, and it is a land that flows with the high protein by-product stolen from voiceless, defenseless, bovine companions

and high-energy, high-calorie nectar unjustly appropriated from innocent (but hardly defenseless) buzzing insects."

- "Oh, you of vertically disadvantaged faith."
- "Money is the root of all behavioral divergence."
- "The harvest is plentiful, but the workers have been downsized."
- "Can the visually impaired lead the visually impaired?"
- "Let him who is ethically unchallenged cast the first stone."

PC is nothing more than a blind adherence to what is deemed acceptable by the social "elite." (Let's not forget that in our world's recent history, the last society to adhere blindly to what its leaders considered acceptable ended up killing millions of Jews.) It's a completely external exercise that has nothing to do with the true, inner state of our lives. It simply enables us to display a false goodness without having to *be* good people. It's all style and no substance.

It was precisely this type of society that the Old Testament prophet Jeremiah found himself living in. In fact, if there ever was a generation of politically correct followers of God, it was Jeremiah's. The Israel of his day was a society of rules, regulations, and religion without reason. It was a society of obedience through sheer will power, of performance without heartfelt involvement. As long as the people said and did the right things on the outside, it didn't matter what was inside, in their hearts.

They had the religious show going on, but the nation was in crisis. The people had drifted far from their former obedience to the God of Abraham. Lawlessness and sin filled the city of Jerusalem. Sacrifices continued to be made in the temple, but Jehovah God was not revered, much less truly worshiped. Personal integrity mattered less than external behavior.

Enter Jeremiah. The state of affairs in Israel gave this prophet of God an awesome opportunity to demonstrate how form follows substance, and not the other way around; how the exterior of a person should truly match the interior; and how important genuine integrity is when it comes to living in agreement with God.

JEREMIAH INTRODUCED THE AGREEMENT WITH BOLDNESS

Reared in a tiny town outside of Jerusalem as the son of a priest, Jeremiah had grown up loving the temple, the traditions, the people, and the God of Abraham and Moses. But on one of his trips to Jerusalem, his integrity was tested, and this test changed his entire life.

He had made the one-hour walk from his home to Jerusalem many times. This time, however, the walk was different. This time he met God. Standing outside the city, overlooking its magnificence and enjoying the sounds and the energy that brought life to the giant walls, Jeremiah heard God: *"I have appointed you a prophet to the nations"* (Jeremiah 1:5).

The dream of every young Jewish man was to meet God personally and, like Moses, speak with Him. The ultimate dream was to be the prophet of God, knowing and communicating His words to the people. Knowing God that closely and being allowed to represent Him and express His desires and demands was the greatest challenge and the most overwhelming honor any Jewish man could receive.

That day on the road to Jerusalem, God specifically chose Jeremiah for this task.

God knew the awesome requirements of the office. He certainly had His pick from among scores of eager young men. Yet without hesitation, He spoke to Jeremiah and declared his destiny: He was to be the prophet of God.

Accepting the role of prophet would forever seal Jeremiah's uniqueness and unleash his greatness. Yet his initial response was not one of excitement and confidence. Instead he muttered, *"I do not know how to speak, because I am a youth"* (Jeremiah 1:6).

How could this remarkable young man who would ultimately possess such prophetic boldness, courage, and tenacity respond to the discovery of his destiny in such a negative way? His struggle centered on his concept of integrity. Jeremiah thought integrity was something a person does. If God called him to be a prophet, he would need to be able to perform in front of crowds as a speaker. But he was young and had no public speaking experience. How could he be a prophet in all integrity if he could not do the one thing a prophet does?

Acknowledging Jeremiah's struggle, God took time to deal with him and to reshape the way he perceived integrity. He showed him that integrity is not about what you do; it's all about who you are. God presented His young prophet with the sole basis for personal integrity: *"Before I formed you in the womb I knew you, and before you were born I consecrated you"* (Jeremiah 1:5).

God was saying, "Jeremiah, I want you to understand that your ability to walk in integrity is not based on any power you possess, any skill you've honed, any office you hold, any fortune you've amassed, or any place of honor you hold among the people. Your worth and intrinsic value come from Me, and I have the right to place demands upon your life. Your integrity is based upon your acceptance of My demands and your willingness to allow My will to be fulfilled in your life. Integrity is not about doing righteous deeds or refusing to do unrighteous deeds; it's about accepting My right to lead your life to complete My purpose.

"Long before I created you inside your mother's womb, I designed a destiny for you that would be valuable and powerful and successful. I knew who you would be. I planned everything about you. I determined your race, your size, your sex, your personality. I consecrated you with My divine purpose. You are great because I have placed value and purpose within you. Now it's critically important that you see what I see in you and imagine what I have imagined about you—and then fully receive it."

God wanted Jeremiah to recognize that his self-worth, his self-esteem, his self-identity, and his self-image needed to come from what God had already done in him on the inside, not from anything he did or didn't do on the outside. Whatever God said about Jeremiah was the truth, regardless of any contradicting verdict handed down by parents, friends, heroes, or enemies. The things God declared about Jeremiah determined his value and worth. His fulfillment of God's verdict determined the level of his integrity!

The problem was, Jeremiah's beliefs, thoughts, emotions, reasoning, and life experiences gave him a perception that was different from

God's. Caught up in the religious culture of his day, Jeremiah believed his identity was defined by what he did. He measured integrity by externals only—by how well he followed the regulations of religious leaders who taught that outward actions determine the content of an individual's life. Jeremiah thought he was pleasing God and living with integrity when he kept the religious rules. As long as he maintained that belief, however, he could not correctly respond to God.

Isn't that the way we are today? We measure our own integrity by the way we act—by how well we keep one set of man-made rules or another. But as long as we define ourselves solely by our actions, we will never be able to deal with the hurts in our lives, confess the needs in our lives, and admit to the failures in our lives. We have a desperate need to be honest with ourselves regarding who we are and who God made us to be.

God wanted Jeremiah to understand that the question of integrity was not "Will you go to the temple and make a sacrifice?" It was "Will you be who God created you to be?" Would Jeremiah live a life of Yes with God and be a prophet? Would he obey?

Will you be whatever God has planned for you to be? This is the central question of agreement integrity. If your answer is yes, you must be willing to stand up and stand out from the culture. Most people today are more focused on *doing* than *being*. But *who we are* is not *what we do*. It's time to stop identifying ourselves on the basis of our behavior, our actions, our accomplishments, and our sins. If we want to be all that God has planned for us to be, we must no longer define ourselves by our behavior; rather, we must define ourselves by who God created us to be.

Do you know who you are? When we find out who we are, then what we do will follow. We will live in integrity when what we do finds its motivation in a clear, godly perspective of who we are.

Like Jeremiah, you and I must find the will of God for our lives and live it out. God told Jeremiah that he was to be a prophet not just to Israel, but to the nations. He would be the one to introduce the concept of a new holy agreement in Christ, and with it, the basis for every person's true integrity. It was through Jeremiah that God said: "*I will put My law within them and on their heart I will write it; and I will be their God, and they shall be My people"* (Jeremiah 31:33).

With God's help, Jeremiah came to see the world in a whole new way. He realized that God had never been served by religious traditions. True integrity was never external, but internal. God wanted to write His will on the hearts of individuals, and this would become their motivation to obey.

Many of us are frustrated today because we're still basing our integrity on our religious behavior and actions rather than on the identity God has written on our hearts. No wonder we have lost integrity! Without this understanding of integrity, we have about as much chance of achieving harmony as O-Town without an effects rack.

JESUS INAUGURATED THE AGREEMENT WITH HIS BLOOD

Jeremiah announced God's new agreement with mankind, but it was Jesus who would inaugurate it. The prophet declared the words of the agreement; the Son would unleash the power of its integrity.

The night the disciples entered the Upper Room to share the Last Supper with Jesus, the table was already set. Jesus passed the bread then took the cup and lifted it, making it the central focus of everyone's attention. He said, *"This is My blood of the covenant, which is poured out for many for forgiveness of sins"* (Matthew 26:28).

The disciples may not have understood what was ahead for Christ, but they were painfully aware of what *"blood of the covenant"* meant. Blood agreements were a part of their heritage and regular worship. In the Old Testament, a blood covenant was used to seal an agreement. It was accomplished by slicing the neck of a heifer, a goat, or a ram on either side. Then the knife would be driven into the animal's breastbone with a downward motion so the bone would crack. The flesh would tear open and the carcass would divide in two, with the pieces falling across from each other and forming a pathway in between.

The disciples also knew that *"it is the blood by reason of the life that makes atonement"* (Leviticus 17:11). Burnt animal sacrifices were offered on a daily basis in the temple in Jerusalem. Once a year, on the Day of Atonement, the high priest carried some of the blood from the sacrifices into an inner room in the temple called the Holy of Holies and sprinkled it on the mercy seat. This annual ritual was commanded by God for the forgiveness of the sins of the nation. Through the blood of the sacrifice, the people's sins were forgiven for that year.

But that night in the Upper Room, Jesus marked Himself as the ultimate sacrifice. He offered Himself without sin to God, and God accepted His death as the total payment for the sin of all mankind. From that point on, it was no longer necessary to offer the blood of animals on the altar, because *"Jesus has become the guarantee of a better covenant"* (Hebrews 7:22). The promise in the Old Testament was realized in the New Testament. Everything God promised through Jeremiah, Jesus fulfilled. The death of Jesus became the foundation of a new, better agreement.

Through His death, Jesus removed the obstacle of sin that separated mankind from God. Now God can reside inside each of us through His Holy Spirit. We no longer have to go to the temple; He makes our bodies His temple. We no longer have to sprinkle blood on the mercy seat; the Holy of Holies is established in our hearts. We no longer have to make sacrifices; the ultimate sacrifice has been made for us.

Jesus' death proclaimed that a new way of living had begun. This new life could not be contained in the old way of following rituals and keeping a code of ethics and laws. This new life required new thinking. The Lord insisted, *"Nor do people put new wine into old wineskins; otherwise the wineskins burst, and the wine pours out and the wineskins are ruined"*—in other words, don't try to live the Christian life by following a set of laws—*"but they put new wine into fresh wineskins, and both are preserved"* (Matthew 9:17).

It doesn't matter what you do for a living; it can be done with integrity from the inside out. Integrity has less to do with what you do and more to do with why you do it. It doesn't matter if you're the person who scrapes dead animals off the highway (pelt wrangler in PC) or the guy who cleans the filter at the local sewage plant (flow facilitation engineer). Maybe all you can do is wash windshields at busy intersections (mobile squeegee technician). Each of us has to know who we are in Christ if what we do is going to have any meaning in the real world.

Integrity is not an issue of keeping the rules or making ourselves look good. Integrity is an issue of living in agreement with the God of the universe who lives on the inside of us. The model for integrity resides in the heart of every newborn believer! Through Christ we can be real people in the real world, because the ultimate reality lives within us. Integrity flows out of who we are—and we are the sons and daughters of God!

PAUL ILLUSTRATED THE AGREEMENT IN THE LIFE OF THE BELIEVER

Paul was an evangelist, preacher, administrator, theologian, and apologist. He filled all these roles because God had called him to defend the teachings of the new agreement. He explained in Galatians 3:8–9: *"The Scripture, foreseeing that God would justify the Gentiles by faith, preached the gospel beforehand to Abraham....So then those who are of faith are blessed with Abraham, the believer."*

Paul argued that before Jesus came to earth, Abraham believed God and was made right with God through his faith. How did Abraham get in on God's covenant agreement? *By faith.* Think with me for a moment: Who was Abraham when God made His agreement with him? Was he a Hebrew? No, he was a man who had come from a land and a people who did not know God. Abraham simply took God at His word. He said yes to God and chose to live in agreement with His will. And because of Abraham's faith, God made an agreement with all mankind. Now those of us *"who are of faith are blessed with* [receive the same blessing as] *Abraham, the believer"* (Galatians 3:9).

Here's another thought: When God made his agreement with Abraham, He promised to bless Abraham and make a great nation from his seed. He told Abraham to seal the agreement through the act of circumcision and to have his descendants seal it in the same way. This simple cutting off of the flesh symbolized that the fulfillment of the agreement couldn't be done by man's best effort; it required faith in God.

Unfortunately, this truth remains an unaccepted, radical idea for many Christians today. A popular and mistaken belief is that salvation is by faith alone, and that afterward we make ourselves better through our own effort. This is foolishness. We can't make ourselves permanently better through our own effort any more than Abraham could make a great nation come from of his descendants. Even if Abraham had lived eight thousand years and enforced a strict code of behavior the entire time, that effort still would not have guaranteed that his offspring would become a great nation.

Most likely Abraham knew nothing of Adam and that first agreement God made with Adam in the Garden. All Abraham knew was that God had made an agreement with him. He simply looked forward to the ultimate fulfillment of his agreement with God. Abraham didn't know the name of the One who would fulfill the agreement, but he did know where He would come from. He would be sent from God.

From the time of Abraham, God went to work calling, preserving, judging, forgiving, and blessing Abraham's descendants—His people, Israel. After God called Moses to lead the Israelites out of Egypt, He gave them an elaborate system of sacrifices, feasts, and rituals to distinguish them from all the other nations. These acts of worship were never intended to enslave the people; God had already released them from Egyptian slavery. Rather, they were intended to help them remember the agreement God had made with Abraham—to paint a daily picture reminding them that One was coming who would fulfill everything God had promised.

Over the years, however, the religious leaders turned these acts of worship into a code of behavior to which all good Hebrews had to conform. As a result, when Jesus came, instead of being recognized as the fulfillment of the agreement with Abraham, he was seen as a threat to the Jewish way of life.

The first-century Christians declared that Jesus had come as the promised Messiah, but most Jews in Israel rejected that claim. (It was this rejection of Jesus as Messiah that resulted in His crucifixion.) The people's dismissal of this message naturally led to the persecution of the early Christians. The assertion that Christ had ended the old agreement and established a new agreement represented a serious challenge to the religious leaders' behavior-oriented standard of goodness.

The early Christians were meek and peaceful and would rather die than live by the sword. The threat the religious leaders sensed was not coming from a holy war of Christian antagonism; the threat came from God Himself. At the very heart of the new agreement was the termination of the old agreement. God had promised that He would write His will on His people's hearts, be their God, and cause them to know Him personally. He would be merciful toward their iniquities and remember their sins no more. The fulfillment of that promise had finally come in the person of Jesus Christ.

If you and I still think we have to do anything to gain favor with God, we are acting in foolishness. Yet our churches are filled with people who want to hold on to a legalistic way of thinking. Many of them are in leadership, and they exercise their authority by demanding and enforcing specific behaviors, claiming that God blesses us when we live holy lives.

In Paul's day this legalistic thinking consumed members of the church at Rome. They insisted that integrity was measured by outward performance. As a result, they were busy judging each other and keeping each other in bondage to the past.

Paul demanded, *"Who are you to judge the servant of another?"* (Romans 14:4). In other words, an individual is responsible to God and God alone for his or her integrity. No person can possibly know or understand what God is doing or demanding in the hearts and lives of other Christians. They are God's servants, and He will take care of them. What a blow to the old, critical way of thinking! Paul was saying to the Romans that integrity is not based upon adherence to an external law; it is based upon being faithful to what God demands of each of us.

In the mid-1990s, we all watched as former President Bill Clinton and Special Prosecutor Ken Starr went head to head. It was the political equivalent of Thunder Dome—two men enter; one man leaves. We saw Clinton struggle when he held a press conference to apologize for his behavior. He ended his apology by saying he wanted to move on. Of course he did—it was getting too hard to think about the truth. So he apologized for four minutes and then went on a vacation.

(It was easy for us, at that time in our nation's history, to say, "He shouldn't have done those things," or, "He lost his integrity." The truth is, he probably lost his integrity when he ran for office.)

As the months passed, Clinton took advantage of every photo opportunity to make his personal life and family life look solid and right. He struck more poses than yearbook photo day at Beverly Hills High School. Each time he went to church, he always spoke to the press outside, as if to remind them, "These windows were stained before I got here." At Chicago's Willow Creek Community Church, he confessed in front of four thousand people that he had submitted his life to pastoral counseling and had begun to work at "restoring his integrity." Did he mean that he was working at not making the same mistakes over again? Probably, but that's not what integrity is.

Integrity is not about behavior; it is about who we are. Do we know who we are in the Lord? If we do, our behavior will fall into line. When we understand that behavior is born out of identity, we will know the significance of Paul's words in Romans 14:12: *So then each one of us will give an account of himself to God.*

Philosophical negativism dominates much of our culture. It's little wonder that we have as much compassion for trees as for people, that we abort children for convenience, and that we fight to save the whales while we throw away our elderly. We have relegated man to an evolved ape and then wonder why crime dominates our streets. If life is only pleasure for a moment, why not push the envelope to the limit? If life is an accident waiting to happen, why not see how close to the edge we can get and still return?

Our Christian response to negativism is as pathetic as the negativism itself. We try to overrun the negativity with positive, superficial thoughts. We believe that if we try hard enough to change the way we think about ourselves, we will change the way we live. But repeating

"I like myself; I'm OK" over and over in front of the mirror isn't going to turn our lives around. Living in agreement with God's perception of who we are and who He created us to be is the only way to permanently change life. Real integrity is found when we accept God's opinion about us and start living according to it.

When we forget who God created us to be, we become capable of performing the pettiest crimes against humanity. We have little difficulty using deception to milk people out of their hard-earned money. We easily choose to lie in order to make ourselves look good. We quickly find loopholes that enable us to escape our liability and create our own style of justice. We become little more than small-time crooks running worn-out scams to get money we didn't earn to support our excessive lifestyles (or to use the PC label, Enron executives).

In order to know who we really are, we must make the choice to walk in agreement with God's will. We must allow this agreement to impact the choices we make. Over time we must recognize more and more the significance God has placed on our lives. Once we begin to accept what God knows to be true about us, we will begin to live lives of integrity based on that truth.

BELIEVERS INTERNALIZE THE AGREEMENT THROUGH THEIR BEHAVIOR

I am amazed at how many ways we still think and act like old-agreement people, enforcing a specific code of behavior selected from a refined list of acceptable choices. I was speaking to a large group of students and made a reference to the warriors who ate at King David's special table. I pointed out that the table was special because that's where the king's gladiators sat to eat. About a week later, I received a letter from one of the group's youth ministers saying that he didn't appreciate my use of a term that referred to a popular movie known for its violent content. I had neither quoted a line from *Gladiator* nor referred to it when giving the illustration about David's warriors. Yet, this man was still offended that I used the word *gladiator* in my sermon.

The nonnegotiable issues of life are relatively few and center on the truth that salvation is by grace through faith and not a result of works. Rather than focus on the essentials, however, we somehow have shifted the greater portion of our attention to the nonessentials—whether or not you go to the movies, what kind of music you listen to, what kind of clothes you wear, what kind of food you eat.

Christians who are strong in their faith disregard as nonessential those prohibitions that are not specifically declared in Scripture. They are strong enough to participate without a guilty conscience in activities that religious people—not God—have deemed wrong. Christians who are weak in their faith have a troubled conscience if they go against these same prohibitions.

As the New Testament church began to grow, conflicts were unavoidable. Some Christians thought they could eat anything served as food, regardless of its source; others did not. Some believed that the Jewish festival days should be kept as holy days; others did not. The strong-faith Christians scoffed at the weak-faith Christians who could not participate in certain things because their consciences were bothered. The weak-faith Christians judged the strong-faith Christians precisely because they participated in those very things. Paul called both attitudes "worldly" and declared that both the strong and the weak in faith have to answer to God.

In Romans 14 Paul introduces the principles that God gives us to guide our behavior in new agreement integrity.

THE STANDARD IS MAGNIFICENT

For not one of us lives for himself, and not one dies for himself; for if we live, we live for the Lord, or if we die, we die for the Lord; therefore whether we live or die, we are the Lord's. (Romans 14:7–8)

Each one of us must choose to value ourselves not for the things that we do but for who we are in Christ. What we do is far different from who we are. What we do can bring some value to our lives, but that value is measured by our own self-interest and the opinions of others. Does what I do bring me honor and recognition? Does what I do bring me an income that allows me to do whatever I desire? Does what I do help me feel good about myself? Does it make me look good in other people's eyes? Such measures are completely external. Let something happen to what we do, and our sense of personal value takes a disastrous hit.

In contrast, when our core value comes from who we are in Christ, then what we do, how much money or recognition we receive, and what other people think of us becomes less important than what we know to be true about ourselves in Christ. In Romans 14:7–8 Paul says that nothing can take that identity away. No matter what happens, good or bad, large or small, whether we live or die, we belong to the Lord. God has placed His life within us—a life of unlimited potential in Him—and nothing can take that life away from us. Understanding, accepting, and living out this reality keeps us real and authentic in our relationships with others.

If we continue to make the mistake of defining ourselves by personal success and failure or by any other external standard, the relationships we build will be based on these external things rather than on the reality of who we are apart from those externals. No one will be able to have a relationship with the real us. If we relate to each other on the basis of who we think the other person ought to be instead of who that person really is, we will be doing nothing more than role playing. The one nonnegotiable standard we must base our behavior upon is who God made us to be, not what other people think about us.

SENSITIVITY IS THE MOTIVATION

> *Who are you to judge the servant of another? To his own master he stands or falls; and he will stand, for the Lord is able to make him stand. One person regards one day above another, another regards every day alike. Each person must be fully convinced in his own mind.* (Romans 14:4–5)

Remember the waitress I told you about in chapter 7 who gave her life to Christ in a Mexican restaurant? I shared that story in a church one evening. Afterward, one of those highly religious, overly "spiritual" (and deeply judgmental) types came up to me and said, "Once you led her to Christ, why didn't you tell her that she was wrong to be dating that guy and she needed to get out of the relationship?" This person was convinced I should have laid down the law to her.

"Well, I don't have that right," I said, "and besides, she just became a believer. Who am I to tell her how to live? She's doing the best she can for where she is in her life with Christ."

It seems we are most comfortable in our Christian lives when we can make other people act a certain way and fit into a certain mold. Agreement integrity is not about *doing* what is right; it's first about *being* what is right. Before integrity can become a behavioral issue, it must first become a heart issue. That waitress had to first realize in her heart what God wanted for her. Only then would she have the strength and the desire to follow through.

Too many Christians try to manipulate people's actions to do what they think is right long before these persons' hearts have been changed. This forceful attitude may bring about a temporary change in external behavior, but it doesn't make people love Jesus. What it really does is makes people hate Christians.

When talking with others, we should stay away from using phrases such as, "I want to exhort you in the Lord," "I want to confront you in brotherly love," or my personal favorite, "The Lord told me to tell you this." These phrases are manipulative and underhanded. They demonstrate control rather than sensitivity. Rather, when we're talking to people who are not at the same place we are spiritually, we should ask ourselves the following questions: What do they know? What do they believe? Where are they weak?

We must learn to give people the right to have God develop integrity on the inside of them. We must extend grace to others and not beat up on them. We must allow the Holy Spirit to work in their lives. It's not our job to change everyone and confront everyone's weaknesses. If there is no personal conviction in their hearts, there will be no change, regardless of what we say to them. Everyone we meet is in a spiritual process. We must never allow the liberty we have received in Christ to become a liability to others.

SPECIFICS MATTER

> *The one who eats is not to regard with contempt the one who does not eat, and the one who does not eat is not to judge the one who eats, for God has accepted him.* (Romans 14:3)

Because of our new agreement identity, we can expect the Holy Spirit to make positive, specific demands upon our lives. His demands are meant to fulfill us, not restrict us; they are given to direct us into the steps of obedience God has planned in order to build more of His character into our lives. His demands go beyond the obvious commands of Scripture. There are some things the Bible tells us not to do: murder, commit adultery, abuse our bodies, steal, gossip, and so on. But the Holy Spirit's demands go beyond these "thou shalt nots." They come into our lives because of our integrity.

In general, our roles determine the demands that are placed upon us. For example, writing this book makes certain moral demands on me. I have to be able to communicate the truths of this book before I can write them. And in order to effectively teach these truths, I cannot give mere intellectual assent to them. Truth must come out of my life; I must live it as well as preach it.

Consider these role-specific demands:

- As a speaker and a teacher, I have to prepare. I do it because of who I am. That's the demand of my role.

- As a new parent, you must take on the demands of that role. You must do without sleep, change dirty diapers, and if necessary, sacrifice what you want so the baby's needs are met.

- As a business professional, you must have complete knowledge of your company's products or services in order to help the customer make the best possible choice.

- As an athlete, you have the demand of practicing hard and avoiding anything that could undermine your performance in the game.
- As a member of a fraternity…well, your demand is *not* knowing which beer funnel to use. You must know who you are and choose how you will live in that environment.

If you are your own person living under the rules you make, there truly are no rules. Anything you choose to do has already been approved by your own personal moral compass. However, if you are representing the Lord and living for Him, your actions have already been determined by the Spirit of Christ living in you.

I have a friend who started a new job and found that she had walked into a cold, unfriendly corporate environment. She felt isolated, self-conscious, and unsure, and she wanted very much to be accepted. So often these kinds of feelings are the ingredients for compromise, but the Lord spoke to her and said, "If they only knew who you really are, they would be talking to you." He reminded her of her identity in the Lord, and she was able to develop work relationships with her integrity intact.

THE STRONG MUST SHOW MATURITY

Now accept the one who is weak in faith, but not for the purpose of passing judgment on his opinions. (Romans 14:1)

Those of us who've walked with God the longest are responsible for the weaker believers. As the mature ones, we must answer the question "Am I willing to limit my freedom so that others might come to Christ?" To choose faith over freedom and self-discipline over self-expression is true maturity.

Jeremiah delivered God's message to a nation that measured people's value based on external behavior. They had long forgotten why they performed their religious rituals. But God came and promised that He would send One who would literally write His law on their hearts. Jesus came and fulfilled this promise through His death on the cross. His death made it possible for God Himself to reside in the heart of every believer. This is why the apostle Paul could say to us that our actions carry the greatest weight in the world when they are chosen and motivated out of a clear conviction of who we are in Christ.

The challenge for those of us who want to live a life of agreement with God is to integrate who we are in Christ with what we do to live out the agreement. For too long we have defined integrity by the activities and behaviors of our life in Christ. It's not that what we do isn't important; it is. But what's more important is to make sure that what we do is initiated out of our realized identity in Christ. When we understand the *why* of integrity, the *what* becomes much more convincing—both to us and to the real world.

In the remainder of this book, we will examine our response to God's agreement in five areas of our lives—purity, spiritual growth, friendship, witnessing, and missions (discussed in chapters 9–13). Saying Yes to God impacts our understanding of these five areas of life and how we live out this agreement in our world. We will see how the four agreements play out in our heart, soul, and body. I will show you that when people use their power of choice to willingly bring all the areas of their lives into agreement, the kingdom of God is indeed extended on earth.

PART THREE

THE HOW
OF YES

So Fresh and So Clean

We all use fashion to attract others and hide our flaws. This is nothing new. Cool coverings have been a concern for mankind ever since Eve turned to Adam and said, "That fig leaf is *so* last season!"

Fashion is now an industry that preys on our insecurities, panders to our pride, and prevails through the envy it creates. Millions of us are seduced to follow fashion trends, believing that if we wear that certain outfit we'll look like the ninety-five pound food-starved zombie strutting down the runway. We are in a constant state of panic because the fashion world tells us, "This is what you need to fit in. You'll be cool if you wear this." Then six months later: "You're a jerk if you wear that. Now you need this!" Those who refuse to follow along with fashion seem to be forever stuck in the '70s—polyester pants, orange and lime green polka-dot shirts, white wing tips. These days it's hard to tell if the person wearing the outfit is a senior citizen or a Gen X'er.

Men don't seem to struggle with fashion as much as women do. Men dress by smell. Their whole wardrobe is sorted into two categories: dirty clothes that must be washed, and dirty clothes that can be worn again. Here's Dave's List of Helpful Fashion Tips:

- Tank tops are only for mobsters and guys without muscles.

- Earrings are to be worn only if you're a pirate.

- Overalls are for planting a crop or working as a rodeo clown; otherwise, take them off.

Men dress for two reasons: protection from the elements and protection from the elements. The closest a man gets to a makeover is buying a new car. Men care about cars for one reason: They know that women love nice cars. If women loved cardboard, men would be cruising around in refrigerator boxes.

Women, on the other hand, have entire sections in stores dedicated to makeovers. (If a guy's not careful, even he will be ambushed by cosmetic sample snipers.) Is it wrong for women to wear makeup? Well, as I once heard a guy say, "If a barn needs painting, paint it." Just remember, ladies: pastels for your eyes, primaries for your lips. Be careful not to reverse it, or you'll look like a clown! And one other thing: It really is excessive for you to carry around tackle boxes filled with paints, brushes, rollers, and spackling knives.

Nowadays the rage is permanent makeup. I know of a lady who shaved her eyebrows and then had them tattooed back onto her head in what she called a "fashionable arch." In my opinion all she accomplished was a look of permanent surprise.

Cosmetic surgery of all kinds is at an all-time high. Today it's possible to have every part of your body altered: calves, thighs, arms, cheekbones, whatever. In most malls in America, people are walking around with more plastic parts on them than Mr. Potato Head. The one problem I see with plastic surgery is that you tend to work only on the body parts that are visible most of the time. My question is, What happens to the rest of you? Don't you think that sooner or later the rest of that saggy, old body will have to be looked at? Yikes!

Fashion role models have firmly established the houses of Gucci, Halston, Channel, and Ralph Lauren in the fashion-conscious public mind-set. Meanwhile, most of us have forgotten that our real Designer works for the house of God. We've made gazing at ourselves in the mirror our favorite pastime, but we've forgotten to look into ourselves. Clothing, cosmetics, and reconstructive surgery can help with our outward appearance, but they will not bring us happiness, meaning, or fulfillment. True happiness cannot be found in a perfect complexion, a new haircut, or a perfectly sculpted body. True happiness springs out of a pure heart that is lived in agreement with the life of Christ that's been placed within us.

It's a true statement: *Purity makes you more attractive.* It's true because a pure heart manifests itself in all parts of your life. The real beauty the world seeks will only be found in purity. Only through purity can the world be returned to its original, God-given beauty.

People struggle more with purity than any other issue in the Christian life. That's because the way we tend to think of purity is debilitating to the soul. Our understanding and expression of purity is often limited to making self-conscious and grand, heroic gestures to say no to certain activities or life choices. We do what's expected: sign the card, make the promise, say the pledge—anything to keep our best foot forward (and our faults hidden). The tragedy is, this self-seeking approach to purity reduces the Christian life to superficial morality. Every choice becomes a platform to flaunt our assumed moral high ground, and we transform ourselves into representatives of heavy-handed legalism. What an adulterated view of purity!

Purity is not earned; it's granted to us at the moment of salvation. We are declared pure at the start of our new life in Christ. From that point on, our focus is not on earning a new pure status but on becoming conformed to God's declaration about us. Purity is not about obeying a handful of rules; it's about enjoying the fullness of our life in Christ. That life makes it possible for the things of God to be personally experienced and demonstrated before others who need to see the purity of life that God intended.

Purity is all about how we view ourselves and how we order our lives as a result. Our God-given call is to live lives that demonstrate the truth of Scripture so that the people around us have a clear view of the benefits that come from life lived in agreement with God's will. Author Terry Crist puts it this way: "God is issuing a mandate for His people to disciple a nation with the Word of God. He is looking for radical followers who will rise a step beyond the limitations of previous powerless generations." [1]

Why is purity such a struggle? Why is it so difficult to order our lives in a way that allows Christ to shine through us? The problem, as we've said, is in the way we tend to view purity. In our society purity is not a compliment; it's spoken of in condemning terms. "He (or she) is too good to be with us." "She's a goody-two-shoes." "He's holier-than-thou." These aren't labels most of us aspire to be known by, are they?

We distort purity by equating it with legalism and forgetting that it is first and foremost a work of the heart. Reducing it to a set of rules trivializes the purpose of purity and creates a veneer of purity without the genuine, underlying character. When purity is reduced to legalism, our hearts are no longer free; they are focused more on maintaining rituals and customs than on living out a genuine character change. The real danger of legalism is that it produces a sense of attainment that short-circuits our call to live the life of Yes through Christ. Self-achievement brings a false sense of assurance that somehow we can live a pure life in our own ability. This attitude ultimately leads us to cut ourselves off from the heart of God and, in turn, to deny our true identity in Christ.

Ultimately, each of us is like a stained-glass window of purity. It is precisely our temptations, conflicts, and limited capabilities that are the fragile pieces through which the purity of Christ is reflected. There is no way we can be perfect in ourselves. We lack the ability. But the perfect Christ who lives in us can shine through all our actions and attitudes.

THE PURITY CYCLE

If we're going to have purity in our lives, it's important that we have a clear understanding of what purity is and what it is not.

WHAT PURITY IS NOT	WHAT PURITY IS
• It's not an elaborate system of dos and don'ts.	• It is a continual attention to the heart, from which springs the purpose for our lives.
• It's not escapism, dividing life into the sacred and the secular.	
• It's not despising the body; this will cause us to disconnect from the pursuit of purity.	• It is doing the mundane magnificently and embracing everyday life.
• It's not perfectionism—the mindset that says, "If I fall, I fail."	• It is physical spirituality; our bodies are marked by the presence of God.
• It's not the loss of identity. We don't become less fake or less human.	• It is a process in progress; we are molding our new identity in Christ into the patterns of our lives.
• It's not self-improvement or refining our inner personalities.	• It is growing and maturing our lives to more closely follow the ways and will of God.
	• It is deliberately focusing on the desire of God, so that our actions are not our main focus but the result of who we are.

Here's how purity works. God singles out an area in our lives to conform to His will. We struggle with this disclosure, make mistakes, and deal with related issues. In the end something is revealed to us about ourselves. When we respond with humility and submission to this revelation from God, we are changed, and we move closer toward God's vision for us.

Essentially, we are in a God-initiated cycle to advance purity in our lives. At first we may cooperate with the cycle; but then, somewhere along the way, we lose sight of the fact that God started the whole thing, and we drop out. If we are to benefit from the cycle process, we must understand its stages, identify where we are in it, and then begin a full-on cooperation with God at each step. Only then will we move forward. Only then will we discover what God has placed within us—something that has been there since the day we accepted Christ but that we've not yet fully experienced. Only then will we discover that purity is not what we do; it's who we are in Christ.

The cycle concept is not something I created. It is found in the life of Israel recorded in the Book of Judges. Israel turned away from God and got into trouble. God sent judges to rescue them, but the Hebrew people never understood what God was doing. Instead they chose to continually repeat a cycle of rebellion, retribution, repentance, restoration, and rest. The following chart illustrates the cycle:

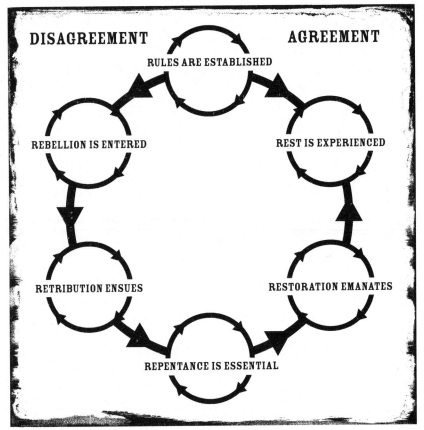

Had the Israelites understood who they were in the Lord, the demands He was placing on them, and what He had in store for them, they might have broken out of the cycle. But instead of experiencing a steady dose of God's blessing and rest, they cycled around and around—committing sin, experiencing the correction of God, repenting, and then repeating the same sin.

CHAPTER NINE: *So Fresh and So Clean*

Before we are too quick to judge the Hebrew people, we must remember that we do the same thing. We don't recognize the stages of the cycle God takes us through. We don't choose the way God provides out of our wrong behavior. We make the same mistakes over and over again. We defend our position, saying, "I can stop and get out of this cycle anytime I want." The clearest sign we're caught in the cycle is when our life in Christ experiences progress for a time, but then the progress fades. Before we know it, we're back where we started.

If the cycle isn't broken, it is inevitably repeated. But at any stage, there is always a way out: choosing the will of God. Instead of cycling into confusion, we can say yes to God and return quickly to His will and design for our lives.

Let's take a closer look at the six stages of the purity cycle.

STAGE 1: RULES ARE ESTABLISHED

> *Now the angel of the LORD came up from Gilgal to Bochim. And he said, "I brought you up out of Egypt and led you into the land which I have sworn to your fathers; and I said, 'I will never break My covenant with you, and as for you, you shall make no covenant with the inhabitants of this land; you shall tear down their altars.'"* (Judges 2:1–2)

When God sent the Hebrew people into the Promised Land, he established one rule: Kill everybody. (Don't take this out of context—remember, we're talking about a specific historical event. There isn't a little voice speaking to you in the back of your head, telling you to do the same thing.) God's desire was that they not entangle themselves with the inhabitants of the land in any way. His purpose was to build purity in His people, because out of that purity, the Messiah would come. God intended for Israel to be a bright and shining light to the nations. If the Israelites didn't destroy their enemies, they would be influenced by them—and then they could never be all that God had called them to be.

There's an important principle here: *We cannot possess what God has for us if we do not dispossess everything that is in the way.* If the will of God is to be firmly established in our lives, it will take work. It doesn't come without a struggle. We have to make choices to drive out the evil that possesses particular areas of our lives. Evil doesn't disappear just because we hit our knees and pray a little prayer. Often it requires a fight.

We need to ask ourselves, "What's in the way of God's will being firmly established in my life? What needs to be driven out before God can dominate a particular area?" We don't have to shrink from the fight; through His Spirit, God has given us the power to possess purity and to dispossess the things in our lives that we have substituted for it.

STAGE 2: REBELLION IS ENTERED

> *But you have not obeyed Me; what is this you have done?* (Judges 2:2)

> *All that generation also were gathered to their fathers; and there arose another generation after them who did not know the LORD, nor yet the work which He had done for Israel. Then the sons of Israel did evil in the sight of the LORD…and they forsook the LORD, the God of their fathers, who had brought them out of the land of Egypt, and followed other gods from among the gods of the peoples who were around them, and bowed themselves down to them.* (Judges 2:10–12)

At this point in history, the people of Israel did whatever seemed right in their own eyes. They had a casual view of the will of God. That's the root of rebellion: an informal mind-set that allows us to flirt with moral danger, believing we can proceed through life unharmed. We think, *What does it matter? It's just the will of God. He'll find someone else to do it.*

We must understand who we are. Purity is not life lived in accordance with law; purity comes from understanding who we are and ordering our lives in a certain way as a result of who we are.

To the degree we do not know who we are in the Lord, we will rebel against the desires of God. We will rebel not because we don't understand the law, but because we don't see ourselves as possessors of the character of God.

Many of us have grown up believing, "Well, I'm just a sinner saved by grace." This is what I call "worm theology." The implication is that we believe in God's forgiveness but not in the new birth. We believe we have been forgiven but not recreated into a new person. We've been taught a new-agreement truth in an old-agreement way. We say we believe in grace, but we define ourselves by our old nature. The problem is, we end up acting the way we think about ourselves. *"For as he thinks within himself, so he is"* (Proverbs 23:7). We believe that our sins are forgiven, but we believe just as strongly that our nature remains unchanged.

You and I have a new identity in Christ! Until we believe that, we will continue to rebel. The old agreement must be mentally removed. It only leads us to focus on performance and legalism—to change our behavior so that we look good on the outside, even though we are still full of death on the inside. Unfortunately, many Christians believe that if they preach the law, it will draw people toward more righteous living, not realizing that focusing on morality alone actually obscures the Gospel.

Most of the people I speak to have had some church experience in which they've heard that living a pure life means keeping a set of dos and don'ts. The closer their lives are lived to this list, the closer they are to a pure life. When this approach to purity is taught, people hear: "You are a bad person, but you can be better." "You are most likely unable to live this kind of life, but go ahead and try harder." "Your life demonstrates that you're not really worthy of God's best blessings."

The message of our new agreement in Christ is quite different: "You are completely loved." "You are totally forgiven." "You are fully and completely pleasing to Me." "You are God's own possession, and He is constantly at work in you to produce His will in and through you."

People say, "You need to take a stand on sin." "You need to tell them what's right and wrong." "You need to lay down the law." The fact is, our new agreement means that we are completely new people. Our new nature is that of sons and daughters of the Most High God. When we really know who we are in Christ and believe what God says about us, it's impossible to say, "I don't know what to do about sex, pornography, and drugs." We *do* know, because God has written His law upon our hearts.

Accepting Christ makes us entirely fresh and new. The Bible speaks of us as a new nation and a new race, not defined by class or color but by the life of Christ in us. What does it mean to be a new race? The answer involves both *content* and *character*.

Content of the New Race

The content of our new race—who we are in Christ—is based on the fact that everything God wants to see in us, He declares us to be. First John 3:1 says, "*See how great a love the Father has bestowed on us, that we would be called children of God; and such we are.*" John wrote this to show us the difference between our old nature and our new nature. Instead of seeing ourselves in light of our past mistakes, we must realize that the mistakes we made before accepting Christ were made by somebody else. That's right. Our old man, our old nature, committed those sins, and now our old nature has died with Christ: "*Even so consider yourselves to be dead to sin, but alive to God in Christ Jesus*" (Romans 6:11).

Many of us believe that we are alive to God. We sing worship songs, read the Bible, and pray. But we refuse to believe that we are dead to sin. We refuse to accept the fact that God has forgiven us and created us to be new beings.

Too often we have excessive guilt over one or two instances of sin in our lives, and we wish God would take the guilt away. The good news is, He already has. The death of Jesus Christ removed the penalty for our past sin. Do you see it? The person who did those things is dead. But many of us don't believe that God really removed our sin. We continue to think that if we just hadn't done that one thing, we would be in right standing before God. That's not an attitude of self-pity; it's self-righteousness. Self-righteousness is thinking that we can be righteous in any way other than how God provided for us to be righteous.

There comes a point when we have to forgive ourselves and walk in our new nature. We have to walk in the new freedom that God has given us. That's why Paul wrote, *"Even so consider yourselves to be dead to sin, but alive to God in Christ Jesus"* (Romans 6:11). We must apply our new God nature to every area of our lives and respond to the new life God has placed within us.

In 2 Corinthians 6:16, God says, *"I WILL DWELL IN THEM AND WALK AMONG THEM; AND I WILL BE THEIR GOD, AND THEY SHALL BE MY PEOPLE."* The life of God is within us. We carry with us the presence of God Himself.

Character of the New Race

The character of the Christian is found in the life of the Spirit. Once we receive Christ as Lord, we follow Him by the power of the Holy Spirit; and as we learn to walk in our new life, we demonstrate the fruit of the Holy Spirit.

Romans 8:14–16 says: *"For all who are being led by the Spirit of God, these are sons of God. For you have not received a spirit of slavery leading to fear again, but you have received a spirit of adoption as sons by which we cry out, 'Abba! Father!' The Spirit Himself testifies with our spirit that we are children of God."* We have been brought into a new family—the family of God—not as slaves, but as sons and daughters. Everything that is His is now ours. There's nothing awkward about our relationship with God. We don't have to wonder whether or not we're good enough or whether or not we have the right to do what He wants us to do. If we are His, and we're empowered by His Spirit, then all the blessings of God rest upon us.

We are His sons and daughters. He is our Father. Our character is shaped by that understanding of who we are in Christ and by our willingness to say yes and allow the Holy Spirit to have His way in us.

STAGE 3: RETRIBUTION ENSUES

> *The anger of the LORD burned against Israel, and He gave them into the hands of plunderers who plundered them* [What were the odds?] *and He sold them into the hands of their enemies*

around them, so that they could no longer stand before their enemies. Wherever they went, the hand of the LORD was against them for evil. (Judges 2:14–15)

As long as the children of Israel remained in agreement with God, they experienced the blessings of God. When they lived in disagreement, they could not prosper, no matter what they did. They refused to say yes to God's will that they get rid of their enemies, so God said, "Fine. Have it your way. But those enemies will pick you apart. They'll plunder you, and you'll be at war your whole life."

I once knew a businessman who went through a period of major rebellion in his personal life. He lived in disagreement with God, thinking his choice wouldn't impact his ability to make money. He had built up a very successful business, but he told me, "No matter what I tried, nothing seemed to work. I made what seemed like good decisions, but my business kept losing money. I knew I was living in disagreement with God, but it took me awhile to understand that my choice had a definite impact on my business."

When we don't see the immediate consequences of our rebellion, we get a false sense of confidence. We think we're getting away with something. We can justify it all we want, but the truth is, our decision to live in disagreement with God *will* catch up with us. There are natural consequences to all the choices we make that are contrary to who we are in Christ.

STAGE 4: REPENTANCE IS ESSENTIAL

The LORD was moved to pity by their groaning because of those who oppressed and afflicted them. (Judges 2:18)

The message of the entire Book of Judges is "Repent!" But many of us have a wrong understanding of what that means. Repentance does not mean saying a little prayer to clean our slates so we can go out and do the same thing again. It's not saying, "God forgive me for what I'm about to do." Repentance is *returning back to* the will of God.

There is a God who has a will. Since we possess the nature of Christ, doing His will is not optional. We might have a thousand good reasons to move in the opposite direction, but His will is still there. We must choose to obey it if we want to experience all the blessings of a life of Yes.

When we choose to disobey, repentance is essential if we want to experience the fullness of God's blessings. Again and again in the life of Israel, we see the same sequence taking place: The people choose to live in disagreement and turn from the things of God. The consequences come. The people repent. Good things happen.

Just because we haven't experienced any major difficulties (yet) from living in disagreement, we shouldn't mistake God's patience for His permission. God may let us go our own way for a while; but ultimately, no one gets away with anything. Hopefully we will come to our senses quickly, repent, and return to the will of God.

STAGE 5: RESTORATION EMANATES

> *Then the LORD raised up judges who delivered them from the hands of those who plundered them....The LORD was with the judge and delivered them from the hand of their enemies all the days of the judge.* (Judges 2:16, 18)

Restoration always comes after repentance. As we've said, repentance is much more than promising not to commit a specific act ever again. Saying, "I'm going to give God's way another try," is like saying, "I'll just practice the law, and maybe I'll get better at it." We must never forget that the law was given to prove to us that we can't make ourselves acceptable to God. Why would we want to keep practicing something we can never succeed at?

The law was given to prove that we could not be perfect. Christ came to fulfill the law, and He's the only one who can live it. Most people have just enough law in them to make them miserable. They know that they shouldn't be doing what they are doing, but they don't know how not to do it. They don't realize that it's only through repentance that they are restored back to the will of God. In order for that restoration to take place, we must:

- Recognize that the law is over; it's been fulfilled in Christ
- Understand who Christ is in us
- Receive His life into the specific area of our lives in which we've been in disagreement
- Recognize that purity is no longer a big struggle—it's automatic
- Live out our new commitment to God's will in that area

When we do this, good things happen. God restores victory and blessing where there used to be struggles and need. We experience an internal cleansing, and purity begins to rise within us. In this stage of the cycle, everything that we've lost, God gives back to us. This fact should be incredibly motivating to us! When we repent, we are once again restored to God's will and energized with His design and desire for our lives.

STAGE 6: REST IS EXPERIENCED

Then the land had rest forty years. (Judges 3:11)

At this point in the cycle, the people of Israel had the truth rooted in their lives; they understood who they were to God, and they understood what they had to do. As long as they lived in agreement and refused to return to idols, there was peace.

The same is true for us. Believing the truth keeps us pure. It's no coincidence that those things that bring us a heightened sense of negative consequences to come also bring us a loss of peace. Stop disturbing the peace! We need to rest in the new nature we've received in Christ and live out of that nature. We don't have to go through these cycles all the time in order to find rest.

Here's the tragedy of this story. Judges 2:17 tells us that the people *"did not listen to their judges, for they played the harlot after other gods."* As soon as a judge was gone, *"they would turn back and act more corruptly than their fathers"* (Judges 2:19). The children of God never got it. In the midst of their sin, they came to God, and God dealt with them through the conviction of His Spirit. In response to this conviction, they made choices they hoped would end the suffering. They realized moments of victory, but they never truly dealt with the areas of their lives that made them bent to repeat the same sins. As a result they just kept cycling down deeper and deeper into the despair that comes as a natural result of living in disagreement with God.

This is exactly what will happen to us without repentance and restoration to the people we truly are. If we do not dispossess the impurity in our lives, we will continue a deepening downward spiral toward greater despair. But if we will live the life of our new nature, we will rise to a higher level—a level where purity is embraced and allowed to flow into the choices of our lives.

CLOSING THE GAP

Perhaps you're thinking, *Now he's going to ask me to find where I am in the purity cycle.* Wrong! It's not a bad idea to think about where you are, but for me to ask that is about as predictable as saying, "I know! I know! The butler killed him in the conservatory with the lead pipe!"

I have another question in mind—a question we always ask about each other, even if we're too shallow to ask it about ourselves: "How are you doing spiritually?" Turn that question inward, and let me give you a simple way I discovered to test how you're doing.

I call it "the gap." I believe that everyone has a gap (and every mall does too). For a long time I struggled with knowing whether or not I was making any progress in my spiritual life. My dad left when I was six, so I never had a man in my life to guide me in my spiritual walk. And even though I've been on the road speaking for the past eleven years, I still sometimes wonder if I'm "getting it" spiritually. Through this type of questioning, I discovered that our spiritual lives can be measured by the time gap between God's conviction and our response to it.

Many times God convicts us of something, but we're slow to

respond. We feel His conviction in a certain area of our lives, but we push it off. At that exact moment, we choose to live in disagreement with God rather than in agreement—and a gap is created that widens with every passing second. Some of us have to measure the gap in months or even years, not hours and minutes.

For Israel the gap was as long as it took them to admit their disagreement with God and repent of it. The Book of Judges records cycle after cycle of Israel's disagreement and repentance, disagreement and repentance. Some cycles were longer than others. But every one of them could have been prevented if only Israel had chosen to agree with God.

We can know that we're growing up in our faith if our gap time—the time between God telling us to do something and our positive response to Him—is narrowing. If we are maturing in our faith, our response time to God will be shorter and shorter with each new opportunity to follow Him. The gap will continue to narrow, and we will be quicker and quicker to dispossess the sin that desperately tries to keep us living in disagreement with God.

The time gap isn't only a measure of our general spiritual condition. It also shows us exactly what things God needs to work on in our lives. Where we have a gap is exactly where God will deal with us. A gap is a call to action. It's an instrument of God's permanent accountability on our lives.

So how do we narrow the gap and begin to grow spiritually? Let's look at three keys.

OBEY THE INSTRUCTIONS

According to the foreknowledge of God the Father, by the sanctifying work of the Spirit, to obey Jesus Christ and be sprinkled with His blood: May grace and peace be yours in the fullest measure. (1 Peter 1:2)

How well do we take the Word of God to heart? It's one thing to read it in the Bible or write it in a notebook; it's another thing to have it written on our hearts. We can have deep quiet times, faithfully uphold the inerrancy of Scripture, and give money to Wycliffe Bible Translators, but unless we submit to all that is written in the Bible, we won't persuade anyone that we believe a single word of it.

Closing the gap means that we obey God's leadership even when we don't want to. It means obeying Him even if it goes against our cheap desire of the moment. We must trust that acting on God's instruction will bring us everything that we want or need. The tragedy is, many of us would prefer to find pleasure in our own ways rather than discover the great freedom and exhilarating joy that is ours if we follow His instruction.

ORDER YOUR INSTINCTS

> *Do not grieve the Holy Spirit....Let all bitterness and wrath and anger and clamor and slander be put away from you, along with all malice. Be kind to one another...forgiving each other.* (Ephesians 4:30–32)

> *But immorality or any impurity or greed must not even be named among you.* (Ephesians 5:3)

We all struggle with our own drives and weaknesses—areas where we're easily taken in by sin. Ordering our instincts means knowing those weaknesses and creating appropriate boundaries. That's difficult for our carnal natures to do, and here's why. First, we've gotten very good at coming up with rationalizations that convince us to sin. Second, we don't like to humble ourselves and say, "Well, I guess I'm not strong enough to resist that thing. What I should do is completely remove myself from the situation."

We narrow the gap by making choices that starve our carnal instincts and feed our spiritual ones. For example, alcoholism has been categorized by psychologists as a disease. It's the only disease I know of that comes with pretzels and chips. But somewhere in the midst of contracting the disease, the choice is made to drink. If this is an area you have difficulty with, get help. If alcoholism runs in your family history, use that fact as motivation to be more cautious, not as an excuse to make wrong choices.

OBTAIN INTEGRITY

The integrity of the upright will guide them, but the crooked-ness of the treacherous will destroy them. (Proverbs 11:3)

In the everyday issues of our lives, we either choose to live the truth that we are a new creation in Christ and go forward, or we choose to live a lie and return to the dead life that we left behind. Integrity is about living in accordance with all that God has made us to be in Christ. It's about saying yes to God and allowing His Spirit to work through us. When we obtain integrity, we narrow the gap. When we turn away from integrity and try to do our own thing, the gap widens; we find we have no power in life, despite whatever talents or skills we possess.

In life's difficult moments, we want to think our struggles come from uncertainty about what we should do. Recently, America's Catholic cardinals traveled to Rome to meet with the pope to decide how to handle the sexual abuse charges being leveled at priests. My question is, why are they looking for an answer in Rome when they have the answer in the Bible?

Far too often the issue is one of integrity. We know what we should do, but we choose not to do it. This choice creates an integrity gap, and you know who always suffers in the gap: We do. The anguish we feel is not from uncertainty; it's from disobedience. We must take hold of integrity and decline the temptation to release it. Refusing to do so will only cause us grief.

By obtaining integrity, we narrow the gap in our lives. We live increasingly on the agreement side of the purity cycle. Purity, after all, is not a destination; it's a journey. The more we live in purity, the more our lives are transformed and empowered by the Holy Spirit. Everything that God wants us to do and to be becomes increasingly more natural to us when we're growing in purity. We respond more quickly to God's conviction and direction because His way pleases us. As if looking at a picture taken by the camera of God, we know who we are—a new creation in Christ—and we know that His way is truly our way.

Advancing the Spirit

Lately I've noticed the weirdest things in stores. I was at a convenience store, and the guy behind the counter had on one of those belts people wear for heavy lifting. I wondered to myself, *What's he lifting behind the counter that's so heavy—lotto tickets, cartons of cigarettes, or packages of gum?*

I saw a sign in a restaurant that read, "This is a drug-free work place." Why put up the sign? Was that a change in policy? Was there a time when the sign could have said, "The whole staff is toasted"? Then there was the sign in the rest room that told employees to wash their hands before returning to work, because it's the law. The law? How about because it's good hygiene? How about saying, "After you've scrubbed the toilet, don't go make a sandwich"?

I was in an electronics store that had a sign out front that read, "These doors will remain unlocked during business hours." Perhaps the owners were talking one day, and one said to the other, "You know, we haven't sold a thing since we started this business. Maybe we should unlock the doors." Then the other one said, "Let's keep them unlocked for as long as we are open. I'll put up a sign so we don't forget."

There's a deli I visited that gives a lie detector test to its employees (I mean, sandwich artists). What is there to lie about in a deli? A customer orders a turkey sandwich and the artist replies, "We don't have any turkey...OK, we do. I admit it, we do!"

Let's face it. People often need to see or hear the most obvious things put in an authoritative statement. It's true today, and it was true in Old Testament times as well.

God put up big signs in the form of religious ordinances and temple sacrifices to show His people how they should live and how they should respond to Him. As a result of what happened in the Garden of Eden, we all need God to show us how to live. We don't have the same religious ordinances or temple sacrifices as the Israelites, but we still need to hear God's most obvious truths stated in a powerful manner.

THE PROBLEM WITH SPIRITUAL GROWTH

Let's say we're escorted to a seat in the theater of human destiny. *In the Beginning* is showing. We sit down and watch as something is formed out of nothing. We see the very beginning of everything and watch it grow as the Creator ushers in Creation by bringing light, order, and life. The show culminates with the creation of man, made in the image of the Author of the universe.

God breathed the very life of Himself into that first man. In Genesis 2:7 the phrase *"breathed...the breath of life,"* literally means, "breathed *lives*," plural, indicating more than one kind of life—that is, Adam had physical, mental, and spiritual substance, and he was given the opportunity to grow creatively in each of those dimensions. Adam was given boundless potential, ability, confidence, satisfaction, and blessing—all found in his relationship with God. He and God had a genuine relationship. They talked, spent time together, and even planned the future of the earth together. God loved Adam, and Adam loved God. God was meticulously concerned about meeting the needs of this new man, and He met them perfectly. The Scripture says that God saw everything He had made, *"and behold, it was very good"* (Genesis 1:31).

CHAPTER TEN: *Advancing the Spirit*

Because God desired a real relationship with Adam and Eve, He placed in them absolute moral freedom. He took a chance on them, giving them the unquestioned right to make their own choices. It was God who restricted His own choice. He refused to make Adam and Eve His robot slaves. He knew that only on the basis of their free ability and power to choose could this new man and woman be truly human. It had to be their choice to love Him and accept Him as God; it couldn't be compulsory. God wanted a real relationship between true, spiritually related souls. And in the beginning, He had that relationship. Together, Adam and Eve had unique positions in the history of mankind. Adam was the only man who could truly say, "You are the only woman for me." Eve was the only woman who could honestly say, "I have nothing to wear."

But Adam and Eve were not gods. Even though they were God's apex of Creation, they were not infinite. All of Creation belonged to them except one tree in the midst of the Garden. God had given them one single restriction: "Don't eat from that tree." I'm sure this single restriction reminded them that they had limitations. I'm also sure it reminded them of God's proper place as the sovereign ruler of the universe.

Tragically, Adam and Eve took the magnificent potential of a perfect, lifelong relationship with God and twisted it, misused it, and finally broke it. When they did, sin entered into the world. Their sin was purposeful; and because they sinned, they lost their perfection.

All sin is a choice to attack the person of God. Adam and Eve not only rejected God; they rejected His rule. They personally chose to believe a satanic lie about the character of God and purposely rejected their relationship with Him. Satan convinced them that they could be God. But as they soon found out, that was a lie.

Now, as a result of their rejection of God, we have a problem. At the heart of human nature (in your heart and my heart), something is radically wrong. Since the sin of Adam and Eve, every human has been born with a spirit that is alienated from God and controlled by sin.

Our first parents were enticed by the idea of not having to depend on God, of making a life for themselves. But once they bit into the empty promises of Satan and rejected God's promise of a full life, they fell. What followed was the end of growth for the human race. Their decision to reject God's standard created an unquenchable desire to determine their own standard of living. This desire has continued to show up in full force within the heart of everyone born after Adam and Eve. It explains mankind's consuming drive toward self-reliance and self-dependence as well as our deeply resentful unwillingness to submit to the will of God.

The fall of mankind in the Garden brought an end to spiritual life and growth. The once perfect relationship God had with the first man and woman was replaced by mankind's indifference, making it possible for people to grow physically but no longer morally or spiritually. In Deuteronomy 29:4, as Moses looked back on his forty-year walk with the Israelites, he wrote, *"To this day the LORD has not given you a heart to know, nor eyes to see, nor ears to hear."*

By default mankind forfeited the ability to know God when Adam made the seemingly insignificant decision to disobey God. Job acknowledged this condition in Job 33:14: *"God speaks once, or twice, yet no one notices it."* Isaiah put it this way: *"Keep on listening, but do not perceive; keep on looking, but do not understand"* (Isaiah 6:9). God's judgment on our condition is clear in Hosea 4:6: *"My people are destroyed for lack of knowledge."* If you're not sure what I've said up to now, you're not listening—and that's my point.

THE PLAN OF SPIRITUAL GROWTH

Throughout the Old Testament, God continued to relate to people through religious practices and spiritual ordinances, which were like the obvious signs posted in restaurants and retail stores. They served to help keep mankind on track until the new agreement could become reality.

CHAPTER TEN: *Advancing the Spirit*

Today those old signposts are no longer necessary. Still, it's easy for us to think that growth in our relationship with God involves a little quiet time spent in self-indulgent, poetic journalizing or reading happy stories about other people's spiritual experiences. For too many of us, spiritual progress spins around the most fashionable, acid-free paper journal; the smoothest flowing writing instrument; and a room saturated with the ambiance of spooky melodies amidst the aroma of fragranced candles—not genuine face time with the Father.

We've all seen the guy sitting in the corner of the coffee shop in his sandals and grey hemp shirt, nursing a tall double mocha caramel latte, intently writing something in a notebook that surely must be deep and illuminating. Of course, when we finally dare to walk by and look over his shoulder, we see that he is filling out a job application.

I know. As good little church people growing up in Sunday school, we were taught that having a daily quiet time would get us a gold star by our name. Because of this emphasis, it has been easy for us to be enamored with the task rather than the point of the task.

But God has a different plan for spiritual growth, and He outlines it in Joshua 3. The people of Israel had been wandering around the wilderness for forty years. (The Bible isn't clear on this point, but I believe they wandered for so long because all of their leaders were men who wouldn't stop and ask for directions. Ladies, can I get an "Amen"?) When they finally made it to the border of the Promised Land, God spoke to them and told them He had one simple task for them to do. They were to follow the ark of the covenant, which represented the presence of God wherever it went.

Under the new agreement, God's presence is not found in a box. We have His Spirit living inside us. Still, our task in spiritual growth is the same: to pursue God wherever He goes. The lighting in the room is irrelevant. The music doesn't matter. The paper in our journals doesn't have to be recycled. Regardless of our season of life, not considering the circumstances surrounding us, no matter what else is happening, the way to spiritual growth is to simply pursue Him.

Nowhere in the Word of God does God ever ask His people to retreat from pursuing Him. It's impossible to pursue God with our backs toward Him. Spiritual growth is never lateral, even though it may seem that way. If we are following God and He seems to stand still or amble around in the same place for a while, it's only His way of leading us deeper into spiritual growth. Spiritual growth is always about being with God more and more. It's about God calling us to a more intimate knowledge of Him, calling us to grow for His greater purpose.

To grow spiritually, there must be a resolve in our hearts that says, "God, I don't know what Your will is. I don't know how all the bad stuff in my life is going to work out. I don't know how all the cool stuff and the successes are going to be factored in. But no matter what, I am committed to You, and I'm committed to grow during the best and the worst times of life." When we make this decision, God moves into our lives and works in three specific ways. These three ways form God's plan for spiritual growth. In a very real sense, these three things are the measure of how real and powerful our pursuit of God is.

In the third chapter of Joshua, the Israelites were moving out of the wilderness and into the Promised Land. They were gaining better ground. It's in this story that we see God's plan of growth for us.

HE EXPANDS HIS PURPOSE

> At the end of three days the officers went through the midst of the camp; and they commanded the people, saying, "When you see the ark of the covenant of the LORD your God with the Levitical priests carrying it, then you shall set out from your place and go after it. However, there shall be between you and it a distance of about 2,000 cubits by measure. [Two thousand cubits is equal to ten football fields.] Do not come near it, that you may know the way by which you shall go, for you have not passed this way before." (Joshua 3:2–4)

In this passage God was taking His people in a new direction to a new destination. Growth is always about moving forward. The common struggle we all seem to have is staying out of the ruts that halt our progress. We find ourselves reading just to get information; praying simply out of duty; or assuming that because we have the basics down, we don't need to know anything else. We get stuck in a holding pattern that prohibits us from moving forward and blocks us from hearing, seeing, or sensing the higher purpose of God for our lives.

I have a friend who is an interior designer. When he refinishes a home, he literally tears the guts out of the house. He redesigns the whole structure and then rebuilds it and redecorates it. I went with him to see one of his projects, and the place was stunning. "Man, who wouldn't want to live here?" I said.

His response surprised me. "Well, I wouldn't want to live here."

When I asked why, he replied, "Because I know that regardless of how good this looks, it's only a small fraction of what I can really do. There is something in me that is much greater than this house."

How true, I thought. We settle for so little, when God has placed so much more within us. The first good spot we arrive at in life, we say, "This is great. Who wouldn't want to live here? Let's stay up here on the mountaintop and watch the sunset." We look at the circumstances and say, "I'll settle here; this will be fine. Later on, if I get tired of this place, I'll follow God a bit further."

But God says, "If you could only catch a glimpse of what I have for you, you would pay any price to get it." It's so easy for us to get caught up in the limited view we have of our dreams. We never dream the dreams of God. We never see all that He has for us. We don't realize that through all the events in our lives, God has a greater purpose in mind. As a result we settle for far less than His best for us.

We think we'll find life when we find the right niche. "I'll meet the right person to love and marry. I'll buy the right house. I'll get the right job and have the right amount of money, so I can afford all the things I want." We believe happiness is finding a plateau where we can live out a future of our own design. We think we'll find life when we settle into an anemic, sitcom kind of happy existence. But the truth is, that's lateral living. It's not the purpose of God. The purpose of

God is for us to get to that place where He can begin to enlarge His purpose for us and grow us up into all that He desires for us to be, to have, and to do.

Following God out of the wilderness and into the Promised Land demands an increasing amount of our personal best. The good news is that as we follow Him, God increases our resolve to follow Him even further. The greater the demands we face, the greater the purpose He instills.

HE ENHANCES OUR PERSPECTIVE

> And they commanded the people, saying, "When you see the ark of the covenant of the LORD your God with the Levitical priests carrying it, then you shall set out from your place and go after it." (Joshua 3:3)

We all have times in our lives when our perspective is challenged, and we get desperate to know the will of God. We want to know every detail of His will for us at that precise moment. But that's not how God works. Our perspective is shaped through a process.

We try to zoom in on God's will as if we were focusing a super Hi8 digital microcamcorder with stereo sound. We push one eye as far as possible into the viewfinder, trying to close out all the sunlight, and work with the image until we think we see it just as it is—only to pull the camera away and see the real scene with all its surrounding beauty. Meanwhile, we've pressed the camera so hard against our face that our eyes bulge out like Marty Feldman's. (If you don't know who that is, log on to www.pixillusion.com/~fredo/marty/index.html and find out.)

Let's look at the three-step process of coming to know God's will for our lives.

It Starts Out Broad

Our knowledge of God's will starts out broad. Israel had followed God for forty years by following a cloud and a pillar of fire. These things would be hard to miss, don't you think? Their relationship with

God was based on the obvious. They knew God was there. They had the cloud, the fire, and the manna with them every day. This corresponds with what I call big-print Christianity: SEE GOD SAVE. SEE GOD LOVE. SEE GOD FEED. SEE US TRUST HIM. GOOD, GOD, GOOD!

This is where all of us begin when it comes to spiritual growth. For us today, following the cloud and the fire means bringing our lives into line with the clear morality God has outlined in Scripture. It means establishing convictions and pursuing the character of Jesus Christ. It means putting His life principles to work in every situation, regardless of how it makes us look.

Too many of us are caught in this starting phase of spiritual growth. We play little beginner games, flirting with actually doing the will of God. But just as with Israel in the wilderness, a day will come when the cloud and the fire will disappear. For the Israelites God replaced the cloud and the fire with a gold-covered box carried by a few men and told the people to follow it. That was God's way of challenging them to grow up.

Keeping the ark in sight wasn't easy. Let me put it in perspective. There were over one million Israelites, and the ark was not much bigger than a tabletop—about four feet long and two feet wide. If you were in a crowd of a million people, how easy would that be to see? A fire suspended high in the sky would be hard to miss. A cloud might take a bit more effort to see, but it could still be viewed pretty easily. The ark, on the other hand, was very small and could only be seen through genuine personal effort.

When God asked the people to follow the ark, He was asking them to follow His presence. That's still our call today. The challenge we face in spiritual growth is that it requires more time and attention than most of us are willing to give.

We cannot physically see God. Our ability to listen to God's voice and obey His leading must be refined. In the beginning stages of knowing God's will, it's important that we understand which of the provisions and the blessings contained in God's agreements with mankind belong to us. Knowing what God has promised us deepens our faith and produces the confidence to move forward.

It Moves into Specifics

In the specific phase of growth, God deals with us in terms of our desires and dreams for the future. He builds in us a specific vision of where our lives are headed. In this phase we must read the Scriptures carefully and pray for greater discernment.

God knew that the task He had prepared for the Israelites—to take complete possession of the Promised Land—was a tremendous calling. He knew that unless they learned how to follow Him even when they couldn't see Him, they would never complete the task. For years the people had lived in the shadow of the cloud by day and the fire by night. Now they had to follow what they could not readily see to a destination they did not know.

This change in God's method of leadership showed the people that if they were to understand the specifics of their future, they would have to focus more purposefully on God's presence. Likewise, if we are to move into a specific understanding of God's will for our lives, it will require us to exercise a greater focus on following God as He leads us through His Spirit.

It Narrows into Details

In the last part of Joshua 3:3, God gave the people directions that told them exactly what to do: *"Then you shall set out from your place and go after it."* He moved them forward by giving them the details they needed. The details phase of growth is the decision stage in which we begin to act on the dreams that God has crafted for us and revealed to us. As we act decisively on what we know to be the will of God, other doors of opportunity open, and the details of God's will for us begin to appear.

It is vital that we pass through each stage of growth in order to live in agreement with God's plan for our spiritual growth. To recap, the pattern by which God sharpens our perspective looks like this:

Our perspective of God's will starts broad, bringing our lives under His rule. It moves into specifics, leading us to dream God's dreams. It narrows into details, giving us specific directions for living in complete agreement with God's will for us.

HE ESTABLISHES OUR PERSEVERANCE

> *This day I will begin to exalt you in the sight of all Israel, that they may know that just as I have been with Moses, I will be with you. You shall, moreover, command the priests who are carrying the ark of the covenant, saying, "When you come to the edge of the waters of the Jordan, you shall stand still in the Jordan."...The waters of the Jordan will be cut off, and the waters which are flowing down from above will stand in one heap.* (Joshua 3:7–8, 13)

When Joshua yelled out the command, "We are going to stand in the water!" Israel entered into a giant game of Pass It On—you know, that game where someone whispers something into another person's ear, and that person whispers what he or she heard into the next person's ear, and so on and so on. By the time it reaches the end of the line, the statement is nothing close to what the originator spoke. When Joshua's words finally reached the back of the crowd, the last guy turned to his wife and asked, "Why are we going to stamp out the otters?"

God was moving the Israelites out of the realm of possibility and into the realm of the impossible. If we limit our understanding of God's will to doing only what is possible, we will never experience the full measure of His will for us. As we grow up in the Lord, God wants to teach us to persevere, to stand where we are, and to obey Him fully in every situation. Perseverance is important because the results of our obedience are not always immediate, and they are not always automatic.

What happened next for the Israelites holds a very important lesson for us: "*And when those who carried the ark came into the Jordan, and the feet of the priests carrying the ark were dipped in the edge of the water (for the Jordan overflows all its banks all the days of harvest), the waters which were flowing down from above stood and rose up in one heap, a great distance away at Adam, the city that is beside Zarethan; and those which were flowing down toward the sea of the Arabah, the Salt Sea, were completely cut off. So the people crossed opposite Jericho*" (Joshua 3:15–16).

There they stood in the cold, murky water, whining to each other, "It's cold! How long do we have to stand here? Where are the otters?" Meanwhile, thirty-one miles upstream at a city called Adam, the water was rising up in a heap. The minute the Israelites stepped into the water, the will of God was accomplished, even though they couldn't see it. They continued to stand in the river until the last of the water that had been cut off at Adam finally flowed past them, and they found themselves standing on dry ground. Now the million-plus people of Israel could cross the river. For hours they'd stood there, waiting for God's will to become evident. That's called persevering.

Perseverance is not our natural inclination. Our culture has so overextended itself that we have PDAs to keep track of our DayTimers. We buy microwave rice because it's ready thirty seconds quicker than the old Minute Rice. Most of us know the anxiety of staring through the tiny holes in the microwave window and shouting, "C'mon, I don't have all nanosecond!" This inability to wait has downloaded itself into our spiritual lives at gigabit speed.

Most of us pray a prayer, give God a try, tip our hat to His leading, wait for just a moment; and when nothing happens, we bail out, thinking we have persevered. We think that if God can't do what He needs to do in the amount of time we give Him, then it's time for us to move on.

A significant part of spiritual growth is coming to the recognition that God wants us to stand, even when we can't see anything happening. He says to us, "You must stand. You must stay faithful, even if you can't see the payoff." Perseverance becomes possible only when our focus is on following God rather than finding the payoff or seeing the results.

THE PROHIBITERS OF SPIRITUAL GROWTH

If you've been in a pillow fight, you know the feeling of being pummeled by a thick, mushy object, leaving you with what can only be described as a dull buzz. That's exactly what happens in the spiritual journey of most Christians. We approach our encounters with God as opportunities to receive either a wink from God or a dull buzz from His heavenly pillow of discipline.

Many of us have become focused on the tasks of reading the Scriptures (a prescribed number of verses—no more, no less), writing in our journals, and praying for others on a daily basis. When we finish, we believe we will have a better day because of our spiritual discipline. That's not spiritual discipline; that's spiritual superstition. We might as well rub Buddha's belly. Neither one, by themselves, will make our day better or worse.

In the midst of the discipline, we lose sight of God. We get so focused on refining our discipline that we drift away from His presence and become blinded to His desires. The only needs we can see are our own. Do you see how easy it can be for just about anyone to blame God for his or her failures?

We are taught "You can be anything you want to be." It's the mantra that generations of American dreamers have grown up with. It's the same thought that has prompted thousands of young men and women to enlist in the army ("You are an army of one"). Self-motivated, self-reliant, self-confident—we are taught to admire these labels. Have we forgotten what these attitudes do to the soul?

Our souls have been suffocated. We no longer have a sense of our own depravity. We no longer see the severity of our need to pursue Jesus or recognize the importance of cultivating a life that intimately knows Him.

Reviving the soul is the first task of spiritual growth. We must recapture the desire for God described in Psalm 42:1: *"As the deer pants for the water brooks, so my soul pants for You, O God."* We can amass as much knowledge as possible, but it will do us little good if we don't have a heart beating in unison with His life in us.

What are the prohibiters of spiritual growth? Dryness, prayerlessness, temptation, and discouragement. These four things can do a number on us—like a professional wrestler wrapping us up in the ropes and turning the entire ring upside down on us.

DRYNESS

Often dryness comes from unconfessed sin. In many ways it reflects a breakdown in our honesty with God. We choose to let things remain as they are without saying a word. We bury things we know are wrong and forget where we buried them.

God calls us to transparency. He gives us permission to be wide open with Him, so He can clear out everything that is harmful in us. Opening our souls to God detoxifies all the poison of buried sin.

PRAYERLESSNESS

Our lives have more distractions than we can possibly handle. We feel overwhelmed with our responsibilities. As a result the quality of our prayer lives is given about as much consideration as Susan Lucci at the Soap Opera Awards. Prayer is at the very bottom of our to-do lists. We assume that prayer doesn't require preparation, but we're wrong. If we are to have a purposeful prayer time, we must eliminate the clutter in our lives and in our homes, so we can have both a time and a place to be with God.

CHAPTER TEN: *Advancing the Spirit*

TEMPTATION

Just because temptation shows up in our lives doesn't mean we're spiritually immature. Everyone struggles with temptation. Temptation isn't sin. If we struggle with it, we're not failures. The struggle isn't the problem; giving in is the problem. We can recognize temptation for what it is, identify it, struggle with it, and admit that it is in our lives. We just have to refuse to give in to it.

The lure hiding behind every temptation we face is the same one that enticed Adam and Eve: the opportunity to live our own way, serving our own desires. Like Adam and Eve, we have a choice. We can give in to temptation, move away from God, and break agreement with Him. Or we can take the same escape route that was available to them in the Garden: Say yes to God and choose to live in agreement.

DISCOURAGEMENT

We've heard the story of Noah and the Flood so many times that we're hardly touched by it anymore. But this story shows us how to combat discouragement with faith. Can you imagine being Noah's wife? Noah went out and preached to thousands of people, but they would not listen; they would not repent. His poor wife stood by every day saying, "Don't worry. Some people will believe you tomorrow. I'm sure tomorrow's the day."

Noah was a man of faith. He knew God would be faithful to the promise He made. When it was all said and done, the ark floated on the water, and Noah was able to look out the window of the ark and say to all the doubters and disbelievers, "Good luck on the swim team! Hope you know the backstroke!"

Recognizing dryness, prayerlessness, temptation, and discouragement as prohibiters of spiritual growth can help us deal with them in such a way that they actually propel us toward greater intimacy with God. A good friend of mine says that a problem well-defined is a problem half-solved. When we can clearly identify the things that prohibit our own personal spiritual growth, we can get about the task of moving beyond them and enhancing our relationship with the Father.

We have to remember that God is on our side, pulling for us and yelling to us, "Come on! Let's keep going!" Whether we walk, stroll, or stumble along in our spiritual journey, God's call is to continue, to keep moving forward, to follow Him wherever He leads.

THE POWER OF SPIRITUAL GROWTH

The overwhelming power of the new agreement comes from the fact that it enables us to know God personally. *"I will put My law within them and on their heart I will write it,"* God said in Jeremiah 31:33. This was the promise that through personal faith in Jesus Christ, the Holy Spirit would come to live within us and teach us the heart of God.

The privilege of intimately knowing the Father is not to be taken lightly. Jesus bought this privilege for us with His death. His death and resurrection provide us with eternal life, and His life inside us gives us the ability to know God and grow in godliness. Jesus makes this clear in His prayer for His disciples: *"This is eternal life, that they may know You, the only true God, and Jesus Christ whom You have sent"* (John 17:3). It is through the leadership and teaching of the Holy Spirit that we are able to touch the very nature of God. Paul tells us in 1 Corinthians 2:12: *"Now we have received...the Spirit who is from God, so that we may know the things freely given to us by God."*

Since the fall of Adam and Eve, mankind has lived with only a limited knowledge of God. Our spirits are dead; so when God speaks, He sounds like one of the adults in a Charlie Brown cartoon. But now Jesus' death has made it possible for us to hear and understand the voice of the Father. Christ has opened up a way for our spirits to become alive for the first time since Adam and Eve chose to disobey God. Through Christ each of us has the opportunity to know God for ourselves. We can know the Father of all creation, learn His will for us, and experience for ourselves the fulfillment of living in agreement with His desires.

Spiritual growth is God's plan for every believer. He wants us to know Him intimately and grow in our relationship with Him. But spiritual growth only happens when we focus on following the Father wherever He goes. The path is not ours to determine. The results are not ours to select. The power for the journey is not even available on our own. No, all these things become ours when we set our focus on the face of the Father. And it's from that day forward that we really begin to live the life of Yes.

CHAPTER ELEVEN

Allies in Agreement

Friendships have always been an important part of life. When we were young, it was easy to pick friends. The main criterion was "anyone who says hi to me first." Those were the days when we could pass out valentines to the whole class without being thought of as weird.

Of course, we had different levels of friendships: best friend, new best friend, friend for now, friend forever—and "Friends are Friends Forever," or so we thought. Most of us probably dedicated that song to at least one person we stopped being friends with a long time ago.

Acceptance is still one of the major criteria for establishing friendships. We think that if someone likes us and he or she seems cool, we've found a friend. But that measure isn't always fail-safe.

Many of us have chosen roommates on that very basis, and before we knew it, they had blown the rent money on QVC; lost their job because they couldn't miss *Jerry Springer*; and eaten all the food, including whatever had our name on it. Then we come home one day to find them sacrificing the cat on the living room coffee table. In a split second of clarity, we realize we're living with someone who is flakier than hot apple pie.

Our need for relationships is intense. We crave friendship but can't seem to find it. Many people are lonelier than Martha Stewart at an RV show. We need friends. Research even shows they can make us healthier (unless we're drinking out of the same glass). Friends accept us. They instill confidence and give us the courage to do things we wouldn't ordinarily do, such as try out for a sport, ask someone out on a date, or drink a six-pack of Scope.

Most of us long for meaningful relationships, but more often than not, we're really only looking out for ourselves. An honest evaluation of most of our relationships would reveal that we use people in hopes of meeting our own needs. Some of us are vaguely aware that there is a higher dimension to friendship, one that could make our relationships more fulfilling. We just don't know how to reach it.

The growing popularity of the Internet has accelerated our loss of relationship skills. On the Internet you can create just about any identity by the user name you choose. At work you may be known as "The Quiet One" who always gets the project done and seldom talks to the person at the next desk. But when you log on, you are known as "Proud_N_Loud@loquatious.com," the marathon chat-session crasher, more obnoxious than smokers in an ice cream parlor. The Internet has made genuineness and openness a challenge. It's easier to open a children's medicine bottle than it is to open up some of us.

As a result, many of us have settled for facsimile relationships and cyber-friendships. We connect with other people in chat rooms, where we have important conversations ("I like green—what's your favorite color?") and intellectually stimulating debates ("Is orange actually a color?"). So many people float alone today in cyberspace that we need a strong reminder that real friendships are both important and necessary.

In fact, this generation thirsts for more than simply a human connection; they thirst for spiritual reality in their relationships. Christians should have a corner on this market, but we really aren't any better at relationships than the rest of the world. Most Christians I know talk about the pastor's sermon like they do his tie. It either matches his suit or it doesn't; it either stays tucked into his coat or it falls out over the button; it looks OK, but it's so last season...doesn't he know? There's neither power nor conviction in our conversations. We aren't challenged to move beyond a superficial level of relating to one another.

As Christians we have all the relationship advantages the new agreement in Christ brings us. Through this agreement we enter into a relationship with God that is more fulfilling than anything else we have ever used to meet our own needs. The Creator of mankind lives within us, and He seeks us out to have a fully intimate relationship with us. It is out of the completeness of this intimacy that we can know how to properly relate to others. And because the Spirit of God lives in us, we have the ability to destroy the faulty relationship habits that have dominated our lives.

Once we understand how much the Spirit of God permeates every part of our lives, we will have a difficult time living with superficial relationships. We will long to have fellowship with others in the same way we have fellowship with God. We will crave human relationships filled with supernatural, powerful meaning.

The agreement God has made with us gives us a new level of safety in the way we relate with others. When we understand that we are completely accepted by Him and can never be rejected, it's easier to open up to others; the fear of ultimate rejection has been eliminated. When we know that God loves us and will continue to love us even when we are unlovely, we can more easily accept others, regardless of the way they behave.

There is a new power in our relationship of agreement with God—a power that comes to us as we learn to trust Him more and more. That power inevitably spills over into our other relationships. The more we walk in agreement with God, the more we can accept others as they are because we know it's not our responsibility to change them. We understand that God is already at work in their lives, bringing about the changes He desires.

There are many ways to approach relationships that don't require God's involvement. Becoming a better listener, learning to affirm another person, becoming more flexible in adjusting to the desires of someone else, learning how to resolve conflicts—all of these can be done with a good self-help book and without the help of God. But the new agreement places God at the very heart of our being. Everything we hope to find in human relationships, all the things we want others to be to us, is found in living the life of Yes with God. The new agreement gives Him the right to invade every one of our relationships and literally energizes every relationship we have.

SET THE PARAMETERS OF FRIENDSHIP

"Let's just be friends." These words have stung the heart of many a man and woman. Even as you read this, you may be having a painful flashback. But as difficult as your memory may be, it brings to the surface something we all know about relationships: They're not all equal.

THE BASICS OF FRIENDSHIP

Without really working at it, we tend to place our friendships in different categories. Let's take a look at some of them.

Acquaintance

These are the people who enter our life at random. Think of that guy with the dreadlocks, orange sunglasses, tie-dyed T-shirt, and ragged jeans who is always standing at the same corner when you go to work. You've bought a flower from him a time or two, hoping that you were helping him out. Then you see him one day while you're walking through the mall parking lot with a friend. You interrupt your friend's enthralling discussion on the biological differences between shrimp and prawns to say, "Hey, I sometimes buy flowers from that guy on my way to work." You don't know his name, and you have no real commitment to him; he's just an acquaintance.

Associate

Specific activities bring us into contact with our associates. These are the people on our team, in our theater group, at the meeting, in the band. They're in our lives because we share common interests, and the majority of the time we see them only in the context of these activities.

Accountability

Close friends, best friends, and perhaps brothers and sisters fall into this category. These are people we have allowed to have access to our heart. They exert incredible influence in our lives because we allow them to impact the choices we make and the directions we take. We take these people with us regardless of where we go. We can pick these relationships right back up even if we've been separated for years.

Agreement

An agreement friendship is in its own category. Please don't make the mistake of thinking it's simply another form of accountability friendship. There is an element of accountability, but it's much more than accountability. An agreement friendship takes place when two people are committed to the design God has for the other person. We need people like pastors, teachers, and mentors to encourage us, but we also very much need agreement friendships.

As you can see from the following chart, agreement friendships influence all of the other friendships we have. The inner circle shapes the way we relate to the outer circles. We carry the connection and commitment we find in this small inner group out into our other relationships.

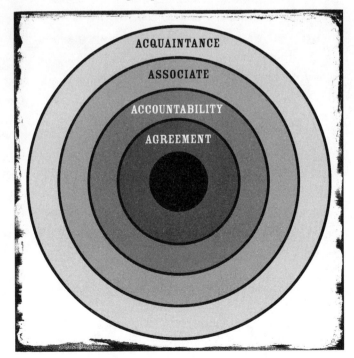

THE BARRIERS TO FRIENDSHIP

The greatest barrier to developing agreement friendships is selfishness. Thinking we deserve more than other people is never a healthy way to make friends. Rather, it's a guaranteed path to isolation and loneliness. Asking "What's in it for me?" is an antirelational approach that creates feelings of rejection in others. Our friends start thinking that we don't care about them—that we only care about what they can do for us.

Christians can be the biggest hypocrites when it comes to relating to others. We believe that the message of Christ's unconditional love and forgiveness should be shared with the whole world, but when it comes to living out that love and forgiveness with our Christian brothers and sisters, we come up short. Most of us value ourselves more than we do other people. This gives our friendships the spiritual strength of a wet paper towel.

Let me go ahead and give you some advice on how to lose the friends you've got, if that's what you want to do.

- *Become stingy with your life.* This is more than not being available to spend time with others. It's having a heart that only does what it wants to do. Just as young children who refuse to share their toys usually end up getting pushed away by the other children, you can expect similar treatment if you choose to be stingy with your life.

- *Never open up.* Some people think this is the safest way not to get hurt in relationships: Just don't open up about how you really feel about things. The problem is, if you aren't honest about how you feel, other people never really get to know you. Sooner or later someone will say something that hurts you. If you've never been open about how you feel, how are you going to be able to constructively tell that person that you're hurt?

- *Talk about yourself all the time.* Know someone who does this? Don't we all! Want to be like him (or her)? Do you want people feeling about you and talking about you the way you feel and talk about that person? Didn't think so. Moving right along...

- *Always have something negative to say.* This is one of the most attractive things about some of the girls I've dated. Notice the emphasis on the past tense.

- *Make your friends feel like they're just a small part of your plan for world domination.* Friends are friends because they get something out of the relationship and because they get to give something to the relationship. If your focus in friendship is solely on what you can get the other person to give you, be ready for mass friend defection.

THE BLUEPRINT FOR FRIENDSHIP

That's enough of what *not* to do in friendship. To understand what *to* do, we need to look in depth at the friendship God has with us. Our relationship with God gives us the pattern for all the relationships we have with others—especially agreement friendships. The driving force behind our agreement friendships should be the same force that drives God to keep all His agreements with us: love.

Jesus defined the essence of agreement love in John 15:12 when He said, *"Love one another, just as I have loved you."* Jesus spoke these words to the twelve disciples He had chosen to love. When Jesus picked the Twelve, He was aware of their potential—and their shortcomings. James and John were ambitious; they tried to promote themselves to the seats right next to Jesus. Peter was impetuous, often shooting off his mouth and making promises he could not fulfill. Matthew struggled with materialism. But Jesus made an agreement to love them unconditionally, no matter what.

Jesus had every reason and right to overlook these guys and disqualify them from having a relationship with Him. Instead, He loved them right where they were, not for where He knew God would take them. He loved them for exactly who and what they were, warts and all. Instead of being judgmental, He involved Himself in their lives. He came to their jobs, their homes; He knew their families. He was interested in everything about them.

In John 15:14 Jesus referred to the disciples as friends, and rightly so. The Twelve had become His friends in agreement, and He modeled that agreement love with His very life. He made the advancement of God's purpose for their lives His focus. He made their deal His deal. His actions said, "I'm interested in what's best for you." All that He taught them—and most importantly, all that He taught them about Himself—set them free and empowered them to Christianize the world.

What are your friendships like? How would you talk to others about them? It's easy to use godly or religious terms to describe an existing, shallow relationship, but that doesn't mean it's an agreement friendship. An agreement friendship is sacrificial; it will cost you something that you value. If it costs you nothing, it's not a sacrifice. Jesus' agreement with His disciples cost Him a great deal. For over three years, He lived with them, ate with them, traveled with them, and shared the same campfire with them at night. Jesus sacrificed Himself and His own personal freedom to keep the agreement of love He made with these twelve men.

Jesus' love was not restricted to the social elite. Jesus offered His agreement friendship to the poor and the weak, the disconnected and the lonely, the homeless and the clueless. He still does. Years after Jesus' death, Paul wrote, *"While we were yet sinners, Christ died for us"* (Romans 5:8). In other words, Jesus doesn't offer His love to people who measure up, because no one ever measures up.

How far are we supposed to take this agreement type of love? Well, Jesus is our example, and He took it all the way to the Cross. That was the ultimate demonstration of His love to the world. We were lost and hopeless without Him. But He loved us in spite of ourselves and made our deal His deal. He kept it His deal all the way to the Cross.

Paul describes the mission of agreement love in Philippians 2:3: *"Do nothing from selfishness or empty conceit...regard one another as more important than yourselves."* Put others first? Yes! That's exactly what Jesus did for us. In the process He demonstrated what real love between human beings is supposed to look like.

Think for a moment about the way God has treated you in Christ. Jesus left the splendor of heaven to come to earth. He put off His eternal shape to put on the mortal shape of a man. He set aside His glory and status to live under the same conditions you do, with the same limitations and restrictions. He faced all the temptations you face; conquered the forces of evil on the cross; and moved into agreement with you. He loves you unconditionally; refuses to judge you, even though you've rebelled against Him; and invites and empowers you to extend His love and grace to others. He does all of this not because you earned it or won the golden ticket; He does it for the same reason He wants you to do it for others: love.

Loving like Jesus loves requires us to step into people's lives and demonstrate love, even when we have no reason to love them. It requires us to invest in others the way we want others to invest in us. This doesn't mean keeping score; it means thinking about others—and ourselves—with the mind of Christ. It means replacing the normal controlling emotions of jealously, bitterness, and revenge with the selfless love of Jesus.

Here are some ways we can demonstrate agreement love from day to day.

- "*Love your enemies.*" (Matthew 5:44)
- "*Husbands, love your wives.*" (Ephesians 5:25)
- "*Wives, be subject to your own husbands.*" (Ephesians 5:22)
- "*Children, obey your parents.*" (Ephesians 6:1)
- "*Regard one another as more important than yourselves.*" (Philippians 2:3)
- "*Put on a heart of compassion…forgiving each other.*" (Colossians 3:12–13)
- "*Be subject to rulers, to authorities.*" (Titus 3:1)
- "*A friend loves at all times, and a brother is born for adversity.*" (Proverbs 17:17)

Our decision to show agreement love is not determined by the other person's character, morality, or sensitivity toward us. These things are not the issue; our agreement to model the love of Christ is.

I was never very good at football, although I played in high school. I was the guy on the team who only had to wash his uniform once a season. I saw less time on the playing field than the mascot (who, by the way, was a sloth). I was very dedicated to working out and going to practice…that's my story, and I'm sticking to it.

Every summer the team prepared for the fall season by doing two-a-days. Working out twice a day—who thought of that? Are two a day really better than one? What about two heart attacks in a day—is that better? Anyway, these plural sessions of torture took place at a nearby state park called Roman Nose. Identifying a state park by referring to someone's nose seemed somewhat cruel to me, if not downright bizarre. Besides, I'd taken a course in Oklahoma history, and I knew for a fact that Romans do not feature prominently in Oklahoma's history.

Back to my story. One afternoon, while the sun was high over Roman's nose, the coach blew his whistle to signal the beginning of a two-mile run. When I began the second mile, I was so far behind everyone else on the racetrack that it looked like I was actually in the lead. Then, as I rounded the backside of my last lap, something strange happened. The track was so hot that the heat melted the glue in one of my shoes, and the sole began to peel away from the upper part of my sneaker. With half of my shoe flopping against the track, adding to my nearly complete lack of physical coordination, I wished I could leave my body and watch myself finish the race from somewhere up above.

That's when the two stars of our team, the quarterback and the running back, noticed my predicament. They were in the lead and would have finished first and second, but they dropped out of their positions and ran back toward me. With one on each side, they held me up by my arms and carried me through to the finish line. They didn't have to give up winning the race to carry the awkward benchwarmer to the finish line—but they did. In a perfect picture of agreement friendship, they gave up their position as starters for the sake of another player. They intentionally finished behind their potential in order to help someone else simply finish the race.

SEE THE PRIORITY OF
AGREEMENT RELATIONSHIPS

The Old Testament book of 1 Samuel tells the story of the agreement friendship that developed between Jonathan and David. Jonathan was the most eligible bachelor in the entire kingdom of Israel. He was King Saul's favored son, which meant that after his father died he would become the next king. Every single day of his life he heard, "Jonathan, learn all you can, because you are going to be king one day." Everything was selected for him on that basis. His teachers were carefully selected, his friends were screened, his itinerary was planned, and even his clothes and meals were chosen for him. Every step that could be taken to prepare him for his future responsibilities was carefully planned and followed. He would have his place in history.

Then one day, while standing on a hillside with his father, everything changed. For days the Israelite army had been camped across the valley from the Philistine forces. Day after day he and his father had watched as the Philistine giant, Goliath, walked out onto the battlefield and issued a challenge to the Hebrew soldiers who were hiding behind the rocks in fear. This day, however, was different. Jonathan watched as a young shepherd named David, a boy who appeared to be about his own age, walked into the valley, accepted Goliath's challenge, and ended up killing the giant.

That act of courage proved to be more than a victory for the Hebrew army. The victory over Goliath gained David the fear and respect of the entire Philistine army, as well as the respect and awe of the people of Israel. And in that brief moment, Jonathan's entire world changed. No longer was he the most popular boy in town; David was.

Sometime later, Jonathan heard a rumor about the shepherd boy. *Could it be true?* he wondered. People were saying that when David was younger, the prophet Samuel had broken open a jar of oil and poured the liquid on David's head, saying, "God has removed his hand from Saul, and David will be the next king of Israel." If the rumor was true, not only was this shepherd a mighty warrior, beloved by the people; not only did he have the obvious presence of God in his life; he was going to be the next king!

If that's not grounds for jealousy, bitterness, and anger, I don't know what is. Jonathan had every reason in the world to hate David. He had every reason to fear him. For all practical purposes, David had ruined his life. From the moment of his royal birth, Jonathan had been raised to be the next king. Now he knew that, sooner or later, David would take even that from him.

But according to the Bible, bitterness and resentment were not Jonathan's response. Somehow Jonathan came to love David so much that none of his own losses mattered. He found a way to work through his personal pain to the point that it became less important to him than his love for his friend. Something other than anger and disillusionment over losing his place in the kingdom became the driving force in his life. That something else was agreement love.

Jonathan and David had a true agreement friendship. Each was committed to the design of God for the other, and they made that commitment a priority. Neither man was the same once they agreed together to help one another achieve God's plan. Every aspect of their lives was impacted. It was out of this friendship that David became a beautiful instrument that God was able to use to accomplish His purpose. He became the greatest king Israel has ever known.

Examples of great agreement friendships are scattered throughout the Scriptures. They're placed there to show us the priority of such friendships and the important and necessary position these special relationships play in our lives. Let's look at a few of them.

NAOMI AND RUTH

Ruth had just lost her husband and the livelihood he provided. She faced an uncertain future and easily could have become a social outcast. But in the midst of the most extreme challenge of her life, Ruth latched on to her mother-in-law and told her, *"Where you go, I will go"* (Ruth 1:16). Any married person can tell you how difficult these words would be to say and mean to an in-law. Most married people think a pleasure cruise is driving the in-laws to the airport. These days the words *"Where you go I will go"* are often spoken by a bride and groom at their wedding ceremony, but they were originally spoken by Ruth to Naomi. God used the agreement friendship between these two women to meet Ruth's needs.

MOSES AND AARON

Moses knew his own weakness when it came to speaking in front of large groups. The task God gave him was an enormous one, and it required a great deal of public speaking. But Moses found his mouth-piece in his brother, Aaron. In becoming Moses' shadow and spokesperson, Aaron sacrificed his own plans and desires for comfort and safety. But that's the mark of an agreement friendship: a deep acceptance of the other person's gifts and a willingness to help that person fulfill his or her God-given purpose.

MOSES AND JETHRO

Moses found himself filling the roles of deliverer, governor, and pastor to the people of Israel. His days were filled with listening to and resolving the people's problems, no matter how small or trivial. Jethro, Moses' father-in-law, spoke to Moses out of his love and concern for him, saying, "You can't do all of this alone. You'll kill yourself." He encouraged Moses to get help.

Agreement friends like Jethro have the ability to see the problems and difficulties inherent in the way we structure our lives. Their criticism isn't negative—it's constructive. They tell us to get rid of certain things, rearrange our priorities, and focus on what we need to be doing. They know they can be totally honest with us without fear of rejection.

ELIJAH AND ELISHA

Agreement friendships inspire sincerity and infuse power into our lives and relationships. Three times Elisha said to Elijah, *"I will not leave you"* (2 Kings 2:2, 4, 6). Because of his commitment to Elijah,

Elisha received a double portion of Elijah's power, enabling him to perform twice as many miracles as Elijah ever did.

Elisha learned how to fulfill his role as a prophet through his close relationship with Elijah. The old saying is true: We become like those we spend the most time with.

JOSHUA AND CALEB

These were two men with a different spirit from the other Israelites who waited at the entrance to the Promised Land. Joshua and Caleb had journeyed with ten other scouts into the region and saw the same things as the other men. Yet when they were asked about the potential dangers of entering the land, their report was favorable, unlike everyone else's. They recognized the design of God at work and sensed that His resources were more than adequate to enable them to take the land they'd seen. In faithfulness to each other and to God, Joshua and Caleb spoke out boldly in spite of the opposition. That's what agreement friends do: They support each other, encouraging one another to be courageous and take a stand for Christ, regardless of the circumstances.

PAUL AND TIMOTHY

From the time he first met Timothy, Paul could see the gift that Timothy carried within him. Again and again Paul stood up for Timothy when his youthfulness caused others to question his ministry. The confidence Paul instilled in Timothy served Timothy well throughout his entire life.

Agreement friends affirm us and build us up by speaking godly wisdom into every area of our lives. But they are more than mentors. They're not there to maximize our potential; they're there to fan into flame the God-things within us.

PAUL AND ONESIMUS

In the small letter Paul wrote to Philemon, we read about the tender concern Paul had for the slave Onesimus. Paul wrote that he was sending Onesimus as if *"sending my very heart"* (Philemon 12), in the hopes that Philemon would be persuaded to give Onesimus his freedom. The kindred spirit Paul felt with Onesimus characterizes agreement friendship. Paul told Philemon, *"If then you regard me a partner, accept him as you would me. But if he has wronged you in any way or owes you anything, charge that to my account"* (Philemon 17–18). Agreement friends aren't the ones who accuse us in public for some wrong we may or may not have done. They're the ones who take the hit for us and stand by us, even when we've made a mistake.

Friends in agreement see the bad in us without being distracted by it; bear the weight of our mistakes; bring honest, penetrating wisdom to the table; and skillfully spot the good in the middle of the chaos and darkness of life. When we have an agreement friendship, we truly have something extraordinary.

SUBMIT TO ANOTHER PERSON IN AGREEMENT

First Samuel 18:3–4 tells us, *"Jonathan made a covenant with David because he loved him as himself. Jonathan stripped himself of the robe that was on him and gave it to David, with his armor, including his sword and his bow and his belt."* There was no question in Jonathan's mind that God intended for David to be king. His actions spoke louder than any words he could have said. He took off his royal robe and placed it on David. Then he took his sword and bow and belt and gave them to David, promising to help his friend fulfill God's decree to become the king of Israel.

Jonathan could have said, "God, why are you punishing me for my father's sin? OK, so my father messed up. But why can't I be king? Don't take the kingdom away from me and my family and give it to this shepherd boy, just because of my dad." Instead he pledged, "All that I have, all that I am, is yours, David." He spoke this to the man who had just derailed his life!

Whether you know it or not, you are an important part of God's plan in someone else's life. Someone needs what you have to offer. But the reason you should submit to another person in agreement is not out of duty or obligation or accountability. The reason you should submit is love. Jonathan loved David as himself.

Most of our best friendships take time to develop; they grow through seasons and stages. But agreement friendships don't always grow that way. Sometimes they grow up in what seems like a moment of time. Jonathan and David hadn't been together long, but they felt as if they had been lifelong friends.

It's possible to miss opportunities for agreement friendships. Unless we're living in agreement with God and know what to look for, an opportunity could stare us in the face, and we would not know it. In general, an agreement friendship should be between two people of the same gender and from a similar age group. It should be a consistent relationship, not hit-or-miss, and it should involve no manipulation.

The temptation is for us to try to make a list of potential candidates we think could fill this role in our lives, narrow it down, and pick the best one. But agreement friendships aren't manufactured. Regardless of how spiritual or ingenious we think we are, we can never bring ourselves together with the people God has designed us to be with. If it's left up to us, we'll pick the person we think can best help us reach God's goals for us.

The reality is, agreement friendship is designed for our submission—not the other person's. In an agreement friendship, our priority is to look out for the other person. At the same time, God uses that person to protect us; to help us become a man or woman of character; to keep us on track to become all God wants us to be; and to hold us back from the things that will destroy us.

By the way, the excuse of not being raised right or having a terrible background doesn't exempt a person from submitting to someone else in an agreement friendship. Look at Jonathan. He did what was right, even though he had a terrible role model. His father, King Saul, had a wrong attitude toward agreement friendship. Saul became angry when he learned that Jonathan had been speaking intimately with David, whom Saul considered an enemy. He screamed at Jonathan, "*You son of a perverse, rebellious woman!*" (1 Samuel 20:30). Of course, you know how we'd say that today. Everything is in the Bible!

I'd hate to have been Jonathan. His father continued, "*Do I not know that you are choosing the son of Jesse to your own shame and to the shame of your mother's nakedness? For as long as the son of Jesse lives on the earth, neither you nor your kingdom will be established. Therefore now, send and bring him to me, for he must surely die!*" (1 Samuel 20:30–31).

Saul was saying, "Do you realize that if David lives, our family will lose the kingdom? You won't be king. David will take what is rightly yours. His death is the only way to protect your throne." Saul didn't want to simply stand by and watch as everything he had lived for was ripped out of his hands by an upstart shepherd who knew how to play the harp. And he couldn't understand why his son would be submitted and devoted to this person instead of sharing his hatred for him.

SUPPORT THE PREROGATIVE OF GOD

Saul died an angry, bitter, and crazy man, because he spent his whole life trying to resist God's plan. But something made Jonathan different from his father. Jonathan knew and believed something that we need to know. What is it? The answer is found in 1 Samuel 20:13. Speaking to David, Jonathan said, "*If it please my father to do you harm, may the LORD do so to Jonathan and more also, if I do not make it known to you and send you away, that you may go in safety.*" In other words, "Even if my dad comes after you, I promise that I am going to protect you in every way I can." Then he added, "*May the LORD be with you as He has been with my father.*"

Jonathan recognized that God had chosen David to be king, just as He had chosen his father at one time. God's decision was made. From that moment on, Jonathan had two choices: submit himself to God's will or resist God Himself. Jonathan chose to submit to God, and from that day forward, he worked toward fulfilling God's intentions for his life, David's life, and the life of the nation of Israel. He devoted himself to David not because David deserved to be the king, but because God had made that choice.

Pride is a subtle enemy of agreement living. It can take the form of jealousy and resentment. We speak of it in terms of getting our feelings hurt, of being angry at someone or something. The curious thing is, we don't speak of being prideful; but isn't that what we are?

Too often we can't be happy for the success of others because, if they're entering our realm, then their success will be our failure. Or if we fail, they will succeed. It becomes impossible for us to be with such people because they threaten the success and security of our world.

Jonathan died in an obscure place, on an obscure battlefield, fighting beside his father for a cause he would never see realized. But he died having surrendered himself to God's choice of David as king. Jonathan had confidence in God's character. He trusted that God was ordering his steps. This trust and confidence gave him purpose, so that even when he died, his death made sense. He didn't have to worry about who would rule the people if he died in battle; he already knew the answer: David.

Both Saul and Jonathan met death in the same way, but their lives were completely different. I don't have to convince you whose life was better. Jonathan died at peace, knowing love and trust. Saul died in a battle he could not win, at odds with his own son, and in rebellion against God, never knowing the peace and comfort of soul that comes from trusting God's decisions.

Jonathan understood three things that his father did not, and these things helped him support the prerogative of God.

GOD HAS MADE EACH OF US DIFFERENT

God has made each of us with our own special blend of gifts and skills. He's made some people to have money and others to be poor. He's given some people abilities in several areas while others are good at only one or two things. We can't decide to be anyone we want to be, and every youth camp talent show proves it. It takes real talent to totally butcher a Point Of Grace song.

I'll never be a rock star. I'll never be a movie star. I'll never play professional basketball. I won't be president of the United States. I wasn't made to be any of those things. I was made to write books, travel the country, and tell people that God loves them. That's what I was made to do.

GOD HAS GIVEN US THE FREEDOM TO CHOOSE

In addition to giving us certain talents that are uniquely ours, God has also given us freedom. People exercise their freedom in many ways, and I am often the beneficiary of the exercise of their freedom. People help me, hurt me, threaten me, encourage me, and discourage me. Hopefully some people out there (Hi, Mom!) even love me. We have the freedom to choose what we will do with the things God has given us—whether we will use them to fulfill His purposes or ours. We can either submit to others in agreement love or live selfish lives. The choice is ours.

GOD HAS A UNIQUE DESTINY FOR EACH OF US

God is behind everything that happens in our lives. It's not that He's at work helping all the people who want to hurt you. But He is at work making everything come out for our good. I don't know how He does it. It's the mystery of the Cross. Wicked men crucified Christ out of jealousy and anger, and God used their act of rage to save us. How powerful a God is that?

We need to pray, "God, I know that nothing comes into my life that You don't take and use in some creative way." If we have this understanding, the power of God will be released in us, and we'll be free to love our enemies. We'll be able to love people who aren't lovable because we'll trust that, at the end of our lives, we will have accomplished all that God wanted us to accomplish—despite all the bitter people who worked so hard to keep us from doing what God set out for us to do.

Now the choice is ours. We can either support God's plan for those around us and work together to fulfill God's purposes in this world, or we can fall apart trying to shake God into submission to our own desires. (A word to the dense: The second option doesn't work.) We must ask ourselves, as Jonathan did, "In light of God's dominion, how should I respond to the situation I'm in? How should I act, trusting in His goodness and relying on His strength? How can I support what He's doing in my life and in the lives of others?"

SERVE ONE ANOTHER PROACTIVELY

To be *proactive* means to act in advance of an expected difficulty; to anticipate what may lie ahead and do something about it. Agreement friends serve one another proactively, working to advance the will of God in each other's lives. Jonathan knew that David was God's anointed one to be king of Israel. Because of their agreement friendship, he made proactive decisions in their relationship so that the greatest good—God's will—would be accomplished in David's life as well as in his own.

Here are five proactive choices Jonathan made in his friendship with David. Through his example we can identify five characteristics of a true agreement friend.

FRIENDS INITIATE—THEY DON'T INVADE

Jonathan said to David, "Come, and let us go out into the field." So both of them went out to the field. (1 Samuel 20:11)

Agreement friends are people who initiate. They initiate conversation; they initiate the relationship with us; but they don't invade our personal space. Agreement friendship has an element of courtship to it. It is purposeful and faithful but never overbearing.

Jonathan knew that David was in a crisis and that King Saul, his father, had something to do with it. So Jonathan took David to a place where they could talk privately. Going *"out into the field"* must have been the ancient equivalent of going to the mall or out for coffee. Jonathan understood the need for confidentiality and the importance of intimacy, so he initiated a meeting with David in a place that would be safe for both of them.

Friendship is always an invitation. It doesn't say, "Do this for me," or, "Here's how you fit into my life." Agreement friendship says,

"*Come, and let us*"—"let us go, let us live, let us cry, let us laugh. But in everything, let us be together." Friends initiate; they don't invade.

FRIENDS QUESTION—THEY DON'T ACCUSE

> *Then David...said to Jonathan, "What have I done? What is my iniquity? And what is my sin before your father, that he is seeking my life?" He said to him, "Far from it, you shall not die. Behold, my father does nothing either great or small without disclosing it to me. So why should my father hide this thing from me? It is not so!"* (1 Samuel 20:1–2)

David asked Jonathan some hard questions, but he didn't get defensive. He was on the run from King Saul, and he wanted to know why. He asked Jonathan if he knew of anything he'd done wrong to cause the situation. David questioned Jonathan, but he didn't accuse.

Jonathan's answer was surprising. If I were Jonathan, I would've said, "Well, of course you should fear for your life. You've turned the people's hearts to yourself, away from my dad, and one day you'll steal the throne away from me." But that wasn't Jonathan's response. He answered David's question with a question of his own. He wasn't trying to be clever or secretive; he honestly didn't know of any plan Saul had to kill David. For David's sake, however, he would find out.

Some arguments we have with our friends are the result of not knowing all the facts, because we're too impatient to learn them. We want to ride into town with both guns blazing, not even waiting for the dust to settle. But that's not agreement friendship. Friends question and get all the facts; they don't accuse.

FRIENDS TELL THE TRUTH—THEY DON'T DENY IT

> *Jonathan said, "Far be it from you! For if I should indeed learn that evil has been decided by my father to come upon you, then would I not tell you about it?"* (1 Samuel 20:9)

As their conversation continued, David's tone intensified. He was under stress. But Jonathan took no offense. He stayed committed to doing the right thing on David's behalf, even though it was going to cost him dearly. Because of his agreement friendship with David, Jonathan became a traitor to his father and to his own hope of being king.

Jonathan was willing to tell the truth, the hard truth. We feel uncomfortable telling someone that we don't like their new shoes, but Jonathan was willing to tell David, "My dad wants you dead." Now that's telling the truth! Honesty is a quality of friendship many of us don't have. We're not willing to be honest with people, and it's quite all right with us if they aren't completely honest with us either. We neither expect honesty nor demand it.

If I say, "Do you like this shirt?" that's not what I'm saying at all. I'm not being honest, because what I really mean is, "Hey, you haven't noticed my new shirt yet, and I want you to compliment me on it." A girl says to her friend, "I went out with John last night. Isn't he great?" She's not convinced that John is all that great; she just doesn't want to hear, "No, he's the antichrist. Stay away from him. He'll ruin your walk with God." As agreement friends we must tell the hard truth in the right way when it's the right time to do so. Friends always tell the truth; they don't deny it.

FRIENDS RESPOND—THEY DON'T RUN AWAY

> Then Jonathan said to David, "Whatever you say, I will do for you." (1 Samuel 20:4)

Jonathan knew that David was in trouble and needed help. He didn't abandon David in his time of need; on the contrary, when David was alone and on the run, Jonathan was there for him. He didn't step in and say, "I'll stick around, but you have to play by my rules." No, he said, "Tell me what you want me to do. I'm willing to help." He understood God's plan for David's future, and he responded by helping him accomplish that plan.

You may be ashamed of your checkered past, embarrassed to tell your Christian friends about the drugs you've done, the people you've slept with, the booze you've chugged, or the places where you've passed out. You shouldn't be. Christ took that shame from you and bore it on the cross. If you need help overcoming a problem, tell an agreement friend. Friends respond; they don't run away.

FRIENDS PROTECT—THEY DON'T EXPOSE

Jonathan made David vow again because of his love for him, because he loved him as he loved his own life. (1 Samuel 20:17)

Something stronger than the urge to protect the family name was at work inside of Jonathan. He chose to protect the very person who threatened his family heritage. Blood is thicker than water, the old saying goes. But Jonathan's example shows us that agreement love is thicker than blood. Jonathan could have exposed David, and he would have been honored by his father for doing it. But Jonathan loved David with his life, and he valued the honor of God over the honor of his father. Not only did Jonathan protect David, he blessed him, saying, "*And may the* LORD *be with you as He has been with my father*" (1 Samuel 20:13). Friends protect, they don't expose.

What would happen if we began to relate to people in all of the arenas of friendship in the five ways Jonathan related to David? Whether they are acquaintances, associates, people to whom we are accountable, or agreement friends, we can begin now to initiate time and involvement with them; to question what we misunderstand; to kindly tell the truth even when it's difficult; to respond to their needs rather than run away when things get tough; and to do everything we can to protect them when others want to see them harmed.

Each of us needs to be in at least one agreement relationship. We've got to stop being superficial Christians and recognize that the characteristics of God's relationship with us are meant to be transferred to our relationships with other people. God is at work in our lives through other people, and we must be willing to submit to His work through them.

We must also be willing to be God's instrument in another person's life. Somewhere, sometime each one of us will come face to face with the reality that God wants us to commit ourselves to the fulfillment of

His design for someone else. We will be forced to face the personal sacrifice this agreement friendship will cost us. If we are to live in agreement with God, we will have to say no to some things in our lives just so we can say yes to this other person. When we recognize God leading us this way, we can expect to see something that's of great value to us appear to die. But as Jonathan and David learned, God is able to make even the appearance of death a good thing in our lives.

Agreement friendship is God's plan for us. It's a major component of the life of Yes. Are you in or out?

CHAPTER TWELVE

Christianizing the World

Christianity has become a subculture of trinkets and gifts displaying Christian slogans. We have pencils imprinted with, "My name is written in the book of life"; erasers that communicate, "He rubs out mistakes"; spinning toy tops embossed with, "Jesus turned my life around." The list is seemingly endless—bookmarks, cards, toys, potpourri. We even have Christian candy, with each piece wrapped in a Scripture verse. Christian candy—as opposed to that evil, secular candy.

The epitome of Christian marketing is WWJD mace. Isn't that story in your illustrated Bible—"Jesus Maces a Leper"?

We have paintings of little cottages that, when hung in a darkened room, seem to have light glowing from the windows. Now I realize that may seem very devotional, but it's nothing new: Back in the sixties, pictures that glowed in the dark were called black-light posters.

Then there's the whole line of Christian clothing: neckties with pictures of Jesus that have eyes that follow you around the room; sunglasses imprinted with, "I worship the Son"; soccer shorts that sport the logo "My Bro"—along with all the other commercial logos we've stolen from Madison Avenue, stripped of any style, and stuffed full of spiritual jargon. Just who are we trying to imitate?

Our clothes should be more than walking billboards bearing cheesy slogans or statements challenging anyone who doesn't believe just like we do to choose an eternity of smoking or nonsmoking. What I'm trying to say is, our clothes should display God as He truly is. There are places that sell good clothes; they're called malls. (Please avoid the kiosks.) I truly believe God is most glorified when we present an image of Christianity that enhances the message of Christ—not mocks it.

That message should be seen in our lives more than on our doormats. I'm not kidding—I once saw a doormat that read, "All who stand here will someday stand before Him up there." I didn't see anyone kneeling on that mat to accept Christ. I do think, however, that the local dog may have used it to mark part of his territory.

We have managed to take the mystery of God, the wonder of Jesus, and the miracle of the Resurrection and reduce them to their shallowest form. We have successfully Christianized everything in life but our own lives and the world we live in. We have managed to write the name of God on everything but the hearts of the people we come in contact with every day.

People don't come to Christ because of what they read on our shirts; they come to Christ because of what they read in our lives. Having His message written on the visual tapestry of daily life is more important than having it written on even the most expensive inanimate objects. What people see in our lives is what convinces them that the message we speak is true.

Christianizing the world is not something we display; it is something we are—and our role as witness is more crucial today than ever. We live in a world that's in the midst of a culture clash. Two worldviews are in a head-to-head, hard-core battle for the heavyweight championship of the world.

"In this corner…" is the world-view of pluralism, with many voices and many gods saying that all gods are equal. Pluralism's gods speak about convenience, power, expediency, and majority opinion, trying their best to get our attention and win our acceptance and loyalty. In pluralism's humanistic culture, mankind creates its own "good." Everything—ethics, rules, integrity, character—is up for grabs. There is no ultimate right or wrong. We make our own rules.

CHAPTER TWELVE: *Christianizing the World*

Humanistic culture imposes its will by either forcing people to cooperate or simply buying them off. It looks to the government to make certain that everything functions well and lives are improved. In fact, pluralists consider politics the ultimate power vehicle for societal change. They have great faith that the state can solve any problem if only certain people who say they will do certain things are elected.

"And in the other corner..." is the Christian world-view, which insists that God is in absolute control of mankind and the world and that nothing works correctly without Him. The Christian world-view deals with absolutes, both rights and wrongs. It demands that people live by the laws of God. It insists that the world, society, and each individual life can only be changed for the better by establishing the will of God as its ruling force.

These two world-views are in constant competition with each other. It is precisely this battle that Christians find themselves in today. To win the culture clash, we must bring more than a tract or an Evangi-cube. In fact, we must do more than *bring* a message; we must *live* the message.

God understands the battle we're up against, and He prepared a strategy long ago to ensure that we win it. He first revealed this strategy in His agreement with Abraham.

Let me summarize for you the story that's told in Genesis chapters 15–22. When Abraham lived in Haran, God came to him and promised to protect him, provide for him, and prosper him. And God kept that promise; but after eighty-plus years of living on the earth, Abraham was still missing something: an heir. Every fiber of Abraham's aging body ached to maintain the fading hope that his wife, Sarah, would bear him a son.

One night God came again to Abraham and said, "Abraham, count the stars."

"Lord, you count them," Abraham replied. "You're already up there. Besides, I can't count that high."

God spoke again: "As many stars as are in the sky, that's how many descendants you shall have."

"Right," Abraham responded with reserved cynicism. "You know, God, there are two words to keep in mind when You make that promise: *without children.*"

"Abraham, just as surely as the sun will rise tomorrow, I will make this agreement with you, and I will not violate it," God continued. "I will make you exceedingly fruitful. I will make nations out of your descendants, and kings will come forth from you."

At that moment Abraham did something quite remarkable. He believed what God said, and the Bible tells us that God counted his belief as righteousness: *"Then he believed in the LORD; and He reckoned it to him as righteousness"* (Genesis 15:6).

But time passed, and an heir didn't appear. Days, weeks, months, and years came and went in a seemingly endless, cruel parade across the childless lives of Abraham and Sarah. Recognizing that her own body wasn't getting any younger, Sarah gave her maidservant, Hagar, to Abraham, and Hagar bore a son named Ishmael. But it didn't take long for Sarah to realize that she hadn't helped God out as she had intended; she had only increased the tension in her own home.

Finally, at the age of ninety, Sarah gave birth to her first and only son, Isaac. Abraham was one hundred when Isaac was born. Isn't it amazing to think that God could make it possible for two people to have a child at such an old age? Abraham and Sarah were ecstatic, of course. They loved Isaac and valued him as God's promised heir.

Several years passed. Then God came to Abraham again and said, "Take your son, the love of your life, and offer him as a sacrifice on Mount Moriah." By this time Abraham was well into his hundreds. Through everything he had experienced in more than a century, he had learned to trust God in ways that might seem impossible to many people. To Abraham, trust in God had become an everyday part of life. So out of his practiced obedience, Abraham made the necessary preparations and set out with Isaac to Mount Moriah.

Early one morning, as the sun broke over the mountain, Isaac lay tied to an altar that Abraham had prepared with wood for burning. Abraham raised a sacrificial knife, intending to kill his promised son with a single stroke. His heart pounded as he watched Isaac's eyes widen. Every scene of his journey of faith with God seemed to flash through Abraham's mind in an instant.

"Abraham!" God called to him.

"Yes, Lord?" Abraham answered, the knife held high over his head.

"Don't hurt the boy."

Abraham looked just beyond the altar and saw that God had provided a ram for the sacrifice. Again the Lord repeated His agreement: "I will bless you and multiply your descendants as the stars. By you and your descendants, all the nations of the earth will be blessed." And from that moment until today, God has provoked the world to jealousy with the blessings that He bestows on the lives of His people.

You and I are heirs to God's great agreement with Abraham, and our role as witnesses to that agreement is just as important as our message. With any message, who the messenger is, how the messenger lives, and what the messenger does has a direct bearing on the impact of the message itself. If our message is to impact the world, we have to live in such a way that we provoke others to want to experience Jesus for themselves.

For many years persuasion has been the primary means the church has used to convert people. What the world needs today is demonstration. First Corinthians 4:20 says, *"The kingdom of God does not consist in words but in power."* The power of God rests on the lives of believers, not in some freaky, weird way, but through the fullness of God in the form of His blessings. That way, the people of the world can see His blessings in our lives and become curious to discover God's goodness for themselves. This curiosity is provoked by five things. It's important that we understand the basis and benefits of each of these and demonstrate them in the way we live.

RESOLVED TO THE RULE OF CHRIST

Abraham was able to do literally anything God asked him to do because he was totally committed to the rule of God in his life. He believed God would bring him an heir and live up to His promise to make his descendants as numerous as the stars. At nearly ninety years old, Abraham knew this was possible only if he trusted God to do what he could never hope to do by himself. Abraham's resolve to believe God and submit to His rule was what God used to build blessings into the lives of Abraham and his descendants. *"Then he believed in the LORD; and He reckoned it to him as righteousness"* (Genesis 15:6).

In Ephesians 4:6 Paul tells us there is *"one God and Father of all who is over all and through all and in all."* A commitment to the rule of Christ in our lives involves the recognition that Jesus is the Son of God and the Savior of all mankind. For believers there is but one King, one leader. This resolve must permeate our lives in the same way it did Abraham's.

As God's witnesses, we don't establish the rule of Christ. That has already been done. Christ already reigns. We're not in love with a Jesus who resides in stained-glass windows, doing His little thing and telling His little stories. No! We are in love with the ruling Christ, the anointed King over all. Regardless of who gets elected to office or what laws are passed, Jesus ultimately rules over all of life. It doesn't matter what stand our society takes on any moral issue; Jesus still rules. We may be voting members of a large, influential church, but this is one thing we don't get to vote on. It is imperative that we be resolved to this fact: Jesus is the ruler of our lives. Everything else that has any authority in our lives must come second.

What I am describing here is a theocracy. A theocracy is the exact opposite of what the world views as valid authority. The world sees authority as generated from the top and delegated downward. In reality authority begins with Christ's rule over creation and then is delegated through His people to be lived and set into motion in the world.

The very essence of a believer's life is the rule of Christ. The benefit of living in agreement with His rule is that the blessings of God rest on us. People ask, "Why do good things happen in your life?" To which we reply, "It's the blessing of God." When people see the blessings of the rule of Christ in our lives, they are drawn to that rule for themselves. This is the first way we Christianize the world.

REGULATED BY THE RULE OF CHRIST

A friend of mine developed a relationship with a very wealthy man who had all the things that "successful" people have: a big house, nice cars, a big bank account. This guy used to drive a Ferrari, so we called him "Ferrari Guy." Through the relationship with my friend, Ferrari Guy received Christ and began attending my friend's Bible study. After several weeks he approached my friend with this observation: "I finally understand that Christ is to rule every facet of my life. I'm having some trouble living this out, though, because I see the lives of other people who have been Christians a lot longer than I have, and they only give lip service to the rule of Christ in their lives. They spend all their time and energy seeking the things that I'm trying to get away from. If I could just see a few of them putting more effort into pursuing the things of God rather than chasing after the things of the world, it would give me the encouragement I need to take greater steps in that direction."

Abraham was able to do what we perceive as unthinkable—offer up his son as a sacrifice—because he had completely adapted his life to the rule of God. He recognized the authority of God's rule and gave more than lip service to it. He didn't know how God would be able to live up to His promise to make his descendants a great nation if Isaac were dead, but he knew that was God's problem. All he needed to do was to regulate his life to cooperate with the complete rule of God—whether or not he understood it. He was willing to do whatever God asked him to do, regardless of what it cost him or what problems his obedience might generate in the future.

In Ephesians 4 Paul not only addresses the rule of Christ over all believers; he also addresses the role of citizens of the kingdom of God. In Ephesians 4:13 he writes that we are to *"attain to the unity of the faith, and of the knowledge of the Son of God, to a mature man, to the measure of the stature which belongs to the fullness of Christ."*

Everybody is regulated by something: emotions, desires, childhood experiences, habits. The temperature in my office is regulated by a thermostat, and since I happen to like it cold, I set the thermostat at just below 70 degrees. I make the choice, and the thermostat regulates the air to whatever temperature I choose. In the same way, we can choose to say yes to God and begin to regulate our lives by the rule of Christ.

When we are regulated by Christ, we learn to control ourselves through the power of His rule and presence in our lives. We no longer display attitudes that say, "Hey, I can do whatever I want," or, "If I want it, I can have it." Instead, we exercise self-control, which means we don't give ourselves free rein. We are His disciples—the "disciplined ones."

When we regulate our lives by the rule of Christ, we are obeying what Paul tells us in Ephesians 4:15: *"Grow up in all aspects."* As Christians we are to live every part of our lives in sync with the rule of Christ. God's desire is to grow us up to the point where we can carry out His agenda on the earth. Being trustworthy and disciplined are the basic building blocks for Christianizing our society.

A disciplined, self-controlled life is a life that can be trusted. It's a life that's regulated by the rule of Christ, not the opportunities of the world. The psalmist had it right when he said, *"Delight yourself in the LORD; and He will give you the desires of your heart"* (Psalm 37:4). Fully give God your heart, and you can trust your heart. That's because your desires will be His desires.

Uncontrolled people, on the other hand, experience life in a random sequence of events that most often have no other meaning than the end they bring them. A nice car, a large house, a thick bank account become ends to these individuals. A party is enjoyed but then has to be recreated or done better the next time. They chase after new experiences, new toys, new people, new conquests—all for the sake of finding the center, the meaning, and the purpose of it all.

The life of Yes is lived by regulating everything by the rule of Christ, who is in and of Himself the meaning and purpose of life. When Christ regulates our lives, our lives are saturated with the blessings of purpose, fulfillment, and meaning—and these things provoke the world to jealousy.

REPRESENTING THE RULE OF CHRIST IN THE WORLD

When God made His agreement with Abraham, He changed his name from Abram, which means "exalted father," to Abraham, which means "father of nations." Many times in Scripture we see that God changed the name of a person with whom He made an agreement in order to signify the importance of the agreement. When God makes an agreement with an individual, the task of his or her life changes. *Abram* was the father of a clan that traveled from place to place to find water and pasture for his flocks. After God made His agreement, *Abraham* became the sire of countless millions of descendents who would bear the blessing of God for all time.

Acts chapter nine tells the story of Saul on the road to Damascus. He was in pursuit of Christians, bent on persecuting them. But then his entire company was stopped by a brilliant white light. God used this experience to blind Saul and speak to him out of the light: *"I am Jesus whom you are persecuting, but get up and enter the city, and it will be told you what you must do"* (Acts 9:5–6). Only Saul heard the voice, and it impacted him to such a degree that his task in life was changed. No longer would he persecute the followers of Christ; instead, he would propagate new believers throughout the known world. Saul's new task brought with it a new name. Now God would lead *Paul* to establish churches throughout Asia Minor and to author over one-half of the New Testament.

Later in his ministry, Paul wrote in Ephesians 4:24: *"Put on the new self, which in the likeness of God has been created in righteousness and holiness of the truth."* When we receive the life of Christ, He becomes our Lord and Master, our Savior. We are adopted into the family of God, and we take on His name for ourselves. With this new name comes our new task: to represent His rule and presence wherever we are and in all we do. The world needs to see believers who are fully committed to living synchronous lives with God. Whatever we choose to do with our lives, whatever role we finally play, that's our primary responsibility.

As God's witnesses, our lives must be characterized by excellence. We represent the King and His kingdom, and He loves work that is well done. After creating the world and all that is in it, He stepped back, looked at what He had created, and called it "good." His desire to recreate the world and bring His people back into a right relationship with Him remains His number-one priority. It has His complete and perfect attention. When we choose to live our lives in agreement with Him, He is able to produce this recreative work in and through us. One day, when the work is done, He will look at it and call it "good."

God is the God of Creation, and He desires for us to be as creative as we can be, regardless of our function in life. Throughout history many great artisans have come from the church. These people used their creativity and talent to provoke others to see and think about God differently. These days the only things Christian artists seem to have given to the world are those little porcelain figurines of children with enlarged craniums and creepy eyes. It's unfortunate, but true: In many ways we have failed to measure up to earlier representations of Christ in visual arts and music. As God's witnesses we must once again creatively represent God in these areas.

A student once told me, "God has gifted me with my talent, so I don't need to practice." The fact that a talent is God-given doesn't free us from the responsibility of practicing and developing it. We must refine what God has given us to make it everything it can be. True faith in God energizes and enhances everything we do. Excellence in the performance of our work or craft will provoke people to want to know our God.

Contemporary Christian music (CCM for short) is often referred to as a ministry of encouragement. Sometimes I think CCM actually stands for "candy-coated ministry." As witnesses of God, we should be doing more than patting other believers on the back. We should be making music that stirs hearts, invades the circumstances of people's lives, and impacts the culture.

Whatever work we do, we should excel. After all, our lives are representative of what life should be like when it is lived in agreement with God. We should be achieving the awards reserved for the best employees. In the corporate world, excellent performance brings expanded influence. When we perform with excellence, we make the blessings of God even more visible to others; and the ears of fellow workers who need to hear the truth of Christ become more attentive to the living message we communicate.

By living in agreement with God, the impact of our lives on others can actually exceed the impact of vocational ministers. I have a friend whose brother, a medical doctor, is currently pursuing an additional degree in philosophy and theology at a prestigious divinity school. He is doing this because he wants to be able to speak to the medical community about ethical issues. He wants to be a voice of Christ to doctors, and he wants to speak as a doctor for Christ.

Here is someone who already spent years in a classroom studying to be a doctor, and now he's there again, seeking to understand how Scripture applies to the moral questions raised by today's medical practice. He could have said, "Being a doctor will give me the chance to meet people, and maybe I'll get a chance to witness to them." But his vision goes beyond that. He sees public speaking as the purpose of his whole life, not just something to do when he's not being a doctor.

Our world is in chaos. Why? Because we have lost the one true standard for living—God's standard. Instead of acknowledging the rule of God, everyone exercises his or her own opinions, ideas, inclinations, and preferences on how to live. It's in the midst of this chaos that you and I must represent the rule of God. We must communicate the truth with our lives and our lips and uphold God's standard. That way people can know what real life is and desire to have His blessings for themselves.

REPLICATING THE RULE OF CHRIST IN SOCIETY

Hundreds of years after Abraham's death, Hebrew society bore the evidence of his faithfulness to replicate the rule of God in his family, his public worship, and the world around him. The lives of the Hebrew people were centered on the celebration of the rule of God. The temple was even erected in the exact center of town. They designated a significant portion of the population to leading worship and offered daily worship and sacrifices to God. Temple taxes took precedence over government taxes. Their calendar, their festivals, and even the harvesting of their crops were all in keeping with the rule of the God of Abraham. In short, Abraham's faithfulness to replicate the rule of God was lived before his family, carried through as he built altars wherever he went, and ultimately demonstrated in the quality of the society God established through him.

We live in a world that celebrates its freedom of choice. In fact, many countries are governed by laws put into place by a vote of the people; we call them democracies or republics. But it's a mistake to think that we have a vote in how God rules. As we said earlier, God's rule is not a democracy; it's a theocracy. We are citizens of a theocracy that is governed by the agreements made by God with His creation.

The rule of God is established on the earth in three areas: family, church, and society's civil government. The following chart shows how this rule operates.

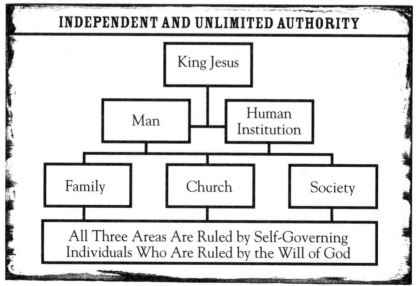

CHAPTER TWELVE: *Christianizing the World*

We don't vote for changes in our families, churches, or government. Real change is only possible in these areas when we as individuals are right before God, ordered by His will, and committed to living out His ways in our personal lives. Without true change on the personal level, there can be no established change on the next level. The theocracy of God is ruled from the top down, but it is carried out from the bottom up. Let's look at the three areas in which God's rule is established.

FAMILY

Anyone who has been on a mission trip to another country will tell you it is far easier to witness to a stranger than to your own family. But God's strategy is for the family to reflect the rule of God on the earth. Ephesians 5:22 says, *"Wives, be subject to your own husbands, as to the Lord."* Verse 25 says, *"Husbands, love your wives, just as Christ also loved the church and gave Himself up for her."* Mutual agreement with the will of God serves to guide and guard the relationship between a husband and wife. The two then raise their children in a way that demonstrates a daily, observable faith. Their common faith and commitment to the will of God is the foundation of their marriage, and that same agreement becomes the foundation for their entire family. This does not guarantee against divorce, but it greatly improves the chances that a strong faith will develop in the lives of all family members.

The family has gone through more shapes and sizes than Oprah. But whatever its size or shape, the ultimate goal of a family living in agreement with God is to make God's blessings visible to other families, who will then desire these blessings for themselves. The same is true for singles. The home of every family-of-one should reflect the same commitment and passion toward God's rule and draw others to want to know God.

CHURCH

We live in a generation that mixes and matches churches, denominations, and religions. We take more samples than Puff Daddy...or is that P-Diddy? We're like the girl who got dressed in the dark, only to arrive at work wearing a navy blue top, black pants, a red belt, and brown shoes. I can't tell you how many times I've spoken in a church and someone says to me, "We came to the early service this morning to hear you." When I say, "That's great! Why not stay around, and we'll go get something to eat after the next service?" the person responds, "No, thanks. We're going to drive across town now to another church, because it has a really good worship leader." People seem to have no problem hearing a speaker at one church, going to sing at different church, then driving back across town to eat lunch with friends from yet another church.

Our generation believes that church is an option, like tinted windows on a new car. They see Christianity as something that is "just between Jesus and me." Many believe, "As long as I am right with Jesus, as long as He and I are OK, then everything else is all right." But that is just not true. God established the church as the worship-evangelism channel to the world. He has initiated His plan for re-creation through the church, and that plan will be completed only as we commit ourselves to replicating His rule in everything the church does.

Our generation needs a better understanding of the church. The church—all those who are truly in Christ Jesus—is His bride, and He takes this relationship quite seriously. He loves, nurtures, and protects His bride. But too many of us play house with God. We "shack up" with Him at one church until we find something there that doesn't meet our expectations. Then we move to another church and "shack up" there for a while. Our focus is on what we can get out of a church rather than what we can do to replicate the rule of God in everything the church does.

The church is not to be treated as just another social club but as an alternate society. The church is the seat of the government of God on the earth. Because of this, our success in life is directly tied to our proper understanding and relationship to the local church. We can only completely replicate the rule of God when we are doing our part to ensure that the church is doing its job.

The church's role is to Christianize the world through its members. These representatives of the agreements of God are to take their drive, zeal, and passion for Christ and His church into their world in such a way that others jealously crave what they have. That is the ultimate witness.

If God had His way, there would be one church and many congregations. There would be one message spoken by many different messengers. The best thing the devil can do is keep the church divided up, because it's only in unity that we win. Can you imagine a football game where everyone runs their own plays and does whatever they want to? Real church is all of us working together, each of us carrying out our own assignment within a specific local body, and all of us moving together toward God's goal of Christianizing the world. Through Christ *"the whole body, being fitted and held together by what every joint supplies, according to the proper working of each individual part, causes the growth of the body for the building up of itself in love"* (Ephesians 4:16).

Much of what God wants to do in our lives can happen only when we are rightly related to His church. We grow and mature when we are connected with the lives of other believers in a local congregation. Some of God's promises and blessings are given to us corporately. When God's blessings reside on the lives of believers living in agreement with a local group of believers, the world can't help but see those blessings and desire a part in God's abundance.

SOCIETY

The extent to which people make decisions based on God's will determines the level of godliness found in a society. Our society is in the shape it is today because Christians have lost their godly influence. Our schools are filled with violence and substance abuse because of the lack of influence held by the Christian students. The businesses of our cities are filled with corruption because the Christians in the workplace have little or no influence. We've lost our influence because we've lost sight of our responsibility to replicate the rule of God in our society.

Godliness is not the by-product of legislation. It is established in direct proportion to the level of influence exercised by God's people.

We have assumed a far too passive role when it comes to influencing our society. God's plan is to re-create our society as He re-creates the world. This can only be done as His rule, based on His agreements, is replicated through our influence as believers.

The core struggle we face today is over who will be in control of our culture. Whenever a society moves away from agreement with God's Word, it begins to mix human laws with God's laws. Human laws are always subjective; God's laws are authentically objective. The two can't be mixed. They're like oil and water; no matter how much you shake them up, the oil is always visible in the water. But while God's rule is established, He doesn't force us to obey. He allows us to choose. He says, "I set before you life and death." It's not difficult to determine which rule—God's or mankind's—ends up in life and which ends up in death.

It takes more than a T-shirt slogan to change our world. We have to put down the gimmicks and the gadgets and come into agreement with the rule of God for our lives. Then we have to replicate that rule before others. When we do, our lives will literally make the world crazy to know our God of blessing. We'll find our influence in society expanding—and see God's plan to re-create and Christianize the world expanding too.

RELATED TO ONE ANOTHER UNDER THE RULE OF CHRIST

Ultimately, our role as representatives of God's agreements is demonstrated in the way we relate person to person. We are intricately related to one another under Christ's rule. This isn't something I made up. It's not something that will take place sometime after Tim LaHaye runs out of things to write. The rule of Christ is very real, very present, and very applicable to the way we relate to each other here and now.

We live in a generation that knows how to hack into the White House database but can't find the right words to ask someone to pass the salt and pepper at the dinner table. It's no surprise that some of our best-selling books are on manners. The fact that we have to be told, "Don't forget to say 'thank you' and 'please,'" shows that we have gotten used to living as a law unto ourselves. We have forgotten that God established a structure for our relationships.

RESOLVING ARGUMENTS

Paul writes about this very thing in Ephesians 4:32: *"Be kind to one another, tender-hearted, forgiving each other, just as God in Christ also has forgiven you."* But living that way isn't easy. Who hasn't been tempted to pull the DMV guy through the little hole in the Plexiglas window just to get him to understand what you're saying? I know Christians who won't speak to one another at church, just because one didn't like something the other said in a Bible study. It's unfortunate that many of the most serious pains we experience in life come as a direct result of conflicts between people in church. The rule of Christ must extend throughout our lives and into the ways we work out our differences.

In Christian homes across the country, husbands and wives must learn how to receive each other in the Lord. What do I mean by that? Men, let's say you're sitting at dinner with your wife, and she suddenly snaps at you, "I hate the way you chew your chicken!" Before you take offense and storm out of the room, receive her. Take responsibility for decoding what her comment really means. Sit there for a moment and carefully, calmly scroll back through your mind: "Let's see…chicken…barbeque…barbeque chicken from Texas…Texas…her parents live in Texas…." Then you'll have it. You'll be able to look across the table and lovingly say to your wife, "You're still mad at your mom, aren't you?"

Paul writes in Romans 12:18, *"If possible, so far as it depends on you, be at peace with all men."* That's the principle Abraham followed in Genesis 13, when he found himself in conflict with his nephew Lot. Both men owned such large herds of livestock that their herdsmen had begun to fight over which animals got to graze where. Abraham approached Lot and said, "Let's not fight over this. Look out over all the land and choose the area you want for yourself. Go ahead and choose the best land. I will gladly let you move there, and I will take whatever is left over."

Abraham knew that God had called him to the place where he was going and that He had promised to meet his every need. He didn't know how everything was going to work out, but he trusted that whatever happened, God would make it right. So Abraham allowed Lot to choose the best, most fruitful land; then, living up to his word, he moved his family and flocks to a place where they wouldn't interfere with Lot's. Scripture records that God blessed Abraham greatly as a result.

When we relate to each other under the rule of Christ, three things happen. First, we bring God into our present circumstances. Regardless of how painful our situation is or how wrong we perceive the other person to be, God is able to step in and change our perspective. Second, peace is established. Pride takes a backseat, and it becomes much easier to relinquish our need to be vindicated or proven right. Third, evil is restrained. When we demand our own way and require others to agree with our perceptions about ourselves, we are easily offended. Relating to each other under the rule of Christ leads us to restrain our fleshly responses of pride and arrogance.

RESPECTING AUTHORITY

The rule of Christ in our relationships teaches us to honor the presence of authority. It blows my mind when I hear young people on daytime talk shows mouth off to their parents and say, "Who died and made you God?" I want to yell, "Well, God did." What the kids are really saying is, "I don't like the way you're always telling me what to do." God knew that we'd all have a tough time dealing with parents. Maybe that's why He doesn't command us to love them; He commands us to honor them.

We don't obey our parents because they are good people or because they are always right. We obey them because they represent the authority of God in our lives. Even if they aren't godly, they still represent the authority of God. When we honor them, we are honoring God.

CHAPTER TWELVE: *Christianizing the World*

We are also honoring God when we honor those people He has placed in authority in the church. You and I aren't free to rail against a pastor or minister and get in his face. We are under his authority. It staggers me when I see people come into a church—even people who are not members of that church—and feel like they have the freedom to condemn, reprove, and critique the person ministering to them. The truth is, the pastor and other ministry leaders represent the authority of God in their lives. Instead of swaggering up to the local minister and yelling, "I don't agree with what you said!" or some other criticism, we must honor the person God has placed in authority over us. If we can't receive the man of God who pastors the church, we can't receive the Man inside of the man of God.

We are all under someone's authority. If it's not a parent, it's a boss. If it's not a pastor, it's someone else. God puts people over us to represent His authority and teach us how to honor authority. When we honor authority, we honor the God who placed it over us.

Each of us will be held personally accountable for the way we respond to the rule and will of God in our relationships. We need to have faith that honoring the authority God places in our lives will result in the holy and practical accomplishment of His purpose: showing the world that living in agreement with God brings blessings far beyond anything we can salvage from this life on our own.

Every Christian is living in hostile, enemy-controlled territory. We have a choice: We can withdraw and live in our own world, do our own thing away from everyone else, allow ourselves to be marginalized, and let our influence be diminished. Or we can enter the struggle and let our lives and our faith engage the culture—something that can only be done as we understand who we are in Christ and the place we hold in His body.

God is building a new nation of new people who will establish the kingdom of God on earth through the example and influence of their lives. Our challenge is to live each day in agreement with that plan. As we do, we become God's instruments for Christianizing the world.

Old Houses, New Stones

When we think of church, it's usually in terms of specific experiences. Occasionally I have flashbacks of potluck dinners. How can so many Christians be against gambling but in favor of potlucks? A potluck is a meal made up of dishes that have been cryogenically entombed in the freezers of church members for decades. People save these dishes for just such an occasion. I think the "pot" in potluck is an acronym for petrified, overcooked, and tasteless. You remember the combinations: lasagna and meat loaf; twenty-bean salad; Spam; cold green beans; and brownies that were actually divots from the men's golf tournament. Such is life in many churches.

Do my memories trigger memories of your own? Maybe church makes you think of overly legalistic, sweaty, yelling preachers. Or maybe you think of some of the mean people you've known in church leadership roles. These are people who never recovered from the humiliation of not being picked first for kickball back in the fourth grade. As high school students, they were never elected to student council, and they weren't accepted by the popular groups. So now, as adults, they come to church and become leaders in a pathetic effort to make up for all the disappointments in their lives. (It's OK to laugh; you've seen the same things I've seen.)

The things about church that make us laugh are too many to mention, but here's one that sticks out in my mind: the church bus that's always in need of repair. Every church has one. No matter how much work is done on that bus before a trip, it always breaks down. Some of my fondest memories from my youth group years are of relationships formed while standing on the side of some random highway, waiting for the tow truck to come.

One other particularly memorable episode from my teenage church years took place when our choir put on a Christmas skit. Someone had decided that live animals would make the scene more realistic. So at the close of the manger scene, when the wise men knelt and laid their gifts at the crib, the camel and the sheep left their "gifts" too.

There are still some things I have never seen but would like to see in church: a shark fin floating behind the pastor while he is baptizing someone; deacons throwing money at the congregation during the offering; people doing the wave during the sermon (somebody else's sermon, please!); bathrooms labeled First John and Second John, with a picture of Charlton Heston hung between the two doors that says, "Let my people go."

The point of this rant (and there is a point) is to say that when we think of church, we tend to think in terms of how we have been affected by it. But this chapter is not about how the church affects us; it's about how we affect the church. It's not about the church ministering to us; it's about us ministering to others through the church.

Here's the focus of this chapter in one sentence: *We cannot understand ministry apart from the view of service given to us in God's agreements.*

In this day and age, ministry has become entrepreneurial. Many people are out there doing their own thing—"for God," they say. But that's not what God means by service. God's picture of service is painted in the agreement He made with David. In fact, service in the kingdom is a continuation of the fulfilling of that agreement.

If our ministry is going to have any impact, it's essential that we understand the elements of service found in God's agreement with David. Here's some history to give us a jump-start.

David had been anointed as the ruler of the Israelites. He had been their warrior and their shepherd, and now he was the king over all the united tribes of Israel. He lived in Hebron, known for its beautiful natural springs, just north of the place where God had spoken to Abraham and Sarah about the birth of their son, Isaac.

David had accomplished much in his short life, and God had blessed him. But as God began stirring more of His dreams and desires in David's heart, David felt a sense of restlessness. God revealed to David that he was to reign over Israel not from Hebron, but from Jerusalem—a fortress city with five-hundred-year-old walls that were high and secure. It had been three hundred years since Joshua led the Hebrew invasion into the Promised Land. In all that time, Israel had never been able to conquer Jerusalem.

Following God's leadership, David led his army into Jerusalem and took the city. From that time on, without question, Jerusalem stood as "the city of God." It was the city of David's throne, the place from which God ruled through him.

David continued to expand his victories throughout the surrounding areas. The people who weren't defeated ultimately surrendered and became Israel's servants. Then finally, after many years of fighting, the king and the kingdom lived in peace.

In the years that followed, David's kingdom became the envy of everyone who saw it. Jerusalem was David's trophy city—a symbol of his personal success and God's blessing on his life. He built a magnificent mansion on the pinnacle of the city's northern ridge as a reflection of his position and accomplishments.

One night as he looked out over his kingdom from his palatial estate, he spoke to the Lord. "I have this wonderful house, with all its beauty, but You dwell in a tent," David said. "I must build a place for You."

But God reversed David's request. "No, David," He said, "I will build a house for you."

The house God had in mind would be far greater than any palace made of stone. Its authority would reach further than any throne David could imagine. That night God made an agreement to establish David's rule throughout all generations. He agreed to raise up a righteous and obedient son, a descendant of David, to take the throne and rule forever after David was gone (see 2 Samuel 7:12–16).

God's agreement with David was a commitment to establish much more than an earthly rule. However strong and powerful an earthly kingdom might become, it could never fulfill the scope of God's agreement. The house that God would build would be more important than a temple where people could go to worship. The house that would fulfill God's agreement would be a kingdom, and that kingdom would be inhabited by God's people. They would fill the earth with God's presence as they recognized and submitted to His rule.

And who would sit on the throne? Only one person could fulfill the agreement and sit forever on the throne of God's eternal kingdom: His own Son, Jesus Christ. And just as God promised, Jesus was born to Mary, the wife of Joseph—a direct descendant of King David. *"The kingdom of the world has become the kingdom of our Lord and of His Christ; and He will reign forever and ever"* (Revelation 11:15).

POLISH UP ON THE STANDARDS

He shall build a house for My name, and I will establish the throne of his kingdom forever. (2 Samuel 7:13)

Let's apply the truth of this agreement to our own lives, particularly in the area of service. God is still in the process of building His house, His kingdom, and He uses materials that are quite different from what we might think. We can try to build a ministry on our own, patterned after our own desires, using materials we believe will make an effective ministry. The end result may look good; it may bring in a lot of money and gain a reputation for greatness. But the reality is, if *we* built the ministry, it's just wood, hay, and stubble. Sooner or later the enemy will come along and huff and puff and blow our house down. If what is built is not built by God, according to His standards, the impact of our service will fall far short of God's desires.

CONCLUSION: *Old Houses, New Stones*

I hear it all the time: "Hey, how do I start a speaking ministry? I've got a testimony, and I believe I can make a difference in the lives of others for God." "I need to be an evangelist, because I want to make an impact in the world—not just in one church." "I'm wasting my talents here in this little church." "There's nothing I love more than singing on stage, worshiping Him. That's what I want to do for God." The most frightening thing about these statements is the number of "I's" used to form the sentences. My optometrist has eye charts with fewer vowels on them.

I can't be too judgmental; after all, I (Oops, there's the "I" again!) have said some of these things myself. In college God placed a desire in me to communicate His Word to others. Taking classes was the last thing I wanted to do. *Maybe I should quit school and go on the road,* I thought. But what road? If I chose a road on my own, where would I go? Fortunately, I sought wise counsel and did the right thing…I stayed in school.

Just because you can get a hamburger any way you want it doesn't mean you can order up ministry on your own terms. Our culture of instant gratification has led us to accept and, in some cases, prefer superficial ministry. After all, it's quicker and easier than the real deal. And it's more fun, because it's up and running in a hurry. Once you get it going, you can make a pretty quick evaluation as to whether or not it's worth it to continue in that direction. If a ministry is no deeper than superficial, and you move on, who really cares? Life as we know it is about as deep as a puddle of mud.

Jesus didn't begin His ministry spouting off profound sayings and going on the road to show off. For the first thirty years of His life, He was tested and tried while doing an ordinary, blue-collar job and studying the Scriptures. Yet, most of us feel that if we haven't made it big by the time we're twenty-five, we've missed our opportunity for greatness.

The moment we feel we can succeed in ministry by our own strength is the moment we begin to worship ourselves and serve for the wrong reasons. Our ambition to "make it," to get that "big break" in ministry, blinds us to the fact that service works on four unchangeable principles. Service apart from these principles misses the purpose of the call of God on our lives.

WE SERVE PEOPLE THROUGH THE CHURCH

When describing service today, the dominant word is *egalitarianism*, which means that everyone is equal. Everyone has the option of seeing themselves as independent, of seeing ministry as "me serving God on my own conditions." But the whole idea behind God's agreement with David was that Jesus Christ, the One who would rule on David's throne forever, would provide the structure for service. And the structure He has established is His church. If we are to live in agreement with God, we cannot serve as independent contractors; we have to serve in the context of God's house. Service done in agreement with God is done through His church.

Agreement service cannot be antichurch and pro-God. The desire of God is to build the church. If we live in agreement with Him, we must be controlled by the Father's desire. This is exactly the example Jesus gave us. Jesus was completely directed by the will of His Father. He would often say, "I can only do what I see my Father doing." Those of us who are Jesus' disciples must follow suit and do only what we see the Son doing.

Many people in this generation see the church as weak and ineffective. They have chosen to go around it and serve through other organizations. The Red Cross, Amnesty International, Greenpeace, UNICEF—these organizations and more exist to help people in need find the necessary resources to get through temporary crises. They provide clothing, food, medications, and legal aid for people who cannot provide for themselves. At best, their services relieve the symptoms of temporary problems.

The structure Jesus established for service may involve similar ingredients and do similar tasks, but the results are much more powerful. They have eternal implications. Jesus established the church as the vehicle through which we are to serve the people of our world. The agreement God made with David ensures that what is done through the church will make an eternal impact on the lives of those who receive the service.

I know this is hard to understand. Our churches are filled with people who have been used and discarded to protect the reputation or promote the dream of a leader. Who wants to be a part of that? Over the past few years, I've seen nearly a thousand students surrender their lives to full-time Christian ministry. Many of these students have told me they want to impact the world through their ministry, but they don't want to serve through the church. I'm sorry to disappoint so many well-intentioned young people, but God's call to serve leads us straight through the church to people who are in need of the eternal difference only the church can make.

It's important to mention here that our reason for serving is not the people in need; it's God. If the motivation for our service is people, we should join the Red Cross. We have grown up in churches thinking that service is going where the people are and finding ways to meet their needs. This narrow view of service is not agreement service. We are people of the agreement. As such, our service is designed and directed toward building the house of God throughout the world.

There will be those who serve in the church but never interact with people. Intercessors may spend their entire ministry lives in prayer and still contribute greatly to the building of the kingdom of God. Theologians may spend their whole lives doing research. Few of us may hear of them before they're dead and gone, but they have served faithfully and built the kingdom.

All service in the kingdom exists to build the house of God. The idea that I am living in agreement with God as long as I am doing *something* is an incorrect notion. This shouldn't offend anyone. God's church is worldwide, and Jesus died to redeem everyone in it. If we're in God's service—if we're serving in agreement with His agreement— we are in the church-building business.

There are many in Christendom today who are building ministries, but they are not church people. They are doing something, but that something is not grounded in a church community. They don't recognize the authority of the church and its place in the world. They are more than willing to use the church for financial gain and to build attendance for their meetings, but they don't want to serve the church. They want to help people, but they don't want to help the church. Every year hundreds of millions of dollars are donated to nonchurch ministries; and as a result, what is built is something independent and separate from the church.

It's entirely possible to build a ministry that looks and feels fantastic. It may even be financially healthy. But because it's not locked into the structure of ministry Jesus gave us, it will always miss the goal of agreement service.

In a perfect agreement world, every ministry would be related to the church. The church would give to it, nurture it, oversee it, and provide a place for it to function. Imagine the impact. No Christian institutions standing in conflict with the church! We don't yet live in that perfect agreement world, but we can. All it will take is a new generation of believers who will say yes to God and serve His purposes in and through the church.

OUR GIFTS ARE CONNECTED TO THE GIFTS OF OTHERS

None of us has everything we need. We are not complete in and of ourselves. We need each other to accomplish the work that God has designed for us to do. The apostle Paul provides clarity on this subject when he says it's *"the proper working of each individual part"* (that's you and me) that *"causes the growth of the body"* (the building of God's house) (Ephesians 4:16). Service in the kingdom of God is not a solo sport. It is always best accomplished when the members of the body of Christ work together, utilizing their gifts in concert for the continual building up of the kingdom.

By God's design our gifts are connected to the gifts of others in the church. The usefulness of these gifts grows only within the context of the church. No one can work effectively in the kingdom by themselves.

CONCLUSION: Old Houses, New Stones

There is a point in service when our gift by itself will not be enough to accomplish what needs to be done. For example, as a speaker I cannot fully function in my gift if someone else doesn't function in his or her gift as an administrator. A worship leader would find it difficult to lead worship without musicians and worshipers.

Our gifts are given to us for a use much greater than our own selfish purposes. They are not our own; they have specific corporate value. Ultimately they exist to benefit God's building plans for the kingdom. Their full value is realized only as they are utilized to advance those plans. When our gifts are put to work outside of God's plan, they don't work as they should; the results are always far less than what God intended.

The extent to which we serve through the church will determine the reach our service will have throughout the rest of the kingdom. The further we get away from the church, however, the more dangerous our gift becomes. Think of Jim Jones, David Koresh, and the Heaven's Gate people...need I say more?

Staying connected to others in the church keeps our doctrine strong and our theology sound. We need people who display God's truth all around us so that we don't start making up our own rules and concocting our own interpretations of what we think God is saying to us. Using our gifts within the context of the church keeps us from believing that if we wear Velcro sneakers, we can get to heaven on a spaceship.

A FULLY FUNCTIONING CHURCH EQUALS CHRIST JESUS IN THE WORLD

Why did Jesus say in John 14:12 that we will do *"greater works"* than He ever did? How is it possible for us to do greater things than Jesus? When Jesus stepped into this world, He limited Himself to time and space, taking on all the restrictions of humanity. He was only able to minister in one place at one time. But now He has given His gifts to the church, and all of us together carry the presence of Jesus into the entire world. Our faithful, continued service through the church allows the ministry of Jesus to take place nearly everywhere on earth at the same time. When all of us are serving, we literally do greater things than Jesus did.

Great emphasis is placed on geography throughout Scripture. We often see God speaking in terms of nations, lands, and borders. This is because within each border, God raises up the church to take the city. In the New Testament, God divided the entire world between two peoples, the Jews and the Gentiles. He sent Peter to the Jews, and He sent Paul to the Gentiles. He told them to go to one city, then another, and build the church. They obeyed, repeating this process throughout the entire world.

When we as believers know our gifts and understand them, when we know what our role is and how our gifts are to be used in the body, then we will see that the goal of our service is to build God's house. And as we serve in the places where God leads us, the ministry and rule of God will be extended throughout the world.

It puzzles me when I hear people say, "I've always known that God wanted me to serve Him, but that call came years ago, and I've had to get on with life." If God really spoke so clearly to them back then, why didn't they do what He told them to do? Why do people draw back from service? The answer is found in one simple yet very powerful word: fear.

We're afraid of service. Fear exaggerates our weaknesses, questions our abilities, and levels accusations that drive us away from serving. It manifests itself in the following common statements.

"Whatever I might do won't be enough—it won't make a difference."

Fear tries to convince us that our lives can't possibly make a difference. After all, there are so many things wrong with the world. What difference can one life make? The truth is, God has equipped you to make a great difference. You have a unique role to fill in the big picture. He has given you gifts and talents that, in connection with the gifts and talents of others, will build His church.

CONCLUSION: *Old Houses, New Stones*

"I don't know if I can do it."

There is an element of risk in serving God. Our success in service comes in facing that risk and saying to God, "I'll go ahead and do it," trusting that He will equip us as we step out. Don't be afraid. Whatever God asks you to do, you can do. It will work. You can't afford to take the bigger risk of being outside of the will of God.

"There are others who can do it better."

This idea holds up about as well as a paper cup in an acid factory. The notion that only "special Christians" can minister and that the average Christian is not called to serve is just not true. This particular fear has its roots in comparison. It exaggerates the abilities of others in our eyes and makes us believe that what we have to offer is not as good. From God's perspective, what's inside of us is unique and important to the kingdom. Stop claiming disqualification. Stop accepting the limitations that others have placed on your life. Believe that you can do what God is asking you to do.

"I know it's important, but it's not my problem."

I took three semesters of Spanish in college, but to this day all I can say is "taco." Why do I remember so little? I never internalized what I heard, that's why. We make the same mistake with service. We intellectualize it, study the statistics, and watch videos of others who are serving, but we fail to make the connection between the act of serving and the heartbeat of God. When Scripture speaks of service, it never gives us the theological explanation only. It always goes straight to the human heart in relationship with God. Your life and your resources are vital to what God is doing on the earth. Building God's house *is* your problem, and you are a vital part of God's solution.

"Hey, I'm doing all I can do."

In one of my favorite worship choruses, "We Are Hungry," there is a line that says, "Lord, I want more of You." We want God to give us all that He has. We want our lives filled with His blessings. Yet, what are we willing to give back to Him? Every time I sing that line, I always imagine God leaning down and saying, "No, I want more of *you*." How much of you does God have? Would you say 74 percent, 85 percent, 96 percent, 100 percent?

Just in case I missed your particular excuse, let me address every other possible reason for not serving this way: If we call ourselves Christians, sons and daughters of God, adopted into God's family, born again, we have the call of our heavenly Father on our lives to advance His kingdom and His rule throughout the earth. He doesn't expect us to do it alone, but He does expect us to serve using the gifts He has given us. He expects us to do this service through the church and make the evidence of Christ's new life in us visible to the world.

PARTICIPATE IN THE PARADIGM SHIFT

You have spoken also of the house of Your servant concerning the distant future. (2 Samuel 7:19)

David knew that the work God was doing would have results that would long outlast his lifetime. He understood that God was establishing a great, future kingdom that would be His eternal house. But if David could have seen into the future, into those early days just after Jesus ascended to heaven, he would have seen a far different picture—nothing that looked like the start of something great and eternal.

Imagine for a moment what it would be like to be homeless, with no real sense of belonging, overlooked and marginalized by a society that considered you useless and outcast. That's what it was like to be a Christian in the days of the apostle Peter. The Jews regarded Christians as nobodies and shunned them because of their beliefs. Jewish society was elitist, and the Christians felt quite alone in their conviction that Jesus was the Messiah. They felt like a people without a home.

Peter wrote to these "homeless" Christians and led them to the new and wonderful discovery of their actual identity in Christ. Throughout Israel the Jerusalem temple was known as God's holy habitation. It was a magnificent structure, with each of the massive stones used in its construction weighing more than a ton. Peter had seen the temple probably thousands of times, and he used its image to develop an extraordinary picture of identity for these struggling believers.

Peter opened his letter by referring to the believing Jews and gentile Christians as "*scattered*" (1 Peter 1:1), which may have been the secret-decoder-ring equivalent of saying they were the "new Israel of God." They were indeed scattered throughout the Roman province like the Jews, God's first Israel, had been. A little later he called them "*living stones...being built up as a spiritual house*" (1 Peter 2:5)—in other words, the new temple of God. These insights must have given these disenfranchised believers an incredible sense of belonging and an excitement about their identity. In Christ they had become both the new Israel and the new temple.

After designating them as "*living stones,*" Peter intentionally used four phrases from the Old Testament to teach the new believers more about who they were. In 1 Peter 2:9 he wrote, "*But you are* A CHOSEN RACE, A *royal* PRIESTHOOD, A HOLY NATION, A PEOPLE FOR God's OWN POSSESSION." These phrases are important because they were originally used to identify Israel as God's people. Here is the paradigm shift that Peter was emphasizing: It's not *physical* Israel but *spiritual* Israel that makes up the living stones. God has not changed His mind, nor has He opted for Plan B. The living stones are the fulfillment of the promise that God gave to David. They are the living stones that God is using to build His eternal house, His kingdom.

Because of our union with Christ, you and I are those living stones—cut, formed, and shaped to fit together as the house of God. We are God's strategy and structure for Christianizing the world. As living stones we must use our status in the service of God's house. Our identity defines our function. First Peter 2:5 explains the purpose of our role: "*to offer up spiritual sacrifices acceptable to God through Jesus Christ.*" We have been recreated as God's living stones to serve.

Once we understand this, the big question is not if we will serve or when we will serve. It's how we will serve, and where.

Recently a friend told me a story that perfectly ties into our understanding of Peter's term *living stones*. It was the beginning of the fall semester, and Architecture 101 had filled room 307A to capacity. In walked a man with silver-grey hair, wearing a weathered blue work shirt, British-made khakis, and brown chukka boots. When he threw his well-worn leather satchel on the desk, it landed with a heavy *thud* that was not the thud of books. All the students turned to look as the teacher unsnapped the flap of the satchel. He removed a brick and held it high over his head with one hand.

"This is a brick," he said. Then, with his other hand, he pointed to a series of lithographs of cathedrals and mansions that hung behind him. "These are all made out of bricks. A brick wants to belong. The primal urge of a brick is to be used as a part of something greater than itself. Ladies and gentleman, your job as future architects is to figure out where the bricks belong. Let's get started."

As living stones the task that lies before us is to figure out where we fit in God's house. What part of the structure do we belong to? God is the architect, and He has a specific plan and a design. We need to know where we fit into that design.

POWER UP FOR SERVICE

Again what more can David say to You? For You know Your servant, O Lord GOD! (2 Samuel 7:20)

Clearly David saw himself as God's servant. He referred to himself that way several times in 2 Samuel 7. There was no question in his mind about who he was. He could describe his identity simply: one who fulfilled God's purposes. We, too, are servants of God, and our identity is the same as David's. We are ones who fulfill the purposes of God in our lives.

Expectancy and trepidation coexist in everyone's call to serve. We look forward to seeing the fulfillment of what God has called us to do, yet we are forced to face up to our own weakness and inexperience. As a result, the call to serve can seem overwhelming to us. Sometimes it can seem easier to quit than to move ahead.

If you have ever felt this way, you are in good company. Timothy had the same feelings. He knew that he was anything but a saint, and he believed that he was unqualified for the heavy task of pastor that Paul had placed on him. At the same time, he knew that God had called him, and he had always longed to serve. His long-term relationship with Paul strengthened that zeal and desire.

You may be thinking, *That's a fine story, but I'm not called to be a pastor.* That doesn't matter. When Paul wrote his letters to Timothy, he was helping one living stone find out what to do and how to do it. The reason these letters are in the Word of God is because what Paul said to Timothy was intended for us as well. The principles found in his letters help us discover our place of service as a stone in God's house. They also show us where we get the power to live out our life of Yes in service to God.

RECOGNIZING THE CALL

> *This command I entrust to you, Timothy, my son, in accordance with the prophecies previously made concerning you, that by them you fight the good fight.* (1 Timothy 1:18)

Ephesus was a city known for its pagan worship. The difficult assignment Timothy had been given was to be the pastor of the church there. Timothy was young and inexperienced, and he could have easily chosen to step away from this task. But in 1 Timothy 1:18, Paul reminded Timothy of the greatness of his destiny. He challenged Timothy to believe what God had said about him when He called him. With the voice of a general speaking to a soldier, Paul told Timothy, "You can do this. Don't forget that you're a man under orders. Obedience is not an option; God has chosen you."

God places a specific call for service on each of our lives. It is for this purpose that we have been born again. Along with the call comes God's supernatural equipping. Our confidence for service comes as we recognize, obey, and embrace this call as our own. God views each of us as individuals, created at a specific time in a particular place and with a definite personality, placed into history at a strategic moment to serve with the unique gift He has given us. Both David and Timothy understood this truth; that's why they found and fulfilled their places in God's kingdom. God's personal call to each of us leads us into His plan for greatness and serves as the road map for our lives.

When I began the Metro Bible Study in Houston, my greatest fear was that no one would come back after the first night. I felt that way every week that followed. Then a man I look to as a spiritual father told me something I have never forgotten. He said, "You must always remember that you are God's man with God's message for that moment, and you must walk confidently in that truth." That advice has helped me to serve faithfully for many years. Only as we recognize our gifts and obey God's call are we able to find and fill our precise position and role in the kingdom of God.

REQUIREMENTS OF SERVICE

You will be a good servant of Christ Jesus, constantly nourished on the words of the faith and of the sound doctrine which you have been following. (1 Timothy 4:6)

Paul recognized the gift that God had placed in Timothy. Still he told Timothy to spend the time that was necessary to nourish and develop his abilities to make them effective for service.

I once had a guy say to me, "You know, I am a really gifted speaker. God just gives me my messages, so I don't need to study." To which I responded, "So you just shoot from the hip and hope you don't blow your foot off?"

Knowing God's call gives us direction and purpose and helps us set the right priorities for our lives. But direction, purpose, and clear priorities are worthless unless we take the actions necessary to nourish and develop the abilities God has given us to fulfill our roles.

The call of God is only a desire and a dream until we conform our lives to the requirements of the call. That means working to develop our gifts in whatever field of service God places us.

Sometimes we have to do things other than our call in order to fulfill that call. Paul was well acquainted with this principle. He was a tentmaker by trade, but he didn't make tents in order to corner the tent market. He made tents to fulfill the apostolic call that was on his life. Paul often had many people traveling with him, and it was his responsibility to provide for them and for himself. He made tents while he filled his role in the kingdom.

When I first surrendered to God's call to be a minister, I thought ministry would just kind of supernaturally happen. I soon realized that in order for me to follow that call, I would need to give it every ounce of energy and every bit of time I could budget. Once I understood my role in service, I found a new clarity in setting my priorities. I knew how many hours to carry at school. The hours I spent at my job had added meaning. I found it much easier to decide what to do with my weekends. I discovered that to be effective in service, we must see our whole lives in relation to the call of God.

REGULATING THE GIFT

> *Take pains with these things; be absorbed in them, so that your progress will be evident to all. Pay close attention to yourself and to your teaching; persevere in these things, for as you do this you will ensure salvation both for yourself and for those who hear you.* (1 Timothy 4:15–16)

Timothy had been given a very difficult ministry for someone so young and inexperienced. So when Paul sent him to Ephesus to pastor the church and take responsibility for the spiritual lives of its members, he reminded Timothy of two things: He had a God-given authority to serve there; and he, too, was a man under authority. Paul knew it was vitally important for Timothy to learn how to regulate his gift so that his youth would not be despised and his ministry would be effective among the various groups within the church. Paul took great care to explain how Timothy could use his gift in ways that would demonstrate that he was a man called to serve under authority, just as the other church members were.

The same principle is important in service today. No individual is a law unto himself or herself. And while the gifts God has deposited in each of us are unique and significant and must be treated with respect, we must be careful not to erect barriers to effective service through cockiness or arrogance. To be positioned for greater use, we must learn how to serve under authority by bringing our gifts and abilities under the leadership of the body of Christ. The further we get away from authority, the more subjective our service becomes. In reality no one rises to prominence in his or her gifting without the permission of God. God promotes from within His house.

We must learn how to serve with our gifts. The true measure of our usefulness as living stones is our faithfulness to use our gifts to serve God's purpose.

The most practical way to tell how well you have been using your gift to serve in your kingdom role is what I call the rocking-chair test. When you are old, sitting on the front porch in your weathered rocking chair, how will you respond to this question: "Am I proud of the way I served?" What answer will flash through your mind? When we serve in such a way that we have no regrets, we can be sure that people are seeing God in us and in our service.

REFINED FOR SERVICE

> But flee from these things, you man of God, and pursue right-eousness, godliness, faith, love, perseverance and gentleness. (1 Timothy 6:11)

In this verse Paul did not call Timothy by name. Instead he addressed him as a man of God. Paul chose to remind Timothy that his effectiveness and continued service were based on the condition of his personal life.

Once we find and develop our gifts and begin to serve in ministry, we begin to pursue a specific ministry. In other words, we now have such clear knowledge of our role and position in the kingdom that we become focused and passionate about seeing our service succeed.

Our pursuit must have its roots firmly planted in an inward quest for continued fellowship with God. Service must be driven by a strong devotional life. Personal, one-on-one time with God and His Word will ensure that our service continues out of a passion to fulfill His purpose, not our own. The standard for our service is the purpose of God; the substance of our service is an authentic life that rises out of our fellowship of agreement with God Himself.

Our living example of life in agreement with God is the most powerful tool we have in service. Without it our work is drained of power, and it becomes hollow. The greatest danger we face in building the kingdom of God is this: that after beginning to serve, we would disqualify ourselves because of our personal lives.

In 1 Timothy 6:11–12, Paul teaches that all of life must be viewed as our platform for service. He challenges us to live in agreement with God and not disqualify ourselves by making choices that could make our service unusable in building the kingdom. In telling us how to win *"the good fight,"* he gives advice in two parts, the negative and the positive.

First the negative: *"Flee from these things"* (1 Timothy 6:11). There is no deep secret to this principle. We are told to get away from evil, to run from it. We are to take constant evasive action. We must know that temptation will come, identify it for what it is, and take measures to find the escape routes God always provides. The problem is, temptation is always focused on something we can actually see ourselves doing. In other words, it's something we want to do. We're never tempted to do something that's not appealing to us. We must develop sensitivity to these subtle traps and see them for what they truly are.

Paul mentions one trap that we often overlook in 1 Timothy

6:20–21: *"avoiding worldly and empty chatter and the opposing arguments of what is falsely called 'knowledge'—which some have professed and thus gone astray from the faith."*

Someone once said, "If you want to deceive a generation, send a philosopher." There has been a long-running debate between Calvinism and Arminianism, between the concepts of free will and sovereign will. I won't get into the discussion here, but suffice it to say that many students have gotten caught up in this debate and have split off into groups. They argue their points but forget the Gospel. Their sole focus in life is to prove that their view is right. Their lives are more about success than service. If your theology makes you spiritually impotent to the point that you can no longer pass on your faith to another person and you have no active role in building God's house, you have chosen to disqualify yourself from service.

Paul commands us to guard what has been entrusted to us—not to debate, not to argue, not to confront, but to guard the truth. We must be careful to avoid the temptation to champion extreme stances and lose the message of the Gospel in the process. Without the Gospel we have nothing to say to the world.

Paul's advice is not all negative, however. He tells us what to flee, but he also tells us the positive things we are to seek: *"Pursue righteousness...fight the good fight...take hold of the eternal life to which you were called"* (1 Timothy 6:11–12). In writing this, Paul wanted to make certain that Timothy understood the importance of being abandoned to the task set before him. Our pursuit of a life of Yes will lead us into roles of service that at times will feel like war. Paul reminds us that we are called to fight the good fight regardless of how we feel. The only way we can fight and never give up is to serve with abandonment. A half-hearted effort or a less than abandoned commitment guarantees that the results of our service will be diluted, diminished, and dismissed for much less than God has planned.

Paul included other words of encouragement throughout his letters to Timothy. They're meant to be encouragement to us as well. Let me share some of them with you.

CONCLUSION: *Old Houses, New Stones*

Be Released to Serve

> *For God has not given us a spirit of timidity, but of power and love and discipline. Therefore do not be ashamed of the testimony of our Lord.* (2 Timothy 1:7–8)

God will do everything He has said He will do, and you must do everything He is telling you to do. Don't let fear dominate you. Expect everything you do in your service to the kingdom to succeed, because God is on your side. He has called you and equipped you. Now go do it!

Know There Is Greatness in You

> *Guard…the treasure which has been entrusted to you.* (2 Timothy 1:14)

What's inside of you is from God. It's His idea; it's His call; it's His talent, and the full measure of His resources comes with it. The gift you carry is bigger than you are. Your service is based on what God has placed in your heart. Accept the call, do it well, and never quit.

Expect Nothing but Success

> *You…be strong in the grace that is in Christ Jesus.* (2 Timothy 2:1)

Your strength and confidence come from having faith in the kind of person God is. He is an enabler; He is your resource, and He works for your good. Whatever God asks you to do, wherever He sends you to serve, go and believe that His favor and His power are on you. What God is doing in you is a spiritual reality. Be prepared for criticism, but don't let anything stop you from serving.

Stay Committed to Your Purpose

> *Be diligent to present yourself approved to God as a workman who does not need to be ashamed.* (2 Timothy 2:15)

During the boring times of your life, when it's not glamorous to serve, remember that your call to service was not manufactured in your own mind. It was born out of God's Spirit. God initiated it. Let that truth explode on the inside of you. Have faith! Stay committed! Keep working, even when it's boring. The success of your service depends on it.

Focus Your Energy

> *Now flee from youthful lusts and pursue righteousness.* (2 Timothy 2:22)

You have unlimited potential but not unlimited energy. Don't place yourself in a position to do anything that will cause you to lose your focus. Living in willful sin will reduce the effectiveness of your service and ultimately lead you to a sense of defeat. Don't get bogged down in defeat. Don't be driven by circumstances. Take hold of your life and make the choices that will help you stay focused on God's gift and your service in His house.

Use Your Gift

> *I solemnly charge you in the presence of God and of Christ Jesus, who is to judge.* (2 Timothy 4:1)

Use your gift for God's purposes, because you will give an account for it. Be bold with the gift God has given you. Jump out and serve. Quit waiting. Turn it loose, get in the battle, and don't quit!

Who are you? Or more accurately, *whose* are you? If you have the name of Christ written on your heart, you have an eternal purpose tied to your life. Your choices, actions, words, and activities count for eternity. God has defined a role and a position for you to fill in His house. And believe it or not, He wants you to know what that role is more than you want to find it. He has already equipped you for it. He has written His purpose on your heart. If you will listen, God will speak, and you will know exactly what your gift and your service are to be.

CONCLUSION: *Old Houses, New Stones*

Service starts in your heart; it functions through His church; and it builds His kingdom.

God has always been about the task of accomplishing His unchanging purpose: to bring mankind and His creation back to Himself. He began His work by making agreements with Adam, Abraham, David, and Jeremiah. In these four lives, He found people who were willing to trust everything they were and everything they could be to God's faithfulness to keep His agreements with them.

None of these men saw the actual fulfillment of their agreements, but each of them lived their lives as if God had already done everything He had said He would do. As a result, they lived in the fullness of God's resources, and God protected them and provided for them.

All four agreements were fulfilled and completed in the life, death, and resurrection of Jesus Christ. We have the privilege of seeing in history what these four men could only see through the eyes of faith. The power that God made active in their lives is the same power He makes available for our lives. The secret of releasing this power is found in living our lives in agreement with God. It's found in living the life of Yes.

God has a purpose, and He has committed Himself to accomplish it through you as you work through His church to build His house. He has promised to make available everything you need to carry out His purpose, and He will not let you down. If you will dare to bring your life into agreement with God, you will discover what Adam, Abraham, David, and Jeremiah knew: that God strongly supports those whose hearts are completely His. God has put His reputation on the line. You can count on His faithfulness. Will you live your life in agreement with Him? Say yes!

Discussion Questions

INTRODUCTION

1. What two or three things do you hope to learn from this book?

2. Do you feel as if life is a yes or a no? In what way?

3. How is it possible for people to look for answers to life's big questions without ever finding them?

4. Can we say yes to God without His working in our lives? Why or why not?

5. Do you know that God is for you? Do you feel it? What makes you think or feel as you do?

6. About which section are you most intrigued: the *heart*, the *hope*, or the *how* of Yes? Why do you think that is?

7. Take time to pray that God would use this book to teach you about Himself and to build in you a life of Yes.

CHAPTER 1: *The God of Yes*

1. Which of the barriers listed in this chapter most keeps you from trusting God? Why?

2. Does God's creative power give you hope as you think about the mistakes that you have made? How?

3. When God loves, does He love in freedom or because He must?

4. Does God respond to what we do? How?

5. How have we as a church misunderstood who God is?

6. In what way can we trust that God is in control?

7. Does God design the circumstances of our lives or simply respond to them—or both?

CHAPTER 2: *Hope, Not Hype*

1. What's the difference between hope and hype?

2. With whom do you identify: Amon, Josiah, or Jeremiah? Why?

3. What brought about the forty-year renewal of the hearts of God's people?

4. How has God proved His faithfulness to you in the last year?

5. Of the four aspects of living life in agreement, which one is the most difficult for you and why?

6. What does God want from you?

7. Who says yes first—you or God?

CHAPTER 3: *God's Four Agreements*

1. Why don't we need to fear God's response?

2. What does the story of Adam teach us about God's justice and mercy?

3. Why did God bless Abraham?

4. Why did God call Abraham "righteous"?

5. To whom or to what should you run "to face the bad news of the moment"?

6. Do you look forward to God's work in your life or does it frighten you? Why?

7. Think about the role of the Trinity in God's yes to us. For example, what does the Holy Spirit do?

CHAPTER 4: *There Is a God, and You're Not Him*

1. Is God still in charge when we sin? when bad things happen? If so, how? If not, why not?

2. Where does God's judgment meet His mercy most powerfully?

3. How has God used your mistakes to advance His purposes?

4. What keeps you from submitting to God's authority?

5. Does God withdraw from you when you sin? Why do you think that?

6. Can anyone or anything keep God for achieving what He wants to do in your life?

7. What causes you to weep will show where your heart is fixed. So what causes you to weep?

CHAPTER 5: *A Promise Kept*

1. What is the only way to reach heaven?

2. How does Jesus bring life to a person today?

3. What aspect of Christ's person most amazes you?

4. How should each attribute of Christ discussed in this chapter impact concerns or worries that you and your friends are facing?

5. Has God touched you with an invitation to know Him, through His Son, Jesus Christ? What will you do?

6. How can God use you to encourage others to say yes?

7. Are you as precious to God as Abraham? Why do you believe what you do about this?

CHAPTER 6: *A Life of Agreement*

1. Does your Christian life *work*? How so, or why not?

2. How did Jesus do the work that you could never do?

3. What was Jesus' greatest desire?

4. What do you need to let go of?

5. Share with a good friend an area of your life where you are struggling.

6. What petty details of life prevent you from living God's grand, bold scheme? What is God's scheme for you?

7. Is your life lived as a life of Yes or No? How so?

CHAPTER 7: *Times of Refreshing*

1. What causes you to drift away from God?

2. What tradition is the Spirit shattering for you?

3. What traditions is the Spirit shattering for your friends and your church?

4. What have you longed for that only God can give you?

5. For what task is the Spirit strengthening you?

6. Of all the works of the Spirit listed, which one is most visible in your life right now? How is it demonstrated?

7. Which is most visible in the lives of your friends and your church? How is it demonstrated?

CHAPTER 8: The Power Line

1. Do you think today's society is similar to the one Jeremiah lived in? Why?

2. In what ways do you see life from your perspective and not from God's?

3. On a scale of one to ten, how well do you know yourself? Why do you say that?

4. Is integrity fundamentally who you are or what you do?

5. When is God most pleased with you? Or is this question even legitimate?

6. What—or who—determines the actions of the fully devoted follower of Christ?

7. Will you choose to be whatever God has planned for you to be? What in your life might stand in the way of God's plans?

CHAPTER 9: So Fresh and So Clean

1. What do you use to hide your flaws?

2. Do you think purity is attractive? Why?

3. Why is it so difficult to order our lives in a way that allows Christ to shine through us?

4. Where are you in the purity cycle?

5. What brought you there?

6. How does God force His will in our lives?

7. In what way is Christian obedience a work of love?

CHAPTER 10: Advancing the Spirit

1. What universal problem resulted from Adam and Eve's sin?

2. What explains humanity's drive toward self-reliance?

3. How has God enhanced the perspective of your community?

4. About what is God asking you to persevere?

5. Is your life consumed with spiritual discipline or spiritual superstition?

6. What keeps you from growing spiritually? What has made you feel dry spiritually?

7. Who does the work of growing believers spiritually?

CHAPTER 11: *Allies in Agreement*

1. Think of your five closest friends. Given what was said in this chapter, are they really your friends?

2. In what way should a relationship with a Christian be different from a relationship with an unbeliever?

3. Do you have an inner circle of friendship?

4. What keeps you from developing true friends?

5. Think of a person who sought your friendship but from whom you pulled away. Why did you do so? Do you think it's time to reevaluate your decision?

6. How can we balance grace and accountability in friendships?

7. At what point should you push someone away from your inner circle toward an outer one?

CHAPTER 12: *Christianizing the World*

1. Can Christian paraphernalia be a cop-out for real witnessing? How?

2. What's at the heart of the Christian world-view?

3. What does today's church need to do as we seek to represent Christ to the world?

4. How do we balance excellence in our jobs with excellence in our Christian lives? Or should we even seek a balance?

5. Do you think living Christianly helps society as a whole? Why or why not?

6. Is control over our culture really important? Or should the church be about something else?

7. What's your greatest hope for your non-Christian friends? What will you do about it?

CONCLUSION: *Old Houses, New Stones*

1. Who builds God's house?

DISCUSSION QUESTIONS

2. Does Jesus' patience in waiting to minister (while He did an ordinary job) encourage you as you wait your turn for service?

3. Why did God equip different people in different ways? Why didn't He give us all the same gifts?

4. Why do you have the gifts you have been given?

5. How will you put them to use?

6. Do you see yourself as "going it alone" or as "part of a team"—why? How should you think?

7. What role should authority play in your desire to serve?

Notes

Introduction

1. Bob Briner, *Final Roar* (Nashville: Broadman & Holman, 2000), 12–13.

CHAPTER ONE: The God of Yes

1. *Changing Lanes*, Paramount Pictures, 2002.

2. Terry M. Crist, *Learning the Language of Babylon* (Grand Rapids: Chosen Books, 2001), 70.

CHAPTER TWO: Hope, Not Hype

1. Arnold B. Rhodes, *The Mighty Acts of God* (Westminster: John Knox Press, 2000), 173.

CHAPTER NINE: So Fresh and So Clean

1. Crist, *Learning the Language of Babylon*, 59.

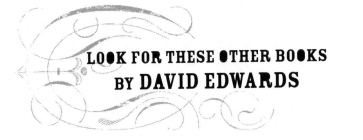

**LOOK FOR THESE OTHER BOOKS
BY DAVID EDWARDS**

Lit

One Step Closer